The Ambiguity
of Teaching
to the Test

Standards, Assessment,
and Educational Reform

The Ambiguity of Teaching to the Test

Standards, Assessment, and Educational Reform

Edited by

William A. Firestone
Roberta Y. Schorr
Lora F. Monfils

LAWRENCE ERLBAUM ASSOCIATES, PUBLISHERS
2004   Mahwah, New Jersey   London

Lawrence Erlbaum Associates, Inc., Publishers
10 Industrial Avenue
Mahwah, New Jersey 07430

Cover design by Sean Trane Sciarrone

Library of Congress Cataloging-in-Publication Data

The ambiguity of teaching to the test : standards, assessment, and edu-
cational reform / edited by William A. Firestone, Lora Frances
Monfils, Roberta Y. Schorr.
    p. cm.
    Includes bibliographical references and index.
ISBN 0-8058-4568-2 (cloth : alk. paper)
ISBN 0-8058-4569-0 (pbk. : alk. paper)
1. Educational tests and measurements—United States. 2. Educa-
tion—Standards—United States. 3. Mathematics—Examina-
tions, questions, etc. 4. Science—Examinations, questions, etc.
I. Firestone, William A. II. Monfils, Lora Frances. III. Schorr,
Roberta Y.

LB3051.A592 2004
371.26'4—dc22   2003054587
                                                            CIP

Books published by Lawrence Erlbaum Associates are printed on acid-
free paper, and their bindings are chosen for strength and durability.

Printed in the United States of America
10 9 8 7 6 5 4 3 2

Contents

Preface

It is difficult to think about educational policy or educational reform without thinking about testing. In practice, all the policy talk about "systemic reform," standards, "No Child Left Behind," and many other rallying cries really revolve in practice around externally imposed tests. Whereas advocates of various ideological stripes argue about whether testing is good or bad, state policymakers, school district leaders, curriculum specialists, and citizens of all sorts are forced to make decisions about how to design and respond to new testing systems, what incentives should accompany those tests, and what educators need to know to make sure that testing helps children rather than keeps them from becoming more successful and better informed adults. Thus a whole range of people need to know much more about the consequences of testing and how those consequences depend on a variety of local decisions.

Over the last 30 years, we have learned a lot about how state testing affects teachers and students, but we lack the kind of scientifically based research that recent federal legislation demands. In fact there is a good deal of ambiguity about the effects of testing. The same test may lead to different consequences in different circumstances; and teachers may use very different strategies to prepare students for tests. To help sort through this ambiguity and provide a firmer basis for decisions, this book provides a hard look at the effects of testing in one state and probes, in detail, the ambiguity of test preparation and how test preparation practices are influenced by what teachers know and the leadership coming from the school and district. By taking a comprehensive look at the variation in practice in one state, we hope to offer many people guidance on how to take steps to ensure that testing helps all children learn more, not less.

This book reports on a 3-year study of New Jersey's testing policy. The first chapter sets the stage by describing the debates surrounding state testing policies: how they should be designed, what they should strive to accomplish, and what local factors affect how teachers respond to state tests. It also describes the policy context in New Jersey.

Chapter 2 provides an overview of the conceptually based perspective that supports recent "inquiry-oriented" approaches that challenge conventional practice and require students to become more active learners. The chapter then explores the current state of mathematics and science instruction by New Jersey's fourth-grade teachers. It relies primarily on interview data and observational data. The interview data show that teachers really believe that they are changing the instructional strategies they use to be more consistent with current inquiry-oriented approaches to teaching and learning. Direct observation suggests that although many teachers "talk the talk" of reform, their actual practices remain much more traditional. Moreover, the teacher surveys show only very modest changes in the amount of time given to various mathematics and science content areas. There is some reduction in the very large amounts of time spent on drill of mathematics facts, but no commensurate increase in some of the newer areas of mathematics.

Chapter 3 uses survey, interview, and observation data to illustrate the fundamental ambiguity of test preparation. New Jersey teachers actually engage in two forms of test preparation. Decontextualized test preparation is what most people criticize when they talk about teaching to the test. It consists of special "cramming" shortly before the test is given and intensification of conventional, didactic practice. However, some teachers also engage in "embedded" test preparation—that is, changes in teaching throughout the year to reflect the state standards and the content of the test. This form of teaching includes inquiry-oriented instruction that challenges students to think more deeply about mathematical and scientific ideas. Teaching to the test is distributed inequitably with districts serving poor students spending more time on specific test preparation activities as compared with those districts serving wealthier students. Ironically, teachers accommodate to the state test more from what they have learned about test items than test results. In fact, teachers have limited access to actual test results and rarely get the information most likely to help them reform their practice.

Chapter 4 explores teachers' perceptions of the pressure and support that they experience. Pressure comes most directly through signals from administrators that raising test scores is very important. Teachers understand that even without state sanctions, low test scores can be damaging to their schools and districts. Under pressure, they are more likely to make short-term accommodations to the state test and use more didactic instructional approaches. Teachers who know more about the state standards, have access to professional development focusing on their subject areas—as opposed to test preparation—and a strong sense of personal efficacy are most likely to try more inquiry-oriented approaches and, to a lesser extent, use longer-term test preparation strategies. Moreover, some events—most notably district professional development—combine pressure and support, offering guidance to teachers on how to teach in different ways while sending a strong message that test scores matter and need to improve.

Chapter 5 explores the special role of the principal in supporting instructional change. Principals' contribution to instructional improvement is different from that of the district office. Whereas the latter provide most of the formal learning opportunities for teachers, the former can support teachers' efforts in important, but less formal, ways. In fact, principal support for standards and assessments contributes to both short- and long-term teaching to the test and more inquiry-oriented instruction. Supportive principals offer teachers advice on how to improve their practice by encouraging participation in learning opportunities even though they rarely know a great deal more about the subjects taught than do teachers. This leadership depends on personal relations more than formal authority. Why some principals become more supportive than others remains a mystery although greater formal accountability for student achievement is not the answer.

Chapter 6 describes seven districts' contribution to improved instruction using interviews with district personnel and teachers along with district records. This chapter suggests that districts that are quite similar in terms of tax base and student characteristics take very different approaches to state tests. Some focus primarily on systemwide reform driven by an image of more challenging teaching and deeper student learning whereas others focus primarily on test besting and still others combine the two approaches. Some districts provide opportunities for teachers to share in the leadership of instructional change—these tend to take the broader view of what the state standards require—whereas others, often those focusing on narrow test preparation, expect district leaders to drive the change effort. Whatever the nature of the student body and financial resources, the district's approach to instruction is shaped substantially by local understandings of the purpose of the state standards and tests. Where leaders do not understand the more challenging vision of reform behind standards like New Jersey's, their responses will encourage a more decontextualized, test-besting approach to the policy.

Chapter 7 explores equity issues by examining changes in New Jersey's fourth-grade test scores over time. These analyses show that student demographic factors—for example, the number of children on free lunch—are much more powerful than any school characteristics measured. Moreover, although test scores have increased slightly over time, scores for African American students have not, suggesting that the complete set of interventions in New Jersey—standards, assessments, whole-school reform programs, changed financing, and so forth—have had very little impact on the underlying complex of factors that maintain inequities in the American educational system.

The conclusion suggests that New Jersey's approach to state testing leads to only modest change. Teacher strategies in response to testing reflect a mixture of decontextualized strategies and a modest amount of intensification of conventional methods on the one hand and embedded use of newer instructional approaches on the other. Our findings offer some suggestions for what principals, district leaders, and teacher educators can do to encourage greater reforms in mathematics and science teaching. However, our suggestions for state policy remain inferences from the variation that we see among schools and districts. Still, the key to improved teaching is the offering of greater opportunities for teacher learning rather than increased pressure on teachers (or administrators). Educators must deepen their understanding of the content they are expected to teach, how children learn that content, and the associated effective pedagogical practices that lead to increased understanding of the content taught and how to teach it before students can actually learn more mathematics and science.

A number of other people contributed to this book in ways that are not obvious from the author list. Gregory Camilli was in at the beginning of this project and led the design of the survey instruments and the quantitative data analysis. Katrina Bulkley oversaw the qualitative data collection and coordinated a great deal of the fieldwork. Both provided much more wisdom and energy to this study than is apparent in their contributions as chapter authors.

David Mayrowetz played a critical role in instrument design, sample selection, the early fieldwork, and qualitative data analysis. Michele Yurecko helped to organize the quantitative data in the early days of the project, and Yasuko Munteneau played a similar role later on. Jim Neuberger and Daniel Garlic helped with the interviews and classroom observations. Sylvia Bulgar, Lesley Lefkowitz, and Trisha Camp coded observation data. Joanne Torok helped develop codes for and coded survey data. Tim Jenkins assisted in the organization of data and provided support to the interview coders. Terri Hawkes and Terrie Polovsky provided editing assistance and project support. Janice Ballou and the Center for Public Interest Polling in the Eagleton Institute of Politics at Rutgers University conducted the teacher surveys. Warren Crown, Sharon Sherman, and John Shaffransky helped to design instruments. Deborah Cook, Jay Doolan, Margaret Goertz, Larry Leverett, Bill Mehrens, Clyde Reese, Joseph Rosenstein, Karen Seashore, Mary Lee Smith, and Carol Stearns served on our advisory committee and provided useful critiques of our conceptualization and methods. Deborah Cook also shared information from New Jersey's State Systemic Initiative (SSI) that was critical for sample selection at several points. Ken Leithwood provided an especially useful review of the chapter on the role of principals. Thanks to Naomi Silverman and Lori Hawver at Lawrence Erlbaum for their help in preparing this book. We would also like to acknowledge the helpful suggestions of Robert E. Floden, of Michigan State University, and an anonymous reviewer, who reviewed the manuscript and helped to make it more cohesive.

We are extremely grateful to the National Science Foundation for financial support for this project through grants 9804925 and 9980458. The opinions expressed here are those of the authors and not those of either the National Science Foundation or Rutgers University.

1

Introduction

William A. Firestone
Roberta Y. Schorr

One day in late spring in a classroom in New Jersey, Ms. Jones put the following problem on the overhead projector along with four possible answers: 56×24. She then told her children to turn off their calculators and said, "Let's just look at the strategy here. You won't have the calculator for this part. You'll get paper and a pencil. You will have a choice on day of the test whether to have lined or unlined paper. I like lines 'cause I like things orderly. So knowing that, let's look at what we have to multiply. We have to multiply by the ones digit. Which one is the ones digit?" The children then identified the six and the four as the being in the ones place and multiplied them together to get 24. At that point, she told the children they could rule out two answers because they didn't end in four. She then passed out paper and had the children follow the conventional steps for multiplying 56 by 24. She then called on one student, Lindsey, who worked aloud on the problem, identifying the steps needed in order to get the solution.

At about the same time in another district, Ms. Smith passed out a bag of M&Ms to each student and asked each one to make a bar graph representing the number of candies of each color in the bag. The students spent about 30 minutes working with partners to sort and count the candies, construct graphs, and consider how they might begin to analyze their own data. Then Ms. Smith asked the students what statements they could make based on the data as displayed in their graphs. When the students reported to the class, one student, Michael, had calculated what turned out to be several different measures of central tendency for the number of M&Ms of each color. For instance, he had found that the mean number of candies of any given color was seven. He also shared that he had calculated what he called "the range" by finding the difference between the predicted total number of candies and the actual total number in his bag. Ms. Smith used this opportunity to build upon Michael's idea, as well as to discuss what the standard mathematical meaning for "the range" is, and how it should be calculated. Other students described the percentage of candies that were particular colors and then used the percentages to make predictions about the likelihood of pulling out an M&M of a particular color from their bags.

Ms. Jones' and Ms. Smith's classrooms illustrate some of the issues surrounding "teaching to the test." This is a term with many meanings, but the implication is, generally speaking, that teachers are doing something special to help students do well on a test, often without helping them to better understand the underlying subject matter. Teaching to the test is decried by testing experts because it artificially inflates test scores so that the measure (the test score) and the construct measured (the child's knowledge of the subject tested) become progressively disconnected. It is abhorred by curriculum experts who believe that testing reduces the quality and quantity of what is taught as commercial test-prep materials are substituted for conventional materials. Students spend too much time learning techniques that help them do nothing more than cope with specific test formats (McNeil, 2000). Those concerned about equity point out that the worst teaching to the test often takes place in the nation's urban schools, where high-quality, intellectually challenging teaching is most needed.

The vignette involving Mrs. Jones illustrates some of these fears about teaching to the test. She was preparing her students by using examples of problems that her math supervisor had downloaded from the state Web site because they were similar to those on the state test. This lesson was a preparation activity for the test, which was to be given in just a few weeks. Ms. Jones indicated that she felt that it was important to help children learn how to quickly eliminate incorrect answers for multiple-choice items in order to save time. Her teaching represents what we have come to call *decontextualized test preparation* because it is a special activity only loosely related to her regular lessons and focused on the test itself.

A more optimistic view of teaching to the test starts from the idea that American education is not sufficiently challenging for any of our students. The curriculum often emphasizes basic facts and skills, and new topics more relevant to the 21st century are sometimes not introduced until later on, if at all. Teaching is all too often organized in a way that treats students as passive receptacles to be filled with knowledge. Teachers drill children on conventional facts and algorithms without seeking to generate any intellectual interest or creative thought or understanding of the algorithms. Often, these tendencies are reinforced by tests that require factual information that can be easily recalled and tested and that fail to tap higher order skills.

In this view, new tests are a way to challenge the status quo and raise the instructional bar. If more thought-provoking tests are given, teachers are expected to rise to the occasion, and improve instruction. If the tests cover more relevant content, the curriculum can be updated. Often, those most identified with the reform movements want to use more authentic or performance-based assessments where children are asked to undertake activities that not only require them to repeat what they have learned but to use that information to construct something that shows that they have a deeper understanding of the subject tested and that they can connect what they know to other problems, including real-world situations. These performance-based assessments, it is argued, may provide more valid measures regarding genuine knowledge of a discipline. They also challenge teachers to teach in more intellectually engaging ways.

Ms. Smith's teaching more closely reflects this view. The content involved graphing, statistics, and probability, topics that had not been prominent in the elementary curriculum before New Jersey introduced its new standards and tests. She also assigned more open-ended activities like making and reading graphs and drawing conclusions from them. Graphical representations, such as those generated by Ms. Smith's students, do indeed often appear on the state test, and students are often asked to make conjectures and write conclusions about similar problems. Though Ms. Smith did not specifically refer to the test, she did feel that doing such activities could prepare students for it, but even more significantly, could help them to understand important content. Ms. Smith represents "embedded" test preparation because activities to prepare students for the test are integrated into her regular instruction, not a special, decontextualized activity.

Critics fear that state tests will reinforce rote teaching methods. Ms. Jones drilled children on the conventional algorithm for multiplying two-digit numbers by hand using a very didactic approach. She felt that the best way to help children prepare for the test was to help them memorize facts. In fact, earlier that period, when a child had forgotten a multiplication fact, she said "I'm a lion. I like to roar. Six times nine is ..." The girl said, "fifty-four." Advocates of reformed assessment hope that new items will lead to more engaging assignments. Ms. Smith gave a much more open-ended, inquiry-oriented task where children could determine what conclusions to draw, and Ms. Smith used their responses to stimulate the development of important mathematical ideas. She felt that it was important for children to use multiple representations. She therefore had them draw graphs, write number sentences, and talk about their mathematical thinking. This strategy is consistent with both National Council of Teachers of Mathematics (NCTM) standards and advances in cognitive science that suggest that understanding comes from building connections between various ideas, facts, representations, and operations (Hiebert & Carpenter, 1992; NCTM, 2000).

Ms. Jones and Ms. Smith illustrate that there are many forms of teaching to the test and many ways that state tests can influence teaching. But single cases can only illustrate possibilities. With so many states testing children in different ways, with different consequences for passing and failing those tests, it is important to understand (a) how teachers respond to different kinds of tests, (b) how other state education policies affect those responses, and (c) what local educators do to ensure that tests will improve instruction, not deaden it.

To explore these issues, we conducted a 3-year study of state testing in New Jersey. Our findings illustrate some of the problems with state tests, but they also suggest some of the ways that tests can be combined with other actions to improve teaching and learning. Our work confirms past studies showing that most elementary math and science teaching follows conventional, less challenging instructional models. However, we also describe the kinds of changes in practice—often just "add-ons" to conventional instruction—that teachers are adopting. We show that teaching consists of a variety of practices and that some are more intellectually challenging than others. The New Jersey story shows that tests with open-ended assessment items encourage more challenging forms of teaching to the test and of instruction in general, but that changing tests alone is not enough to bring about such changes. With the need for additional measures to change instruction in mind, we explore how school administrators support or undermine more constructive versions of teaching to the test through principal leadership and district professional development. Finally, we clarify how standards-based testing can help or harm educational equity by examining how student characteristics and a variety of policy variables affect achievement on the new tests over their 3-year history.

STATE TESTING AND THE STANDARDS MOVEMENT

Although New York's Regents tests go back to the 19th century, most people date the beginning of modern state testing with the passage of Florida's Education Accountability Act in 1971. Eleven years later, 36 states mandated some kind of testing program (Odden & Dougherty, 1982); by 2000, almost every state tested students at one or more grade levels, and testing was spreading from the most central subjects like language arts and mathematics to science and social studies (Editorial Projects in Education, 2001).

Several factors promoted this growth in state testing. One was the expansion of state government during the 1960s and 1970s. State departments of education grew more than threefold between 1957 and 1986 and the policy staff serving state legislatures more than doubled between 1968 and 1979. These larger agencies had more capacity to think about, monitor, and govern education (Firestone, 1990).

Another was the change in educational financing. Constitutionally, education is a state function, but it had been locally governed and funded throughout the 19th century with little state oversight. The state share of school funding increased gradually after World War I through the 1980s.

Since then, the proportions have been fairly consistent with state and local governments each contributing 42% with the balance coming from the federal government (National Center for Education Statistics, 2000a). As states paid more of the costs of schooling, they expected local districts to be more accountable for how these funds were spent. This was especially true when increased state funding was mandated by courts to equalize funding in rich and poor school districts.

A third reason was the concern throughout the postwar period about inadequate educational performance. An important milestone was publicity about dramatic declines in Scholastic Achievement Test (SAT) scores between 1963 and 1977. Another was the publication of *A Nation at Risk* (National Commission on Excellence in Education, 1983) and a spate of other commission reports in 1983, all decrying the poor achievement of American schools and offering a variety of remedies. Though some have challenged this overwhelmingly bleak view of the effectiveness of American schools (Berliner & Biddle, 1995), the consensus was that American schools were performing poorly, that something had to be done, and that a great deal of responsibility for leading the improvement effort rested with state government.

Meanwhile, state government began borrowing business ideas about efficient management. The first efforts included planning, programming, budgeting systems, and management by objectives. When these strategies did not work well in schools (Wolcott, 1977), states and business groups refined their approaches. They consistently pushed for specifying goals, measuring outputs to ascertain whether the government was spending money wisely, and holding educators and students accountable for their performance. The first recommendation of a recent report from the National Alliance of Business (2000), for instance, was to "enact a wide range of measures that give schools, educators, and students the strongest possible incentives to perform at high levels" (p. 1) and to link those incentives to "high, clearly defined, and publicly supported academic standards" (p. 1).

Over time, these business-based ideas, often refined by economists and political scientists, became the basis for current thinking about how the state should develop standards of educational performance and use them to design tests to hold schools and districts accountable. In rough outline, a standards-based accountability system was likely to include four elements:

- Content standards that set out the knowledge and skills children are expected to learn.
- Tests or assessments to measure those content standards.
- Student performance standards that define proficient performance in terms of the official assessments.
- Rewards provided to students or schools that meet or exceed the standards and punishments or remediation activities for those that do not.

A strong system would have all four elements. The theory of action behind such a system is that the formal sanctions linked to meeting standards motivate educators and students to learn what is tested. A weak system would certainly not have the last two elements and might not have the first—many states began testing without any guidance from standards. The theory then is that the publication of test scores will motivate improvement by appealing either to professional pride or indirectly to the public which will use political pressure to promote improvement (Firestone, 2003).

Meanwhile, the federal government was influenced by the same ideas about efficient management that were affecting thought at the state level. These ideas progressively influenced the main federal legislation affecting schools, the Elementary and Secondary Education Act (ESEA). Early requirements that ESEA be evaluated influenced the use of testing, stimulating school districts to test more (Linn, 2000). Revisions in 1994 required states to establish content standards, to implement assessments that assessed students against those standards by testing students in mathematics and reading at least once each in Grades 3–8, and to hold schools accountable for the achievement of all students (Goertz, 2002).

Led by governors and state legislators, state governments adopted and elaborated standards and accountability systems in the 1990s. In addition, they defined state standards, developed and refined tests, and considered the alignment between the two. Slowly, they moved toward stronger accountability systems by linking consequences to meeting (or failing to meet) performance standards. At the same time, along with this growing focus on tested outcomes, they de-emphasized, without totally removing, older forms of accountability (Adams & Kirst, 1999).

Every indication is that this movement to increase accountability will continue in the coming years. For instance, the reauthorization of the Elementary and Secondary Education Act of 2001, now referred to as "No Child Left Behind," mandates that states increase their testing requirements substantially beyond what was required by earlier legislation. Specifically, states are required to conduct statewide assessments in reading and mathematics in every grade from third through eighth and assess students in science at least once in the elementary, middle, and high school years. Each child must complete the full assessment—no matrix sampling of items is allowed—and results must be broken out by race, income, and other categories. For schools that do not achieve proficiency or make adequate yearly progress toward proficiency,[1] penalties include a parental option to move their children to a different school. These requirements will increase the sheer quantity of state testing because very few states tested in all the grades specified by ESEA at the time the legislation was passed (Robelen, 2002).

DEFINING STANDARDS IN MATH AND SCIENCE

The movement to increase state testing and accountability comes largely from outside of education. Though it lauds high standards, it says relatively little about what those standards should be. In math and science especially, most of the work in defining standards has been led by subject matter specialists in government, schools, and universities.

This movement is in part a reaction to the remarkable sameness of American teaching in schools over the last hundred or more years. Cuban (1993) described the consistent pattern of teacher-centered teaching in which adults dominate whole-class discussion, make assignments, rely on textbooks, and treat knowledge as relatively fixed, and as something to be given to students. At all grade levels, but most particularly in the elementary grades, there have been some modifications in the way content is taught. For example, our research shows that more teachers are using small-group instruction, at least some of the time. However, the basic pattern of teacher-as-authority telling children is extraordinarily constant.

This pattern limits the intellectual activity of the students and the content that is actually understood. American math teachers, for instance, tend to focus on definitions and procedures with limited exploration of mathematical ideas, discussion involving proof and justification, or use of multiple media to help students see the connections between different representations of an idea (Stigler & Hiebert, 1999). Mrs. Smith's use of M&Ms to analyze data is not typical of classroom activity. Many teachers may do the same or similar activities, but do so in a relatively traditional manner where children have little or no opportunity to explore ideas in a meaningful way. Moreover, Americans break topics into small, discrete units, which may make sense to an experienced mathematician, or educator, but works against helping students to understand the content or see the interconnections among mathematical ideas (W. H. Schmidt, McKnight, & Raizen, 1996). In science, topics are also broken into small units. Elementary students have few opportunities to design their own research problems, use scientific materials to see how ideas work concretely, or conduct any form of investigation—or in short, think like a scientist (Razze, 2001).

Each content area in the American elementary curriculum includes a wide range of topics. In science there is very little focus until high school. In mathematics, many topics are taught superficially one year, repeated the next, and again the following year. Although the intent may be to make the content increasingly complex, this rarely happens. The multitude of topics that are covered results in superficial attention to any one "big idea." Worse yet, the focus is still primarily on numerical operations and procedures in a way that encourages facility with algorithms and operations without deep understanding (W. H. Schmidt et al., 1996). The NCTM suggests that although students should have fluency with algorithms and procedures, they must also learn mathematics with understanding and actively build knowledge from experience and prior knowledge (NCTM, 2000).

Attempts to reform American mathematics and science in the postwar world began with curriculum. This effort started with the introduction of the "new math" and science curricula between the mid-1950s and the mid-1970s. These programs were intended to modernize the content covered, provide a variety of instructional media beyond books, and get children actively involved with scientific experiments. Though several curricula were distributed widely, the consensus is that classroom practice changed very little because of these programs (Welch, 1979).

Another effort began in the 1990s. The National Science Foundation again invested in developing research-based, field-tested materials such as Everyday Mathematics (University of Chicago), Investigations (Technology Education Research Center), Mathematics in Context (University of Wisconsin), and Connected Mathematics (Michigan State University). The intention of these programs was to provide materials that would introduce content in a more unified, coordinated manner. Like the earlier materials, these were very different from traditional conventional book series, and demanded greater content and pedagogic competency from teachers. Like their predecessors, these programs had some success in changing the content taught. In addition, commercial textbooks also began to incorporate these ideas on a broader scale.

In part because of the limitations of curriculum writing as a reform strategy, but also because of a growing interest in defining and mandating educational standards, professional associations began providing statements describing what such standards should include. The NCTM standards, which defined mathematical power as the "abilities to explore, conjecture, and reason logically, as well as the ability to use a variety of mathematical methods effectively to solve nonroutine problems" (NCTM, 1989, p. 5) provided a critical impetus for this effort. This was a much more intellectually challenging conception of knowing mathematics than was used in most American classrooms. It also challenged the notion of mathematical achievement operationalized by the standardized tests that dominated the elementary curriculum, calling instead for more authentic forms of assessment through performance tasks and student portfolios. Similar documents also appeared, setting standards for science (National Research Council, 1996), and the original documents were updated over time (NCTM, 2000).

The existence of broad content standards adopted by professional associations provided useful guidance to several states that were developing their own standards in the 1990s and also created a demand for assessments that would reflect the ideas embedded in the standards rather than older conceptions of learning (Resnick & Resnick, 1992).

EQUITY

Schools have been a major arena in efforts to build a more equitable society. In fact, some have argued that the biggest problem American schools face is not overall poor performance, but inequity as reflected in the disparity of educational outcomes between rich and poor children and minorities and the White majority (Berliner & Biddle, 1995). With the *Brown v. Board of Education* decision in 1957, schools became a central tool for eliminating desegregation. It quickly became clear that desegregating schools did not ensure equal outcomes in terms of achievement, access to higher education, or high-paying jobs.

Equity has always been a central issue in discussions of standards and assessments. From the beginning, advocates of strong standards have argued that if fairly administered, such standards could become a key to equity by ensuring that all children had access to the same curriculum and equally skilled instruction (O'Day & M. S. Smith, 1993). Indeed, the NCTM's first principle in its revised standards is that excellence in mathematics requires high expectations and strong support for all students (NCTM, 2000).

In practice, however, state standards and assessment systems have not always had the intended results. The effects of Texas' program in particular, though debated, have been widely criticized as reducing equity in access to intellectually challenging instruction and in educational achievement. In that state and elsewhere, researchers have argued that the quality of instruction has deteriorated after higher standards, new tests, and strong sanctions were introduced. The result has been that content taught was limited to what was tested, instructional materials began to mimic test items, and teachers spent much of their time on preparing students for the test. Such findings have been used to argue that changing state testing systems and incentives will not promote equity without simultaneously providing adequate resources in schools serving poor and minority children (McNeil, 2000). In some other states, the achievement gap between White and minority students has been reduced, but rarely, if ever, has it been eliminated.

These failures of standards to achieve greater levels of equity may reflect a number of factors. One is the difficulty of getting adequate resources and substantively changing instructional practice in schools serving poor and minority students. Another is popular sentiment whereby most adults see education as a way to help their children get ahead and therefore are loath to invest heavily in policies that would help children from poor urban schools do better in school or the job market (Labaree, 2000).

In some circumstances, higher standards may contribute to educational equity, but only if those standards prompt teachers to consider new content, delivered in new ways. When teachers learn how to give students the opportunity to study important content in classrooms that are conducive to learning and in ways that promote deep understanding, students can display talents and abilities that might have gone unnoticed otherwise. In these contexts, children that have traditionally done poorly can learn powerful ideas (Campbell, 1995; Silver & M. K. Stein, 1996). It remains to be determined however, how much high standards contribute to such instances, how much these instances reflect other interventions in the environment, and whether they can become common responses to high standards.

TEACHING TO THE TEST: THE EVIDENCE TO DATE

We now have about 30 years of experience with state testing programs, but relatively little evidence about how those programs have affected teaching. The first round of research on this issue focused on the multiple-choice, basic-skills tests that were first used by most states and continue to be employed extensively today. The consensus is that those tests have had largely negative effects. Teachers focus the curriculum on the content covered in the tests, which necessarily narrows the range and breadth of topics covered. Often this means that mathematics and reading are taught to the exclusion of other subjects and that the conception of mathematics and reading is quite different from that suggested by recent standards documents. These tests reinforce and intensify conventional teacher-centered, didactic instruction with an emphasis on repetition. Often the teaching materials rely heavily upon test-like items. Teachers and students are said to be demoralized, and observers complain about the "dumbing down" of instruction as teachers lose discretion and the opportunity to use their knowledge and skills (Corbett & Wilson, 1991; McNeil, 2000; M. L. Smith, 1991b). At least one reviewer, however, suggests that these conclusions are not as well established as many observers have argued (Mehrens, 1998).

Though multiple-choice items have dominated state tests, the same forces that promoted interest in new mathematics and science standards also encouraged new approaches to assessment. State educators and assessment experts have experimented with several alternatives. One of the first, and more rare, is the use of portfolios or collections of student work. Often teachers are given instructions as to what kinds of tasks or assignments should be included in students' portfolios. Student work is then collected, and most typically scored by trained raters using a common rubric or set of scoring criteria. Another alternative is the use of performance items. During a testing session, students are given a common prompt and expected to create a response, usually in the form of a written product. This may include an extended answer to a question about mathematics where students show their work and justify their solution strategy or a description of some kind of science task and its results.

These new approaches to assessments have been suggested as more valid measures of the more complex skills represented in the new standards and better models for teachers of effective instructional tasks. However, these approaches raise a number of problems. One is that performance assessment items take more time and cost more to administer than multiple choice or true–false items. Another is their limited reliability or consistency in scoring, whereas another is generating comparable items over time—both of which are especially important in strong accountability systems where sanctions are linked to test scores. Yet another is that such items remain unfamiliar to the public and many educators, a situation that is enough to provoke opposition. Thus, few states have adopted portfolios, and even fewer have kept them. Full-fledged performance tasks have been rarer than a variety of open-ended items that require more writing than multiple-choice items but are still limited in terms of the length and complexity of response required (Editorial Projects in Education, 2001).

Nevertheless, studies of the states that do or have had alternative formats geared to more challenging standards—especially Kentucky, Maryland, and Vermont—suggest some patterns and raise some questions. For instance, it is fairly clear that these assessments influence the content taught, although the consequences of that influence are not as clear. When Kentucky was testing language arts and science in fourth and seventh grade and mathematics and social studies in fifth and sixth grades, teachers spent substantially more time on the subjects tested in their grade level, often skimping on those subjects not tested. This led to inconsistencies in content coverage across teachers, schools, and districts (Stecher & Barron, 1999). On the other hand, in keeping with the new mathematics standards, Vermont's portfolios promoted more emphasis on complex problem solving with corresponding de-emphasis on straight calculation (Stecher & Mitchell, 1995). In Maryland, too, teachers emphasized tested subjects although whether on balance this was positive or negative was not entirely clear (Koretz, Mitchell, Barron, & Keith, 1996).

Similarly, teachers use materials like the assessments for teaching purposes. In Vermont, teachers made students familiar with the scoring rubric that would be used and had children score each other's work (Stecher & Mitchell, 1995). In Maryland, "MSPAP activities," extended mathematics questions like those on the state test, became common (Firestone, Mayrowetz, & Fairman, 1998). The benefits of this development are debatable. To some extent, the use of learning materials modeled on the state test was anticipated by the advocates of alternative assessments who thought that assessments with good instructional models would improve teaching. However, teachers may use a variety of mixes of general teaching and focused test preparation. Though reformers have hoped that general teaching would become more intellectually challenging as a result of these new assessments, it is possible that teaching could remain in the didactic style that has been so common for so long. Stecher and Barron (1999) emphasized the short-term adjustments teachers make that allow them to help students do well on the tests without changing their fundamental approaches to teaching. The literature includes instances of alternative assessments moving teachers closer to more challenging instruction but also instances when assessments have gotten in the way of more demanding teaching (Borko & Elliott, 1999; Firestone et al., 1998).

PRESSURE AND SUPPORT

State tests rarely lead directly to changes in the broad strategies teachers employ. Whatever the tests, teachers adjust the curriculum and use materials like those on the tests. The issue is whether changes in curriculum and materials lead to more challenging instruction in areas that have been neglected in the past or simply to the intensification of didactic instruction in the same old material. Which way teachers go may depend on other factors besides the design of tests that might push instructional changes in one direction or another.

Two factors that can influence teaching practice are pressure and support, both of which can come from a variety of sources. Fullan (1991) suggested that any serious change requires a combination of both, but others question how compatible pressure and support are (Berman, 1986).

Accountability systems are designed to build pressure for change in two ways. Simply making test scores public creates some pressure to work to improve them through a mix of professional pride, concern of top administrators communicated to teachers, and public demand. When state tests are linked to rewards and punishments, the stakes can be much higher. Most of the research on teaching to the test suggests that the pressure of high stakes contributes to the negative effects that have been frequently documented: focusing on short-term strategies for scoring well, focusing the curriculum overly narrowly on tested topics, repetitive drill, and so forth (Borko & Elliott, 1999; M. L. Smith, 1996; Whitford & Jones, 2000). However, there are also instances where teachers ignore state tests because the attention paid to test scores is so low that no one seems to care (Firestone & Mayrowetz, 2000). Thus, the challenge may be getting the stakes high enough to get teachers to pay attention without leading to unintended negative consequences—if possible.

Motivation to comply with central policies is most likely to occur in schools and districts that have their own internal accountability "system" that is aligned with policymakers' external accountability system. An internal accountability system is not so much a formal set of standards, measures, and incentives, as a part of the local culture. In such a culture, staff agree on what is expected of children and will help each other meet those expectations, seek out and acquire appropriate help, work together to improve practice, and formally or informally discipline slackers within their midst. These cultures can be very powerful. Such internal accountability systems have their own history. They precede external accountability mechanisms, and state standards and incentives are only one influence among many to which they might respond. Because internal accountability can be so strong, local leadership is crucial to the alignment of internal and external accountability, when such alignment is possible at all (Abelman & Elmore, 1999; Newmann, King, & Rigdon, 1997).

All the pressure in the world seems unlikely to change practice, however, if educators do not receive adequate support to make the changes demanded by higher standards and more challenging tests. The necessary support includes knowledge of the content being taught, an understanding of the ways in which children learn the content, effective strategies for teaching it, the social supports to help teachers learn new instructional approaches, materials aligned with the new assessments, and the time and other financial resources to support change (Schorr & Lesh, 2003; Spillane & Thompson, 1997). Knowledge and some of the social support can come through professional-development programs that are offered by states, districts, universities, and special programs. We are coming to understand better how effective professional development programs are designed, but they appear still to be rare events (Loucks-Horsley, Hewson, Love, & Stiles, 1998). Cultures stressing strong internal accountability usually provide support to their members, as well as pressure. When local cultures do not stress internal accountability, it is especially important for school and district leadership to develop such cultures (Leithwood, Jantzi, & Steinbach, 1999).

TESTING IN NEW JERSEY

New Jersey provides an interesting setting to study the effects of state testing because it is neither one of the trend-setting states like Maryland or Kentucky, nor among those that stick to more basic skills-oriented or multiple-choice tests. Although it was one of the earlier states to adopt minimum basic-skills testing, it has not stayed with that approach. In 1996, the state began its second round of assessment revision when it adopted its core curriculum content standards in seven areas, including mathematics and science (New Jersey State Department of Education, 1996). These standards are consistent with the most challenging national standards for mathematics and science (NCTM, 2000; National Research Council, 1996). Within 2 years, the state began giving tests in the 4th, 8th, and 11th grades that were aligned with these standards. The fourth-grade Elementary School Performance Assessment (ESPA) was first piloted in mathematics and language arts testing in 1997, and science in 1998. The first operational administration of the mathematics, science, and language arts tests occurred statewide in spring 1999. Students spend about half their time answering multiple-choice items and the other half answering relatively short open-ended items. The test specifications emphasize "knowledge and skills" as well as "conceptual understanding," "procedural knowledge," and "problem-solving skills."

At first blush, the test appears to encourage instructional approaches where students are actively engaged in inquiry, and the test does not appear to stress direct teaching as much as some other states. In interviews associated with the larger study, teachers reported that they prepared students for the math and science ESPA by having students explain their thinking, work with open-ended problems, keep journals, and do less drill on straight computation. Thus, although not among the most performance-oriented state tests, ESPA seemed to influence teachers in a direction very different from that seen in Texas (McNeil, 2000) and some other states.

At the same time, New Jersey has had a weak accountability system. In fact, using data collected before New Jersey adopted its core curriculum content standards in 1996, the state was rated in the bottom quartile for activism in adopting standards policies (Swanson & Stevenson, 2002). The absence of strong accountability has been especially apparent with regard to the fourth-grade test. Test scores are released annually and published in the newspapers. However, these scores have had no bearing on student promotion.[2] There is little if any relationship to remuneration for teachers or administrators. Although the state has a law allowing for district takeover and has already taken over three districts, criticism of that program suggests that it would be unlikely to take over any more districts. Moreover, there is no provision for taking over individual schools. Schools that do not have the requisite number of students achieving proficiency on the state test would, however, be subject to more intensive monitoring and required to fill out more paperwork by the state.

New Jersey has a rather underdeveloped system for addressing other elements that might constitute a systemic strategy for shaping instruction. For instance, unlike California and Texas, the state has no centralized textbook or materials approval system. Nor does it have an elaborate system for offering professional development to support the new standards and assessments. The state recently adopted a requirement that teachers receive 100 hours of professional development every 5 years, but the range of activities that count as professional development is quite broad, sanctions for not doing the professional development are unclear, and even the means of monitoring compliance are quite vague. Nor does the state have the kind of professional-development networks that a few other states have had at various times (Pennell & Firestone, 1997).

On the other hand, as a result of ongoing school finance litigation, New Jersey has taken special steps to address inequities in its educational system (*Abbott v. Burke*). A 1997 decision (*Abbott IV*) required the state to immediately provide funding for 30 urban school districts[3] that would match the per pupil expenditure in the state's wealthiest districts, substantially increasing the operating budgets of those urban districts. The next year, in *Abbott V*, the court called for the implementation of whole-school reform (WSR) programs in all the schools in those urban districts. The idea of comprehensive or whole-school reform programs had grown out of dissatisfaction with federal Title I legislation, which, by targeting funding on a limited number of low-achieving children in schools serving poverty-ridden areas, tended to fragment educational programs. Evaluations of Title I suggested that it did not do enough to reduce the achievement gap between majority and minority children. At about the time, the U.S. Congress was passing legislation to allow Title I schools serving large numbers of poor children to adopt "comprehensive school reform" programs (Erlichson & Goertz, 2001). WSR programs generally were supposed to provide coherent ways for urban schools to increase their focus on raising achievement in literacy and mathematics. Often, they did so by providing intensive professional development around those subject areas. However, the extent to which programs focused on professional development in specific content areas or—for that matter—the extent to which that professional development was aligned with state standards varied considerably. In some cases, the fit was quite good, whereas in others, the programs had other implicit theories about the barriers to achievement in schools serving poor children and took time away from improving instruction in content areas.

This state policy focus on poor, urban schools reflects a paradox in New Jersey: It has a history of funding education very well in the aggregate but very inequitably. A recent report on state education ranks New Jersey in the top 10 for adequacy of resources for education (highest state expenditure per pupil), but in the bottom 10 in equity of resource distribution in spite of recent court decisions intended to equalize expenditures between the state's wealthiest districts and its poorest cities (Editorial Projects in Education, 2001). Nationally, about 19% of children ages 5–17 live in poverty, whereas in New Jersey, the poverty rate is about 14% (National Center for Education Statistics, 1998). Approximately 38% of the elementary and secondary students in New Jersey are members of minority populations, and those students comprise 78% of all students enrolled in urban schools (National Center for Education Statistics, 2000b).

STUDY DATA

This study began with the intention to learn how fourth-grade teachers were changing their instructional practice in mathematics and science as the ESPA was being implemented. We also wanted to understand what factors influenced teachers to maintain or change their practice. Finally, we recognized a major dilemma for those studying changes in teaching. Often the changes are subtle so self-reports are not always reliable. Even if teachers do not give socially acceptable responses, they may not understand some of the terminology used to describe new practices, so their reports may not be accurate. In addition, even when teachers use a common vocabulary, one may not necessarily conclude that they have all attached the same meaning to it. Thus, it is important to get into classrooms and observe teaching directly. Yet, it is impossible to observe enough classrooms to generalize to all of New Jersey and get a good understanding of how the new test is affecting practice overall. A large enough sample almost requires surveying teachers. Moreover, neither teacher surveys nor classroom observations throw light on how schools and districts interpret state policies, support teacher change, or increase the stakes they face.

Over time, we collected four kinds of data. First, we surveyed teachers by telephone. For 3 years, beginning in the spring of 1999, we interviewed or observed a sample of fourth-grade teachers. We asked about their responses to the ESPA in mathematics and science as well about changes in curriculum, instructional practices, and various sources of pressure and support. These samples are highly representative with regard to geographic and district wealth and demographics (see Appendix A).

We also observed some teachers every year (information about sampling of teachers for observation is described in Appendix A). Typically, we observed teachers in two math classes and one science class. We also spoke to them at length about how they felt the observed lessons had gone and why they taught the way they did. At the same time, we asked them for their opinions about ESPA and to describe the pressure and support they received in their own schools and districts.

To learn more about the context in which teachers worked we surveyed the principals of the teachers included in the survey study. These telephone surveys had a mix of open-ended and fixed-choice responses about their beliefs about New Jersey's standards and assessments, their supervisory practices, and school and district policies.

Finally, we conducted case studies of six districts. These districts were working with New Jersey's State Systemic Initiative, a National Science Foundation–supported program to improve the quality of mathematics and science teaching in the state. One way to do so was to broker technical assistance to school districts through regional centers in state colleges, universities, and community colleges. The research team asked the three centers that worked with elementary pupils to identify districts that were among their more active ones. Working with these centers, we identified districts that varied in their wealth (including two Abbott districts—urban districts designated by the state supreme court as so impoverished that they needed special financial support and programs to help their large populations of poor and minority students achieve at levels more comparable to the rest of the state), location, and size. We visited each district during the second and third year of the project; interviewed the superintendent, mathematics, science, and testing specialists; collected information on curriculum; and in the year 2000–2001, collected records data on the number, content, and attendance of professional-development activities offered to elementary teachers in mathematics and science.

In the remainder of the book, we share what we learned.

ENDNOTES

1. These terms are not clearly defined in the legislation and are the subject of a great deal of debate as regulations are being formulated.

2. Students did have to pass the previous 11th grade to graduate from high school. This test has been phased out and replaced by a new test aligned to New Jersey's content standards.

3. The court specified 28 districts, and the legislature extended coverage to two more districts.

2

Teaching Mathematics and Science

Roberta Y. Schorr
Sylvia Bulgar
Janet Stickle Razze
Lora F. Monfils
William A. Firestone

In this chapter we explore the impact of testing on teachers' actual instructional practices and the content that they report they are teaching in math and science classes. This analysis is done in the context of state and national reform efforts, which provides a backdrop for considering teaching, learning, and testing.

Recent state and national standards documents (AAAS Project 2061, 1993; National Council of Teachers of Mathematics [NCTM], 1989, 2000; National Research Council [NRC], 1996; Rosenstein, Caldwell, & Crown, 1997) set forth a vision of science and mathematics instruction in which the development of conceptual understanding in students is of paramount importance. These documents, combined with current findings from the mathematics and science education research literature, state that learning involves the active participation of students; that is, students are not simply passive recipients of knowledge (Cobb, Wood, & Yackel, 1990; Davis, 1984; Schorr, 2000; Schorr & Koellner-Clark, 2003; Schorr & Lesh, 2003; Schorr, Maher, & Davis, 1997). Active participation occurs when students conduct thoughtful investigations with their peers using appropriate materials in a supportive environment (Bulgar, Schorr, & Maher, 2002; Maher, Martino, & Davis, 1994; NCTM, 2000; Schorr, 2000). In such an environment, students experience mathematics and science as processes that demand thought, creativity, and understanding (Davis, 1984; Schorr &

Koellner-Clark,2003). This is in sharp contrast to having students participate only in activities that involve seat work on algorithms or procedures
with which they may or may not already be familiar, and whose meanings
they do not know and may never learn (Carpenter & Lehrer, 1999; Schorr et
al., 1997). The type of environment described earlier, in which students are
actively involved in solving problems, if often referred to as being more "student centered" or "standards based" (NCTM, 2000; Rosenstein et al.,
1997). In such classrooms, teachers listen closely to the explanations of
their students, probe them for justifications, encourage them to share their
solutions with their peers, and provide opportunities for students to work in-
dividually and collaboratively to refine, revise, test, and extend their solutions (Davis & Maher, 1997; Maher, 1998; Schorr, 2000; Schorr & Lesh,
2003; Shafer & Romberg, 1999).

Few would argue that all instructional practices are enhanced when
teachers have a high degree of content and pedagogical competence. Instructional approaches that emphasize understanding, however, make additional demands on teachers for a deep sensitivity toward students' thinking
and reasoning, and the ability to build instruction based on that (Cobb,
Wood, Yackel, & McNeal, 1993; Davis & Maher, 1997; Fennema, Sowder,
& Carpenter, 1999; Maher, 1998; NCTM, 2000; Schorr, 2000; Schorr &
Lesh, 2003; Sowder & Phillip, 1999). To help teachers acquire the knowledge needed to teach in more student-centered ways, many different professional-development projects and policy initiatives have been implemented.
However, many researchers report that the type of instructional environment described previously is still relatively rare (Schorr & Firestone, 2001;
Spillane & Zeulli, 1999; Stigler & Hiebert, 1999). Furthermore, the very
meaning and manifestation of teaching in a "standards-based" or "student-
centered" manner, as interpreted by many teachers, teacher educators, and
researchers, is not always consistent in terms of both intent and implementation in classrooms.

For instance, one teacher educator, who herself was involved in a substantial amount of professional development, said that she could identify a standards-based classroom by noting several things. The first involved the
physical appearance of the room. The state standards would be posted on the
bulletin boards; student work would be displayed; pictures of mathematicians
and scientists would be hanging on the walls; and, key words and formulas in
math and science would be posted. Second, students would use manipulatives
and work in small groups. Finally, she noted that the classroom teacher would
be "open" or willing to try new methods. Absent in her remarks was any mention of the deeper aspects of standards-based instructional practice focusing
on increased conceptual understanding for students.

The remarks of this teacher educator refer more to strategies, techniques,
or more surface level characteristics that tend to be associated with reform
(such as having children work in small groups, using hands-on materials,

solving "open-ended" problems) rather than with fundamental changes in practice. Simon and Tzur (1999) and Simon, Tzur, Heinz, Kinzel, and Schwan-Smith (2000) suggested that teachers often have a limited understanding of what the changes advocated by mathematics education researchers and the standards really mean. They say that many teachers interpret the changes that are needed as discouraging telling and showing, using manipulatives, or having students work in small groups, for example. Though all of these strategies may well contribute to a better teaching environment, taken alone, or even in combination, such strategies may not necessarily lead to greater student learning (Boaler, 2002; Schorr, 2002; Schorr & Firestone, 2001; Schorr & Koellner-Clark, 2003; Simon & Tzur, 1999; Spillane & Zeulli, 1999). These strategies may represent a step in the right direction, but the authors of the *Principles and Standards for School Mathematics* caution that many of the pedagogical ideas from the NCTM Standards—such as the emphasis on discourse, worthwhile mathematical tasks, or learning through problem solving—have been enacted without deeper changes in actual classroom practices (NCTM, 2000).

Goldsmith and Shifter (1993) pointed out that developing a better form of teaching requires more than the acquisition of some new instructional techniques or strategies. It demands a reconceptualization of the entire process of teaching and learning, and this entails substantive change in teachers' knowledge and beliefs about instruction and content (Schorr, 2002; Schorr & Lesh, 2003; Simon et al., 2000; Simon & Tzur, 1999). But, teaching practices are not easily modified or revised. Stigler and Hiebert (1999) argued that teaching is a cultural activity, and cultural activities "evolve over long periods of time in ways that are consistent with the stable web of beliefs and assumptions that are part of the culture ... and rest on a relatively small and tacit set of core beliefs about the nature of the subject, about how students learn, and about the role that a teacher should play in the classroom" (p. 87). Given the long history of relatively stable instructional practices in this country (cf. Cuban, 1993), it is not surprising that the changes that have been reported are more akin to the adoption of new strategies or techniques rather than fundamental shifts in practices.

In addition to setting forth a vision emphasizing understanding and inquiry-based learning, state and national standards (AAAS Project 2061, 1993; NCTM, 1989, 2000; NRC, 1996; Rosenstein et al., 1997) also emphasize new content (e.g., discrete mathematics). Some proponents of testing consider tests to be the best hope for using the authority of the state to improve teaching and learning. They believe that standards, and associated standards-based tests, used effectively, can steer teachers and students to content areas that are important for modern society but have received inadequate attention in the past (NCTM, 2000). Others at least hope that tests may prompt teachers to consider more challenging content and activities that provide an opportunity for students to develop an understanding of mathematical and scientific concepts and the connections between them (Resnick & Resnick, 1992). Some opponents believe the opposite. They claim that testing will inevitably "dumb-down" teaching, encourage the measurement of less relevant skills, and reinforce the educational status quo (McNeil, 2000).

New Jersey's Elementary School Performance Assessment (ESPA) is intended to be aligned with the state's Core Curriculum Content Standards, which are closely aligned with national standards. These standards emphasize modernizing the content taught and using instructional methods that require student inquiry, leading to a deeper understanding of content with no loss of facility in executing basic mathematical operations. The test itself is designed so that students would spend about half their time answering multiple-choice items and the other half answering short, constructed response items. The test specifications placed items in a grid where one dimension was labeled "knowledge and skills" with categories for "conceptual understanding," "procedural knowledge," and "problem-solving skills." The following two items, though not on the actual test, are considered to be representative of the short, constructed response items that do appear on the test. These items were taken directly from the state Web site.

Example 1. Veronica is making a rectangular garden. She plans to put a fence around the garden using 28 feet of fencing, and she wants the garden to be 8 feet long. How wide will Veronica's garden be? Show how you got your answer. If Veronica is going to put fence posts two feet apart around the outside of the garden, how many fence posts will she need? Show all of your work and explain your answer.

Example 2. On Friday, your class will have a party after lunch. Each of the 30 students in your class has chosen one party activity. Here are the results: 1/2 of the class chose outdoor relay races. 1/3 of the class chose indoor games. The rest of the class chose to watch a movie. How many students chose to watch a movie? Show all of your work and explain your answer.

The change in New Jersey's standards and tests have raised two questions, which are addressed in this chapter. First, are teachers using more challenging instructional approaches, and second, are teachers teaching different content?

The research reported in this chapter documents both teachers' actual practices and the content that they report they are teaching, in an effort to better understand what teachers are actually doing in math and science class. This chapter focuses on the sample of teachers observed and interviewed as part of the larger study. The interview and survey data suggest that the teachers believe that they are incorporating standards-based approaches into the teaching of science and mathematics. Indeed, observations suggest that they are doing what they say they are doing. They *are* using more manipulatives, open-ended problems, and group work. However, their overall approach to teaching and learning still appears to reflect the view that Cuban (1993) referred to as teacher centered or a "hybrid" of teacher centered and student centered. Furthermore, their incorporation of new content, particularly content emphasized in the standards, has not changed much.

In the sections that follow, we report on the teaching practices of the teachers observed, and on the changes that teachers reported in the content that they taught.

METHODS AND PROCEDURES

Observations

A total of 63 teachers were observed teaching mathematics. Fifty-eight of the 63 teachers were observed for two math lessons and 5 teachers were observed once for a total of 121 classroom observations. In science, 5 teachers were observed twice whereas 49 teachers were observed once. These observations were intended to provide a window or picture in time of their actual practices. The classroom researcher kept a running record of the events in the classroom, focusing on the activities of the teacher as well as capturing the activities of students. The field notes recorded all problem activities and explorations, the materials used, the questions that were posed, the responses that were given—whether by students or teachers—the overall atmosphere of the classroom environment, and any other aspects of the class that the researchers were able to gather. (For further information on sample selection, see Appendix A.) All of the teachers in the second year's sample (28 teachers) were observed twice in mathematics. No additional observations were made in science.

Interviews

At the conclusion of each lesson, all of the teachers were asked to respond to a series of open-ended questions about the observed lesson. These included:

- What were you trying to accomplish for today's lesson?
- What concept or ideas were you focusing on? What, if anything, would you change about today's lesson, and why?
- Why did you do this, or how did you feel about that (referring to a particular instance or to a particular event or activity).

Teachers were also asked how state testing affected their teaching. Sample questions included:

- What kinds of things do you generally do to help your students get ready for the Elementary School Performance Assessment (ESPA)?
- Considering either the ESPA or the Content Standards, how, if at all, has that affected the topics you teach?
- How have you changed the teaching strategies you use in response to the ESPA and/or the Content Standards?

(For the complete interview guide, see Appendix D.)

Coding

While observations were under way, researchers conducted detailed reports of records of classroom observations, and adapted several preexisting coding schemes to be used for coding the classroom data. These were based on the works of Stein, Smith, Henningsen, and Silver (2000); Stein and Smith (1998); Stigler and Hiebert (1997, 1999); Davis, Wagner, and Shafer (1997); Hiebert and Wearne (1993); and Stein and Smith (1998). These codes were selected because they reflected ideas about effective mathematics instruction as indicated in national and state standards (they were later modified to accommodate the science observations). They included attention to the mathematical and/or science discourse that emerged, the opportunity for conceptual understanding to take place, the nature of student conjectures, the opportunities students had to share ideas and defend and justify solutions, and so on. They were also chosen because it was felt that they would supply information on the nature and implementation of teaching strategies most generally associated with the Standards (i.e., hands-on manipulatives, small-group instruction, use of different types of problems and activities, questioning strategies, classroom discourse, etc.). Collectively, they provided a "window" into the classroom instructional environment.

A preliminary coding scheme was tried out on six observations before being agreed upon by the researchers. A sheet of code definitions was created and a training session was held for coders involved in the activity. Ultimately, a coding instrument was developed that incorporated the dimensions in Appendix F. This was accompanied by a detailed list of descriptors of each coding category.

Six members of the research team who collectively represent a wealth of educational experience, including elementary and mathematics classroom teaching, supervision, teacher training, and mathematics education research, conducted coding of the classroom observations in mathematics. Two individuals independently coded each observation—at least one coder was an experienced mathematics education researcher. The other coder also had extensive experience in elementary education. After independent coding, raters sought to reconcile their differences. When that was not possible, another mathematics education researcher discussed differences with the raters and helped them to reach agreement. Appendix F provides a summary of all codes, along with descriptors that identify each option. Similarly, in science two individuals independently coded each observation and at least one coder was an experienced science educator.

Interviews from 58 of the 63 first-year teachers and all 28 of the second-year teachers were available for analysis in mathematics, and interviews for all teachers were available for science.

Surveys

Every year, the survey included questions asking teachers how many lessons they devoted to 17 specific topics in mathematics and 17 in science (see Appendix B). Data from the longitudinal sample were used to explore changes in the amount of time devoted to specific topics from year to year (see Appendix B, Sections D-2 and D-3).

INSTRUCTION

Reported Practices

In this section, we describe what teachers said they were doing and compare it to observed practice. We begin by noting that many teachers reported that they were now implementing more inquiry-oriented instructional practices. One teacher explained, "It's become my philosophy to teach them the concepts before, just, you know, ramming these rote facts down their throats." In the interviews, teachers mentioned four general changes they were making: having students explain their own thought processes; using manipulatives; problem solving; and, including students' writing in activities. Many teachers (43% in the initial set of data) talked about trying to get students to explain their thinking in more detail. According to one teacher, "[the part] that I guess I really didn't do a lot of before is really to get the students to start to learn how to explain their thinking, to explain what they were doing. Sometimes they do it in writing; sometimes they do it to a partner; sometimes they do it to me." One strategy designed to encourage student explanation was the use of more open-ended questions on tests and in class, and was mentioned by 33% of the teachers in this data set. Fourteen percent of these teachers talked about using more "how" and "why" questions in their whole-group teaching. One described this as working on "critical thinking skills" instead of "feeding them the answer." Eight also talked about using small-group instruction so students would explain their work to each other.

Another theme that emerged involved using manipulatives, and was mentioned by 45% of these teachers. The ESPA has questions that involve at least written or pictorial descriptions of manipulatives. Many teachers felt that students who are more familiar with some of the manipulatives referred to on the test could better respond to the questions.

A third theme was a greater emphasis on problem solving (mentioned by 38% of this set of teachers), though the actual meaning of "problem solving" was not always clear. One teacher noted, "We do a lot of work with problem-solving skills, just the basic skills of how you read a problem, how do you find the question, how do you find the information that you need, how do you check to see whether your solution is logical and can solve it [sic] a couple of different ways."

Finally, 40% of these teachers said that they emphasize writing to prepare their students for the ESPA. One teacher said that she now had her students "write all the time for all subjects." Some teachers noted that they have begun to encourage students to document their thinking processes in mathematics on a regular basis. In fact several teachers said they now have students keep journals in math as well as other subjects.

Observed Practice

The observations confirm that teachers are making some changes. Manipulatives were used in about 63% of all observed mathematics lessons. Similarly, students worked in groups for at least a portion of the time, in almost 64% of all observed mathematics lessons. Teachers made an effort to connect the lessons to the students' real-life experiences in well more than half of all observed mathematics classrooms.

The adoption of specific strategies was not necessarily accompanied by a change in overall approach to teaching, however. For example, though manipulatives were used extensively, they were used in a nonalgorithmic manner in only about 20% of all observed mathematics lessons. Algorithmic, in this case, essentially means that the manipulatives were used in ways that were prescribed by the teacher without allowing the students to have the opportunity to consider the relationship between the problem and the materials as they developed their own personally relevant solutions. In fact, in almost two thirds of the lessons where manipulatives were used, they were used in a very procedural manner, where the teacher generally told the students exactly what to do with the materials, and the students did it as best they could. Other times, teachers used manipulatives to demonstrate a particular procedure to the class. In many lessons, though teachers had students physically touch concrete manipulatives, there was little or no opportunity for the students to develop their own solutions to the problem. Consequently, students often did not see the relationship between the problem activity and the concrete (or alternative such as written, symbolic, pictorial, etc.) representations.

As with mathematics, it has been commonly accepted as part of reform practice that textbooks should not be the only source for elementary science instruction (Lazarowitz & Tamir, cited in Razze, 2001; Tobin, Tippins, & Gallard, 1994). It is felt that elementary science should have a concrete basis that is relevant to the student (Hammrich, cited in Razze, 2001), and science learning can be enhanced by the appropriate use of materials, laboratory equipment, videotapes, computer software, and other printed materials such as reference books and trade books (Fallon, cited in Razze, 2001). As with mathematics, many of the teachers reported in their interviews that they felt that they were incorporating reform practices when they had students use concrete objects, or work with each other in a small-group setting.

Our observations and interviews suggest that both the mathematics and science teachers did not notice whether or not the students were connecting the concrete or hands-on experiences to the problem situation or symbolic representations that were used. The fact that the students had used concrete materials or equipment appeared to be what mattered most, not how they were used, nor the level of understanding that was elicited.

As an example, in one classroom, the teacher supplied the students with pretzels to be used as concrete manipulatives in order to make parallel lines. She demonstrated exactly how she wanted the students to position the pretzels. Indeed, her demonstration left little to the imagination. All the students had to do was to take the pretzels and form the shapes that she described and demonstrated. In this example, the students had a concrete material (the pretzels), but they were only allowed to do what the teacher wanted them to do. In essence, their role was simply to follow her instructions.

This example represents a common thread: The teacher gave the children a physical material, but also told the children exactly what to do with it, and how to use it. Other examples indicate that even when children were given more freedom, the teacher often stopped them without ever asking what they had built, how it connected to the problem or some other representation, or how it compared to what others had built.

We found that in science classrooms, materials were often used for simple demonstration. In one lesson that dealt with the rotation and revolution of the earth, moon, and sun, the teacher used the text and corresponding published worksheets throughout the lesson. The teacher alone handled the materials, as she demonstrated concepts from the readings using a globe and balls. The only actual student involvement consisted of a student who was chosen to represent a stationary body as the teacher moved around him. Her stated purpose was to demonstrate the definitions of the vocabulary terms, *rotation* and *revolution*. This particular incident represented a very small portion of the lesson. The balance consisted of students reading from the textbook. The worksheet that the textbook manufacturer created to correlate with this lesson was copied onto an overhead transparency and all students were expected to replicate the answers that the teacher wrote and projected. The teacher highlighted the importance of spelling and understanding the definitions of vocabulary words, rather than emphasizing rich concepts.

Students were rarely provided with opportunities to use equipment and materials for experimentation testing and/or application. In the few lessons where this occurred (only 10% of the observed science lessons), students had the chance to find different ways to solve problems and also discovered different solutions.

As previously mentioned, we were also interested in the extent to which teachers used group work as part of their classroom instruction. We found that some of the teachers who used group work did so in ways that encouraged the students to actually work together to solve problems. Others merely had students sitting near each other and never actually interacting with each other. Some teachers used the term *group work* to denote a form of student-to-student tutoring. For example, one teacher noted during her interview that she "like[s] everything as a group." As an example, she noted that she likes to have children work on problems "And then when they're done, if they're confident, they go around and help the other children." In mathematics classes, group work occurred in 64% of all observed classes. However, when working together in groups, students only discussed alternative strategies with their peers in about 11% of the observations. In science classes we observed little or no actual student collaboration taking place in 32% of all classes, occasional or modest collaboration occurring in 32% of the classes, and extensive collaboration in 36% of all observed science classes.

Beyond looking at specific practices and materials, we also examined the mathematical tasks that students were asked to perform. Romberg and Kaput (1999) emphasized the role that tasks play in effective instruction. They outlined five key questions to consider in the selection of tasks: Do the tasks lead anywhere; do the tasks lead to model building; do the tasks lead to inquiry and justification; do the tasks involve flexible use of technology (technology includes the use of concrete materials, calculators, and other types of materials); and are the tasks relevant to students? They stated, "Although students cannot be expected to reinvent all mathematics, they should be expected to invent routines, formulas, or expressions as a consequence of their investigations" (p. 11). With this in mind, we now share our results relating to the mathematical tasks that were observed.

In almost all cases, the tasks that we observed violated several if not all of the criteria listed by Romberg and Kaput (1999). Students had few opportunities to engage in the type of inquiry that would potentially enhance deep conceptual understanding. One code categorized tasks as memorization only, doing procedures where the focus was on producing correct answers rather than developing mathematical understanding, doing procedures to develop a deeper understanding of mathematical concepts or ideas, or doing a mathematical task that requires complex and nonalgorithmic thinking (Stein & Smith, 1998). An example of nonalgorithmic thinking can occur when students are building a representation of the problem situation that extends beyond the execution of rules or procedures, and involves an understanding of the mathematical and/or scientific principles or concepts. Seventy-seven percent of all tasks fell into the first two categories (memorization or doing procedures in an algorithmic manner). Only 4% of all observed mathematics lessons involved situations where students were required to do nonalgorithmic thinking.

We also examined whether the mathematical tasks, as implemented, involved practice or nonpractice activities. With practice tasks, the teacher demonstrates or develops a procedure, such as long division, and then assigns a number of similar problems on which students are to repeat the same procedure (Stigler & Hiebert, 1999). In a nonpractice task, the student may be required to invent a new solution method, analyze a mathematical situation, or generate a proof. We found that practice tasks predominated, constituting almost 80% of the observed mathematics lessons.

We also examined classroom discourse and teacher questioning. Cobb, Boufi, McClain, and Whitenack (1997) said that reflective discourse can help students build mathematical ideas and develop a general orientation to mathematical activity. It is therefore important for teachers to know how to deal effectively with the discourse that is occurring. We found that in the mathematics classrooms we observed, classroom discourse rarely focused on substantive conversations between and among students. Though many teachers said they wanted students to explain their reasoning and find and understand multiple strategies for solving problems, such activity rarely took place. One code documented whether or not the teacher encouraged students to reflect on the reasonableness of their responses. In almost 78% of all mathematics observations, the teacher rarely asked students whether their answers were reasonable. If a student gave an incorrect response, another student provided, or was asked to provide, a correct answer, but there was little discussion of an appropriate strategy to solve the problem. Additionally, in 16% of all mathematics observations, the teacher may have asked students if they checked whether their answers were reasonable, but did not promote discussion that emphasized conceptual understanding.

In nearly half of the science lessons observed (47%), students talked directly to the teacher and not to each other. Indeed, the teacher controlled all aspects of the classroom discourse. In many instances, students were not given the opportunity to reflect on a question long enough to come up with an answer. For example, in the following excerpt, the teacher asked the students one question followed immediately by another. This type of rapid-fire questioning directed students to the answer the teacher wanted but did not give the students the opportunity to think about or expand upon any particular answer (Razze, 2001):

T: What were some things you could tell about the Ping-Pong
      ball or the checkers by looking at them?
S: The Play-Dough was lumpy.
S: The checker had a crown on it.
T: What did you know about the checker by feeling it?
S: It was smooth.
S: It was smooth also.
T: Did you notice anything about the checker? Was it heavy?
S: It was light.
T: What did you notice about the Play-Dough?
S: It was mushy.
T: That's right. It was soft and you could squeeze it. There's a
      word for that. It was pliable.
S: It was moist.
T: Very good word. You could tell that by feeling it.
S: It was heavy.
T: Heavier than the checker?
S: Yes.
T: What about the chalk?
S: It was hard.
T: Think about the checker, the chalk, and the Play-Dough.
      Which one was the heaviest? You're on the ball. That matter is
      anything that has mass and takes up space. Another way to say
      that is that matter is anything that has mass and has volume.

In this instance, the children did not have the opportunity to carefully
consider the relationships between the types of substances, and students
were rarely asked to explain how they got their answers, or how they developed their particular strategies.

In our analysis we were also very interested in how and when students
shared their solutions. Davis and Maher (1997) stressed that it is important
for teachers to understand the representations that students construct and
to channel the discourse so that they can help students to build upon these
ideas. They imply that it is very important for students to have the opportunity to justify and explain their solutions. Cobb, Wood, Yackel, and McNeal
(1993) also noted the importance of justification and explanation in helping
students to deepen their understanding of a concept. In our observations,
we found that when students *had* opportunities to talk about their answers
or strategies, they typically stated answers, without elaborating on their solutions. When a student was asked to share his solution, often he would respond with a numerical answer such as "5" or a procedure such as "you
should add." Students were rarely asked to explain how they got their answer, or how they developed their particular strategy. In fact, students only
explained their responses or solution strategies in a way that went beyond

the execution of procedures in 6% of the observed lessons. Sometimes teachers would ask for an explanation about the use of a particular operation, but would not encourage students to expand upon their answers, or move beyond simplistic responses.

Similarly, students did not have many opportunities to share their thinking in science classes. In fact, more than half of the teachers taught their lessons (54%) in ways that appeared to send the message that science is primarily about following correct procedures. Generally speaking students were allowed to explore only one solution or method. Students were usually expected to use a predetermined procedure and follow directions explicitly. In most cases, teachers did not connect the activity to real-world situations or to students' experiences and did not make connections among other related science topics. The overwhelming emphasis was on having all students arrive at the same answers and the same results. An example can be found in a lesson in which students were going to make electromagnets. The requisite materials were prepared in advance and left in each work area. Students were directed to wrap a wire exactly 20 times around a rivet. The teacher demonstrated exactly where to start and finish. All students were expected to be working on the same step at the same time. They were asked to repeat the process with 40 winds and then 30 winds. The teacher asked the students to predict the number of washers that could be picked up by the rivet, but this was done on the board and all students were directed to write down the prediction. All switches on the circuit were turned on and off at the same time. Students were not allowed to turn on the circuit at any other time. The teacher highlighted careful note taking and organization in writing logs at the conclusion of the activity.

Our coding also focused on the use of teacher questioning. Many studies have emphasized the importance of teacher questioning in helping children advance their mathematical thinking (cf. Bulgar, 2002; Klinzing, Klinzing-Eurich, & Teicher, 1985; Martino & Maher, 1999; Pirie & Kieren, 1994; Sullivan & Clarke, 1992). These studies underscore the notion that asking more "open-ended questions aimed at conceptual knowledge and problem-solving strategies can contribute to the construction of more sophisticated mathematical knowledge by students" (Martino & Maher, 1999, p. 55).

Teacher questions were coded according to whether they required a student to recite previously learned facts or recall procedures (recall questions), create a story to match a number sentence or create a problem to fit given constraints (generate questions), describe a strategy or describe an alternative strategy (describe questions), and explain why a procedure is chosen or consider the nature of a problem or solution strategy (examine questions). In mathematics, only 12% of all teacher questions fell into the last category. In many cases, even teachers who asked examine and describe types of questions did not give students enough time to answer. Often, the teacher would follow up with a recall question or answer the question him or herself.

As an example, in one classroom, the students were investigating the probability of landing on a particular color on a spinner. The teacher allowed the students to explore the number of times they landed on each of the different colors. However, instead of allowing the students to discuss what had happened, the teacher simply stated the conclusion that she wanted them to reach:

> T: I don't think that we want to play with that spinner. Right?
> Class: No.
> T: Of course, because many times you will finish in blue. Right?

On the bright side, some teachers did ask questions that resulted in classroom discussion. In the following excerpt (relating to fractions), one student made a conjecture about the similarity between her own solution and that of another student.

> T: What made you decide to make 8 groups?
> Girl 1:   I thought that if we were saying 1/8, there should be 8 groups.
> T: Did anybody else do it another way?
> Girl 2:   I knew that 1/8 of 24 is 3 so I set up 3 groups and divided all the M&Ms and checked to see if there really were 8 in each group.
> T: That's a good way. Is there somebody with another way?
> Girl 3:   I know that a lot of numbers go into 24. So I set up 8 groups and I tried 2 in each group. That didn't work because I still had some left. So I kept trying until I used up all of the M&Ms.

In the preceding excerpt, the teacher's questioning and reiteration helps students to express their ideas to the class. In addition, by encouraging alternate strategies, the teacher has shown students that their ideas are valued.

We also found that several teachers had misconceptions about the mathematics they taught. At times, teachers misinterpreted or misunderstood definitions. For example, one teacher appears to have confused the term *mixed number* with *improper fraction:*

> Student: Aren't there some times when the higher number's on top?
> T: Right, and we talked about that, a mixed number.

In another instance, the teacher implies that all hexagons are regular hexagons when she discusses the perimeter of a hexagon. She erroneously told that students that in order to calculate the perimeter of any hexagon, they need only find one side and multiply that by six:

> T: So what we really need to do is measure one [side] and mul-
>   tiply by 6. What would we have to do for a square though?
>   We measure one [side] and multiply by what?

In yet another case a teacher repeatedly referred to a sector of a circle as triangle:

> T: Think this through, how many green triangles do you think it
>   would take to cover that entire circle?

She then proceeded to repeat the same mistake with a slightly different shape triangle.

> T: All right, here's our red triangles. Think, how many reds
>   would it take to cover that circle?

Examples of misinformation or incorrect information given to students varied across science topics. For example, one teacher reversed the root with the plant as the first part to germinate out of a seed. Another teacher reversed the meaning of veins and arteries. Our observations in science also show that many teachers also missed opportunities to share important information with students. One teacher never linked an in-crease in breathing rate to an increase in physical activity. Another teacher did not take the time to fully explain that static electricity does not flow and is essentially at rest, leading students to believe it flowed like current electricity.

CONTENT COVERED

The surveys indicate that the changes in content covered have been mod-est, at best. The teachers who participated in all 3 years of the survey re-ported that they did change the amount of time they spent on most topics. Teachers were asked to report how many lessons they devoted to 17 topics. In math there were reported changes in four areas. The first two were re-lated to teaching whole-number operations including addition, subtrac-tion, multiplication, and division (see Fig. 2.1). Time spent on these topics declined across the 3 years. Interviews confirmed that teachers reduced the amount of time spent on basic operations. Unfortunately, we do not see a comparable increase in some of the areas suggested by national standards, including geometry, analyzing data, and so on. There was an increase in the use of open sentences, which in some instances can be related to early alge-

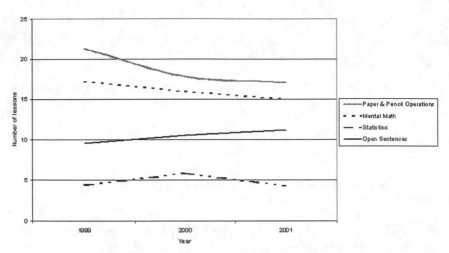

FIG. 2.1.   Math content—longitudinal sample: change in number of lessons spent on each topic in mathematics.

braic reasoning. Time spent on statistics increased between 1999 and 2000 but then declined.

In science, we see a 3-year decline in five topics with most of the decline between 1999 and 2000 (see Fig. 2.2). This is somewhat misleading. Our interviews suggest that teachers increased the amount of science they taught in preparation for the new tests that started in 1999. However, when the percentage of students passing the science tests was quite high (higher, for example, than in the language arts), attention shifted to other areas. In sum, the fourth-grade test appeared to reduce the teaching of basic mathematical operations but did not encourage the introduction of new mathematical or scientific topics or concepts.

CONCLUSION

The aforementioned data highlight some of the instructional practices that we saw in the classrooms. Overall, the data suggest that there is indeed widespread use of some of the specific strategies often associated with reform. However, these strategies were rarely accompanied by changes in the ways in which teachers organized their overall approach to their subjects. Moreover, math and science teachers reported that they are not significantly changing the content that they teach. Although they are de-empha-

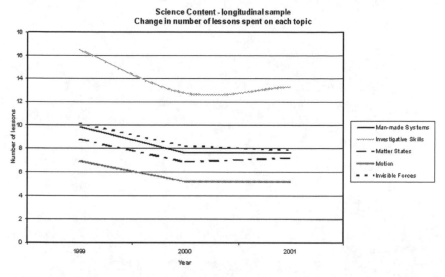

FIG. 2.2. Science content—longitudinal sample: change in number of lessons spent on each topic in science.

sizing, to some extent, practice on basic numerical operations like addition, subtraction, multiplication, and division of whole numbers, they are not necessarily introducing new mathematical topics or maintaining a sustained interest in science.

The teachers involved in this research have indicated that they have been motivated to change their styles of teaching and the content that they emphasize as a result of the ESPA test. Indeed, our observations confirm that they do incorporate many of the strategies and techniques that they reported in our interviews (such as small-group instruction and the use of manipulatives). This research does not and cannot document just when these strategies first became part of their practice; we can only note that the teachers attribute the implementation of many of them to the test. This study provides evidence that the teaching practices that we noted in our observations, however, are not focused on the more conceptually oriented aspects of instruction referred to in the mathematics and science standards. On the positive side, perhaps with appropriate support, teachers who are ready and willing to make changes in their teaching will be able to incorporate practices that will enable children to have access to mathematical and scientific instruction that fosters the growth of conceptual learning.

Though we have examined teachers' general approaches to mathematics and science, we have not yet focused on teaching to the test. That is the subject of the next chapter.

3

Teaching to the Test

Lora F. Monfils
William A. Firestone
Jennifer E. Hicks
M. Cecilia Martinez
Roberta Y. Schorr
Gregory Camilli

We suggested in chapter 2 that the effects of state testing on teaching practice were mixed in New Jersey. Some of the benefits included sensitizing teachers to the types of classroom and assessment practices associated with reform in math and science (e.g., rubric scoring, use of manipulatives, use of open-ended items in math and science, emphasis on written and spoken discourse and justification), as well as the introduction of topics covered with low historical frequency in the fourth-grade math/science curriculum (e.g., probability, statistics, and data analysis in math; and physical properties of matter, and forces and motion in science).

In this chapter, we explore the effects of testing more fully by asking how test scores are being used to inform teaching practice in general across the state in general and within selected districts. We note as others have (e.g., Madaus & Clarke, 2001; McNeil, 2000; M. L. Smith, 1996) that instruction may be differentially impacted by state testing, and that equity issues may arise in terms of amount and types of test preparation occurring in schools serving disadvantaged students, as well as how test scores are used to influence instruction. Because New Jersey is a state with extremes of district wealth and a history of fiscal inequity (now mediated to some extent by court mandated state funding conditional on whole school reform), we were especially interested in comparing practices in the lowest and highest wealth districts.

Specifically we ask:

1. Have test preparation practices changed in the 3 years since the implementation of the Elementary School Performance Assessment
   (ESPA)?
2. What is the relationship between pedagogy and test preparation?
3. To what extent does teaching to the test contribute to educational inequities?
4. How are test scores being used to inform instruction?

METHODS

To explore these questions, we use data from the statewide survey as well as
classroom observations and post-observation interviews described in chapter
2. In this section, we provide a general description, first of the quantitative
methodology and then of the qualitative methods used (a more detailed technical discussion of methodology is given in Appendix A).

Quantitative Methods

The survey data come from the most recent (2001) cross-sectional sample
of 301 teachers and the 3-year longitudinal sample of 119 teachers from the
3-year research study (see Appendix A). To use the survey to explore teaching to the test more thoroughly, we borrowed and revised a "teaching to the
test" scale that had been developed for a study of Maryland's state testing
program (Koretz, Mitchell, Barron, & Keith, 1996), which uses test items
that are even more performance oriented than those used in New Jersey.
Hence, the scale items referred to a number of activities that would not be
included in the more critical definitions of teaching to the test suggested by
M. L. Smith (1991b) and McNeil (2000). The revised scale contained items
assessing how often teachers did the following things:

- Motivate students to make their best effort on the ESPA, like suggesting they prepare by getting a good night's sleep or encouraging them to
  try hard.
- Teach test-taking mechanics like filling in bubbles, how to put your
  name on the test, or how to pace yourself during the test.
- Teach test-besting skills like methods for turning story problems into
  arithmetic calculations or how much to write after an open-ended
  math item.
- Use commercial test preparation materials like "Scoring High" and
  "Measuring Up on the ESPA."
- Give practice tests with items similar to those on the ESPA.
- Teach the regular curriculum using performance-based exercises simi-
  lar to ESPA.
- Have students use rubrics to grade each other's work.

These items represent a range of test preparation activities that are roughly ordered from content-free activities directly linked to the test (e.g., motivating students to do their best) to those that are embedded in the curriculum. For example, having students use rubrics to grade each other's work is an instructional activity that may promote learning through peer review and self-assessment. If used effectively, it may provide opportunities for students to judge the reasonableness of solution paths in comparison to other possible strategies (National Council of Teachers of Mathematics [NCTM], 1995). Moreover, this activity has the potential to provide a context in which students talk about important differences and similarities between their own and their peers' work, as they explain their reasoning and defend and justify their solution strategies. We asked teachers how often they did these various activities throughout the year and during the month just before the test was given.

We were interested in the association between teaching to the test and pedagogy, categorized broadly as didactic- or inquiry-oriented instruction (Smerdon, Burkam, & Lee, 1999). Inquiry-oriented instruction is more closely related to the kind of instruction encouraged by the NCTM standards. As described in chapter 2, in this approach students have considerable opportunity to explore ideas in meaningful ways to build knowledge and understanding of the content (Cohen & Hill, 1998; Newmann & Associates, 1996). Didactic instruction is closer to conventional teaching. Teachers are active, and students tend to be engaged in more practice types of activities rather than investigations in which they discover a rule or principle for themselves (Brophy & Good, 1986; Cuban, 1993). Measures of didactic and inquiry-oriented teaching were developed as part of the 3-year study (Monfils, Camilli, Firestone, Yurecko, & Mayrowetz, 2000), and revised in 2001 to include only the most salient items that characterized the two types of instruction.

The revised didactic instruction scales have six items, and asked teachers how often they did things such as "emphasize the importance of following procedures in solving math problems" and "begin each unit by describing scientific terms." The revised inquiry-oriented instruction scales have eight items. Teachers were asked how often they did things such as have students "show or explain a concept in more than one way," "work on problems for which there is no immediately obvious method of solution," and "design their own science experiments."

To learn more about how test scores influenced instruction, we introduced a set of questions included on the 2001 survey that asked what information teachers had received about the math or science ESPA scores from the spring 2000 administration. We also asked whether teachers had met with anyone to discuss these scores, if teachers felt that the scores were used in their evaluations, and how teachers used these scores to change their teaching practices in math and science. We also asked whether teachers felt the scores reflected their students' knowledge of math and science.

With an eye toward equity, all analyses included a comparison of results for schools in four broad categories based on state district factor groups (DFGs), a composite measure of district wealth that includes indicators of district wealth such as family income, occupations, the amount of poverty, and several measures of education. New Jersey has eight DFGs that range from poorest (A) to wealthiest (J). We collapsed these ratings into four contiguous wealth categories (A/B, CD/DE, FG/GH, I/J) to obtain reasonable frequencies in each category.

An analysis of the longitudinal sample explored the change in amount and type of test preparation, generally for the complete longitudinal sample and across district wealth categories. A repeated measures analysis of variance (ANOVA) was conducted on the test preparation scales as well as individual items for the month before ESPA and throughout the year. For the DFG analysis, post hoc multiple comparisons used Bonferroni tests to control family-wise error rates at the .05 alpha level.

With respect to the use of test scores to inform instruction, a question of interest concerns differences by district wealth. Summary statistics provided a general impression of how teachers throughout the state changed their instruction in response to the previous year's (2000) ESPA scores. A one-way ANOVA and post hoc multiple comparisons were conducted with district wealth categories as the grouping variable to explore the question of differences based on district wealth.

To extend previous work on the relationship between pedagogy and test preparation, we sought to uncover an interpretable dimensional structure by conducting exploratory factor analysis (EFA) on the 2001 survey responses to the pedagogy and test preparation items. Factors were estimated with principal axis factoring of the correlation matrix, with orthogonal rotation of the factor solution. Separate analyses were conducted for math and science because prior correlational and regression analyses showed different results for the two subjects. To compare factor scores across wealth districts, one-way ANOVA was conducted with district wealth categories as the grouping variable, followed by post hoc comparisons using Bonferroni tests to control family-wise error rates at the .05 alpha level.

Qualitative Methods

The interview guide used after teacher observations included a number of questions that gave teachers the opportunity to describe how they had responded to the state test. Specifically they were asked:

- What things, if any, are you doing to help your children learn the Core Curriculum Content Standards in math and science?
- What kinds of things do you generally do to help your students get ready for ESPA?

- What are you doing specifically to prepare students for the ESPA (i.e., test preparation)?

Occasionally, discussion of ESPA arose in response to other, more general questions. The complete set of postobservation interview questions is included in Appendix D.

The coding scheme, developed from emergent themes, included nodes for retrieving teachers' perceptions about the positive and negative aspects of the test and about changes teachers made in response to the test. With these nodes, we could pull together teachers' perceptions and reports even when they were stimulated by different questions. (Observation codes are included in Appendix E.) We also reviewed the observation data to find instances of teaching to the test that became apparent either because of what was in the observation record or because of what the teachers said during their interviews.

RESULTS

To contextualize our findings regarding our four research questions, we begin this section by reviewing teachers' comments on the quality of ESPA drawn from 3 years of teacher postobservation interviews. Next, we give findings regarding our four research questions. As appropriate, we integrate the quantitative and qualitative data to illustrate our results.

Teachers' Perceptions of the Quality of ESPA

In keeping with our theme of ambiguity, the 75 teachers who commented on the quality of the ESPA gave the test mixed reviews with 41 making positive comments and 51 making negative ones, so a large number made some of both. The general question allowed teachers to comment on any element of the ESPA including the math, science, and language arts sections. The positive comments focused on two main themes. The first tapped the general idea that ESPA was better than other tests because it was more valid or assessed more important aspects of achievement. Often teachers' statements were very general. Some were clearly positive as with the teacher who said, "I can understand why [ESPA] matches, you know, the demands that are placed on these kids for the future. I can understand the need to enhance communication and problem solving." Other positive comments were more guarded, as illustrated by one teacher who said, "I think that the intent of the ESPAs are well-meant …. I think that the idea to test in a way that children learn is good, but I don't think that today's ESPAs do that."

The second theme focused on how the content and format of ESPA changed what was taught in positive ways—that is, teaching to this test was a good thing. Some teachers made more specific observations. For instance, 28 teachers thought that requiring students to explain their thinking was a good idea, making statements such as, "It's, you know, a good idea to get kids to be able to think about their math, to be able to write something down. Their reasoning behind it." Seven appreciated that ESPA required students to apply what they learn because the test is "more focused on getting students to apply their knowledge instead of just to regurgitate information." Though teachers were generally critical of the language arts section—the one on which children's scores were consistently lowest—they were more supportive of the other two sections with 15 making positive comments about the science section and 12 making similar comments about the math section. For example, teachers said, "[ESPA] really got at what you want kids to do in science and figure things out and see how the world works" or "if there's any section that I think is reasonable in the ESPA, I think it's the math because they do put some computation in there, [but] they [also] put some higher-level thinking which we've always tried to infiltrate in mathematics."

Eighteen made general comments to the effect that "[ESPA is] forcing teachers who may have gotten caught in a rut to evaluate their teaching style because they just won't be able to do it if they don't teach to standards. They just can't get kids up to par." A few made more specific comments that the presence of ESPA was encouraging them to use alternative teaching methodologies like manipulatives in mathematics (mentioned by 4) or have children respond to more open-ended questions (mentioned by 10).

In sum, many teachers referred to the ESPA as a catalyst for change ("the test is fueling change") and cited ways in which their practice has changed in response to the test. For example, one teacher stated, "I like the way the questions are challenging and make them think. I think it certainly has affected the way that I've taught, I teach, and that I'm very, I'm always looking for opportunities to have an open-ended question somewhere and that's good."

The following quote from a teacher in a progressive, high-wealth district summarizes much of what teachers across the state told us about the test, both good and bad, and about differential impact across districts:

> The main thrust of the test is to change the way teachers are teaching in the classroom to match the skills that are needed for the students of today. We can't teach knowledge. We have to teach skills for getting knowledge. That was what the test was supposed to drive—this kind of teaching in the classroom …. I do think that the test is reflecting more of the methods we were already using in the classroom. I think that change had taken place before we ever got to the test in many districts. I'm sure there are districts that still aren't up to that point yet but they are evolving towards that …. I felt like our students were pretty prepared before we even got the ESPA and saw it for the first time. Much more so. Again, we have made those changes in our curriculum to reflect the ESPA. So, is the test pushing us in a right direction or are we pushing ourselves to match these standardized tests for fourth and eighth

grade? … I will say that I think it is difficult to teach to the test. It probably must be easier to do with other standardized tests like the Iowa and the CAT. Those type of tests lend themselves to teachers teaching to the test. Whereas, this was much more difficult to do that. If you don't have it in place all year long and in previous years they are not going to be able to do it.

Although many teachers believed that ESPA was encouraging constructive changes, they also pointed to difficulties. The most commonly mentioned difficulty was simply that the test was too long (mentioned by 32). Almost as many teachers (30) felt that the test was too difficult. As one explained, "It's asking a fourth grader to do something that a sixth grader should be doing. And it's a very good test for a [gifted] student." Another reflected the sentiments of many teachers in our study when she stated, "I agree with raising the standards and expectations, you know. And I want my children to achieve. But to raise them so high …." A related concern was that the math portion of the test was difficult for students with limited literacy skills. In both cases, it is difficult to know whether the test really was too hard or whether it was successfully raising expectations.

Although many positive comments focused on the open-ended items, these items raised concerns that scoring might be too subjective (mentioned by 18 teachers). One teacher described his experience at a workshop where he had to score responses like those on ESPA:

There were many times I'd disagree. Say that kid got a zero. I'd say, well, you know, in my reading and looking at what he did, it's pretty clear to me that he understands what he's doing. And maybe he hasn't fully explained it …. So maybe I was easy on the kid, the kids, I don't know. But I just … to me it leaves something open, wide open to your interpretation or my interpretation.

In addition to concerns about subjectivity, 14 teachers felt under more pressure because of ESPA. Some described a general sense that too much was expected of them: Three mentioned that pressure came from parents, and six said that it came from administrators. Seventeen teachers expressed concern about the pressure put on students, stating, "I had kids in tears the first year and … it was very frustrating," or "the publicity level of ESPA is a problem. And I think that by the time our children sit down to take it, they're a mess. They're a basket case." One teacher summed up the sentiments of many when she stated:

And some of them [the standards] are really too high. We're not going to be able to meet those, you know. And a frustration—you know, I want to be honest. And I see in overall the faculty, you know, the stress it puts on the faculty, the stress it puts on the child, you know. And we demand so much of these children.

Taken together, these comments suggest that ESPA is encouraging teachers to introduce new content and to rethink their teaching methods in the way some reformers suggest. However, it is also putting teachers and perhaps students under more pressure than they have felt in the past and it takes up a certain amount of time that could be used for instruction. We now turn to our four research questions and explore these findings with greater specificity.

Changes in Test Preparation Practices

We looked for change in the reported frequency of test preparation practices among the 119 teachers in our longitudinal sample. For the most part, reported levels of test preparation remained stable with a slight decrease from 1999 to 2001 (see Figs. 3.1 and 3.2) in all but a few practices (student use of rubrics, teaching test-besting skills, and giving practice tests with ESPA-like items in the month before ESPA), suggesting somewhat less attention to state testing overall as the novelty effect wore off. Among the significant trends for test preparation in the month before ESPA were three practices that decreased from 1999 to 2000, and then increased in 2001 (teaching test mechanics, teaching the regular curriculum using performance-based exercises similar to the ESPA, and teaching test-besting skills) and one practice that decreased significantly in each year (motivating students to make their best effort). Practices throughout the year changed little from 1999 to 2001, but one practice (teaching the regular curriculum using performance-based exercises similar to the ESPA) had a significant, though minimal linear decrease, and one practice (using commercial test prep materials) had a significant though mild trend of decrease followed by increase. Figures 3.1 and 3.2 illustrate significant trends for test prep the month before ESPA and throughout the year.

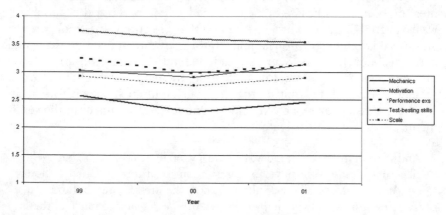

FIG. 3.1.   Trends in test prep the month before ESPA.

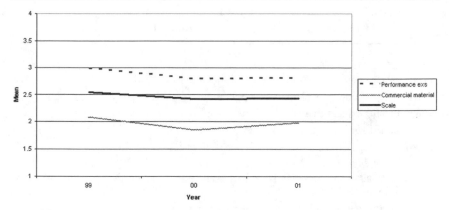

FIG. 3.2. Trends in test prep throughout the year.

Relationship Between Pedagogy and Test Preparation

In our previous research, we noted the association of certain types of test preparation (e.g., student use of rubrics, use of performance-based items) with inquiry-oriented instruction. On the other hand didactic instructional approaches were associated with more decontextualized test preparation (giving practice tests, use of commercial test prep materials, teaching test mechanics) especially in the month before ESPA (Firestone et al., 2002).

Results from the exploratory factor analysis, given in Tables 3.1 and 3.2, suggest that this is indeed the case but that there are some differences for mathematics and science. In the analysis for mathematics, two dominant factors emerged that correspond to the two pedagogy scales. Although several of the test preparation activities loaded on both factors, a pattern emerged that suggests a strong association of direct or decontextualized test preparation activities with didactic instruction but not inquiry-oriented instruction. When including factor loadings of .3 or higher, loading solely on the first and dominant factor are most of the inquiry-oriented instructional items and having students use rubrics to grade each other's work throughout the year and in the month before ESPA. Loading solely on the second factor are didactic instruction items and the more decontextualized or direct test prep items such as teaching test mechanics throughout the year, using commercial test prep materials like "Scoring High" throughout the year and the month before ESPA, and having practice sessions with ESPA-like items the month before ESPA. Loading about equally on both factors are test preparation items such as teaching the regular curriculum using performance-based exercises similar to ESPA the month before ESPA and holding practice sessions with ESPA-like items throughout the year. Of interest is the fact that teaching test-besting skills throughout the year loads more

TABLE 3.1
Math Pedagogy and Test Prep Items Rotated Factor Loadings

Item	F1	F2
Have students complete mathematics worksheets on their own.		
Have students show or explain a concept in more than one way.	0.42	
Have students explain their ideas in pairs or triplets.	0.51	
Use a rubric to grade written work or student projects.	0.52	
Begin each unit by having students practice skills necessary for the understanding of concepts.		0.34
Supply detailed procedures in order to keep students focused in mathematics lessons.		0.46
Use manipulatives to explain new mathematical ideas.	0.37	
Use lecturing as the main method of instruction.		0.38
Allow students to invent their own procedures for solving a math problem.		
Step back and let students discuss or argue their own ideas.	0.51	
Give model problems for which there is a clear easiest approach.		0.41
Emphasize the importance of following procedures in solving math problems.		0.62
Have students explain conclusions or solutions in writing.	0.53	
Review student portfolios or math journals to identify misunderstandings.	0.49	
M: Teach test-taking mechanics.	0.30	0.43
M: Motivate students to make their best effort on the ESPA.		0.37
M: Have students use rubrics to grade each other's work.	0.61	
M: Teach the regular curriculum using performance-based exercises similar to the ESPA.	0.44	0.42
M: Teaching test-besting skills.	0.42	0.51
M: Use commercial test preparation materials.		0.57
M: Have practice sessions with ESPA-like items.		0.62
Y: Teach test-taking mechanics.		0.37
Y: Motivate students to make their best effort on the ESPA.		0.30
Y: Have students use rubrics to grade each other's work.	0.64	
Y: Teach the regular curriculum using performance-based exercises similar to the ESPA.	0.52	0.30
Y: Teach test-besting skills.	0.52	0.36
Y: Use commercial test preparation materials.		0.55
Y: Have practice sessions with ESPA-like items.	0.46	0.43

Note. Extraction method principal axis factoring with varimax rotation. $N = 259$.

TABLE 3.2
Science Pedagogy and Test Prep Items Rotated Factor Loadings

Item	F1	F2
Have students complete science worksheets on their own.		
Have students show or explain a scientific concept in more than one way.		0.42
Have students explain their ideas to each other in pairs or triplets.		0.37
Use a rubric to grade written work or student projects.		0.47
Begin each new unit by defining scientific terms.		
Give a short-answer or a multiple-choice test.		
Use scientific models or realistic demonstrations to explain new ideas.		0.37
Use lecturing as the main method of instruction.	0.32	
Allow students to design their own science experiment.		0.55
Step back and let students discuss or argue their own ideas.		0.47
Give model problems for which there is a clear easiest approach.		
Emphasize the importance of following procedures in science investigations.		
Have students explain conclusions or solutions in writing.		0.52
Review student portfolios or journals to identify misunderstandings.		0.51
M: Teach test-taking mechanics.	0.54	
M: Motivate students to make their best effort on the ESPA.	0.45	
M: Have students use rubrics to grade each other's work.		0.58
M: Teach the regular curriculum using performance-based exercises similar to the ESPA.	0.48	0.32
M: Teaching test-besting skills.	0.66	
M: Use commercial test preparation materials.	0.63	
M: Have practice sessions with ESPA-like items.	0.67	
Y: Teach test-taking mechanics	0.11	
Y: Motivate students to make their best effort on the ESPA.	0.30	
Y: Have students use rubrics to grade each other's work.		0.65
Y: Teach the regular curriculum using performance-based exercises similar to the ESPA.		
Y: Teach the regular curriculum using performance-based exercises similar to the ESPA.	0.38	0.40
Y: Teach test-besting skills.	0.52	0.32
Y: Use commercial test preparation materials.	0.59	
Y: Have practice sessions with ESPA-like items.	0.53	0.32

Note. Extraction method principal axis factoring with varimax rotation. $N = 260$.

highly with the inquiry-oriented pedagogy items, but teaching test-besting skills during the month before ESPA loads more highly with the didactic pedagogy items.

A different factor structure emerged in science (Table 3.2). Loading most strongly on the dominant factor are three test prep items for the month before the test is given. Teaching test-besting skills the month before the test is given, using commercial test preparation materials, and practicing with ESPA-like items right before the test is given all suggest decontextualized practice for the test. Most of the other test preparation items load somewhere on this factor. The use of lecture as the main method of instruction, a defining characteristic of didactic instruction, also loads on this factor albeit rather weakly. Loading especially high on the second factor are test preparation items having to do with the use of student rubrics and such inquiry-oriented items as allowing students to design their own experiments and having students explain their solutions and conclusions in writing.

The factor structure also highlights the complex relationship between pedagogy and test preparation. Some practices load on both factors, suggesting the pervasiveness of teaching test-besting skills and use of ESPA-like items either for practice sessions or for the regular curriculum throughout the year, and the use of ESPA-like performance items for the regular curriculum the month before ESPA. In earlier postobservation interviews, most teachers (37 out of the 58 questioned on how they prepare their students specifically for the ESPA) referred to use of test preparation materials that contain ESPA-like items. Specifically, 20 said they use commercial ESPA prep books, such as "Scoring High," "Measuring Up on ESPA," and "Blast Off." The amount of time spent on such workbooks ranged from strictly the month before the exam to once a week starting in September. Another 17 said they use their own sample problems or sample problems or tests they received from the state or downloaded from the state's Web site.

Most of these teachers mentioned that they use these sample questions or tests so that their students can "get a feel" for what the exam will be like in May. Some teachers use ESPA questions as a "problem of the day" throughout the year, whereas others use them closer to the exam as a means for their students to practice a "timed" test. In the 2001 interviews, when we asked specifically about test prep in the few weeks before ESPA, 19 of the 27 teachers said that they used commercially prepared materials or sample problems released by the state, and 12 stated that they taught test-taking skills; only 10 stated that they reviewed the curriculum.

In spite of some areas of overlap, the two approaches to pedagogy and test preparation suggested by the factor structure are apparent in the classroom observations. Consider the lessons of two mathematics teachers observed in the weeks prior to ESPA as they each prepared their students for the computation and geometry test questions. The first teacher taught a lesson designed to reinforce definitions like acute, right, and obtuse angles, and parallel and perpendicular lines. After a verbal review of definitions, the rest of the lesson involved students in answering questions from a worksheet on an overhead projector. The questions were narrow in scope and had one correct answer, such as identifying whether each of four pairs of lines were perpendicular or not. Discussion centered on how to remember definitions and procedures to follow for obtaining the correct answer. Two days later, the lesson was devoted to ESPA review. As a warm-up students answered multiplication problems drawn from a set of flash cards, and then "tested" their calculators by checking answers. For the remainder of the lesson, the teacher guided students through a series of ESPA-like multiple-choice items, and directed them in test-besting techniques, like how to eliminate answer choices and how use their rulers to extend lines in diagrams. Both lessons were teacher directed and emphasized following procedures for getting the single correct answer.

In contrast, we observed a more inquiry-oriented and embedded approach to preparing for ESPA. When we arrived, students were practicing their computational skills by playing the 24-game, the object of which is to find multiple ways to get 24 by adding, subtracting, multiplying, and dividing four single-digit numbers given on a card. Next, the students used pattern blocks to give students an opportunity to consider the concept of symmetry. To begin, the teacher asked students to classify five plane figures placed on the overhead. After whole-class discussion about different methods students had used to group the objects, they moved into a discussion of how some students categorized the objects by the number of lines of symmetry. Students broke into groups and worked on an activity in which they used pattern blocks to "build a mirror image below a dotted line." Then they created similar problems and worked on each other's problems. Students were required to justify their answers by explaining their reasoning. Incorrect responses were tested by students moving objects on the overhead or by paper folding.

The two approaches to instruction were also apparent in responses to interview questions about preparing students for ESPA. They roughly parallel the factor structure discussed previously. On the one hand, most teachers referred to a more embedded approach to preparing their students for ESPA, using phrases like "teaching life skills," "teaching that reflects the standards," "critical thinking," "yearlong preparation," and stating that by covering the curriculum they were preparing their students for ESPA. For example, one teacher said, "My classroom is set up to work with ESPA, not separate that I'm gonna stop and train for. My writing folders, right from the beginning my math portfolios—everything is open-ended questions, rubrics are used from the beginning, language is used. Its just part of our way of life in here."

Many of the teachers who profess a more embedded approach do use practice items from commercial materials, especially the open-ended items, but do so to familiarize their students with the format of ESPA or as end-of-unit review. One teacher described how she used practice problems from the

"Coach book" for each content cluster after students had learned most of the skills in their regular instruction from the math text:

> So what I do is I take that review part at the end of each cluster, and when I feel like the class has, you know, that we've done many of the things in that cluster, then I'll pull out that review and so they'll get used to some of the types of questions that are on the ESPA. And the biggest ones that I do are those open-ended questions … I like the open-ended questions because … I am really big on kids figuring things out and seeing the relationships of stuff. And an open-ended question will let them explore and do that. So I like those.

The open-ended items were mentioned by almost all of our teachers as providing opportunities for worthwhile instruction in terms of getting their students to think more and explain their answers. These teachers tend to talk more about teaching their students about process rather than particular content just for the test. States one teacher:

> I don't believe in teaching to the test. But the kinds of skills—if I can incorporate something in a lesson that they need on a test, to me that's a life skill; it's not a test skill. And I know that there is a lot of, you know, open-ended questions on tests, or writing paragraphs, explaining. So that's also like embedded. The practice is kind of embedded in the activity. But they're still getting something out of the activity. It's not a separate lesson for test taking.

Lessons typifying this embedded approach to test preparation were observed in a number of classrooms. One teacher, who explained that her preservice education had stressed the Core Curriculum Content Standards whereas her school stressed the ESPA, developed standards-based math activities based on ESPA problems that students worked on every day throughout the year. Observed a few weeks after ESPA, her students worked in groups on a combinatorics ESPA-like problem of the day: "Tonight I'm making dinner for guests. The three main dishes include chicken, beef, or turkey. Each can have a side dish of mashed potatoes or corn. Also, some of the guests can have this meal either with or without dessert. How many different meals do my guests have to choose from?"

In their groups, students interpreted the question, discussed different solution methods, and began to solve the problem together. They used different representations (pictoral, graphical, numerical) as they wrote up their solutions. Often students debated among themselves about the defensibility of assertions, and about appropriateness of representations and solution strategies raised within the group. The teacher said that students had been taught to use rubrics to score their own work, and it was clear throughout the lesson that students were aware of the criteria for good work. At the end of the lesson, students presented their work for class discussion at the overhead. Their homework was to create their own ESPA-like "problem of the day." Other lessons observed in this class were similar centering on large, open-ended problems that required student collaboration and justification of solutions.

The second approach was a more direct or decontextualized teaching to the test, communicated by teachers who said that their teaching was "molded by," "focused on," or "geared toward" the ESPA, and others who stated that they teach "ESPA Math" or that their science is "mostly the ESPA." Some teachers directly stated that they "teach to the test" or that they "teach the ESPA." In fact, one said, "There is nothing wrong with teaching to the test. I'm teaching to that test. That's what you're supposed to do … I have to teach to it to get the results." We observed one teacher a few weeks before ESPA who used multiple-choice items from a test preparation book as a way to bring closure to a math lesson on standard and metric units of measurement. In this lesson the teacher used containers of water to demonstrate conversion between scales of measurement during which he asked students discrete, single-response questions. There was little room for student inquiry, and students were not given the opportunity to explore by working with the materials themselves. In the last 10 minutes of class, the teacher read aloud from the students' ESPA practice books multiple-choice items on units of measurement such as "What would you use to measure how much water is in a bathtub?" Although the teacher held up materials used earlier in his demonstration to assist students who were struggling, there was little discussion of the reasoning behind answer choices, and students were not encouraged to do anything but go on to the next question.

Teachers in districts that experienced a drop in scores often referred to a more decontextualized test preparation, one that involved use of commercial materials in the period preceding ESPA, use of item clones, and the direct drilling of students on test-besting techniques. In one district a third grade teacher said, "We got our results back from last year. Apparently, the district wasn't very happy with them…. So, ah, because of that, they ordered us books. So I guess we're going to be asked to teach ESPA stuff from an ESPA book." A fourth grade teacher from the same school stated that the pressure to raise scores is "just plain ridiculous." Another, when told they probably wouldn't get the ESPA scores back until January, replied, "Just in time to start test besting again." A teacher in another district lamented his and his colleagues' pervasive use of item clones or "problems that are very similar [to the ESPA], and it's not that you're teaching to the test, but you're prepping for the test. And that is a downside …."

The difference in factor structures suggests that there are some differences in how New Jersey elementary teachers link test preparation and instruction in mathematic and science. In mathematics, inquiry-oriented instruction is associated with long-term, embedded test preparation and strategies like having children use rubrics to grade each other's work that require more student judgment. Short-term, decontextualized test preparation is associated with didactic instruction. The link between short-term test preparation and didactic instruction is not as strong in science. Test preparation seems to be more an activity unto itself, and the didactic test items do not show up as strongly in the factor analysis. Inquiry-oriented instruction in science is not so clearly linked to long-term, embedded test preparation, but it is still tied to having students use rubrics.

More generally, these analyses suggest two important points. First, test preparation is not a uniform thing. There are different ways to prepare children for a test. Some are closer to more inquiry-oriented instruction and may even reflect some ideas about national reforms in mathematics and science. These integrate year-long curriculum-based test preparation into the regular practice of inquiry-oriented teaching. Others are short-term strategies for raising test scores that at best intensify conventional didactic instruction and at worst undermine the validity of tests by helping children raise their scores while having little educational value.

Second, a point that has not been adequately explored in the past is that test preparation may differ in substantial ways across subjects. As a field of study, teachers perceive mathematics to be more defined, sequential, and relatively static than science, and report more standardization and less autonomy. Language arts, although not a focus of our research, is even less clearly defined and sequential (Stodolsky & Grossman, 1995). How these differences in the content taught affect test preparation is an area that has not been extensively explored, but these analyses suggest that there are important differences between subjects.

Test Preparation and Educational Inequities

Before discussing how test preparation differs between rich and poor schools, it is worth remembering that New Jersey is among the states with the greatest inequities between districts (Editorial Projects in Education, 2001a). Chapter 7 will show that inequities in student achievement strongly reflected the family background of students and did not decline during the 3 years when ESPA was being administered

In this context, it is perhaps not surprising that ESPA affected teaching more in the poorer schools than the richest ones. For example, teachers in the longitudinal sample reported very little change in the amount of time they spent on various test preparation practices during the 3 years of the study. However, differences in the use of various practices were marked, and these differences too were very stable. Reported use of commercial test preparation materials in A/B districts exceeded I/J districts both throughout the year and the month before ESPA by a 3-year average of 0.525 ($p = .019$) and 0.655 ($p = .036$) points respectively on a 4-point Likert scale. This means that teachers in the lowest wealth districts used commercial test preparation materials significantly more than teachers in the highest wealth districts during all 3 years of operational ESPA testing. Figures 3.3 and 3.4 illustrate the DFG differences for use of commercial test prep materials throughout the year and during the month before ESPA.

In the postobservation interviews, teachers in the higher wealth districts, but not the lower wealth districts, reported that some of the instructional strategies required to help children do well on ESPA were already part of their practice long before the Core Curriculum Content Standards and the

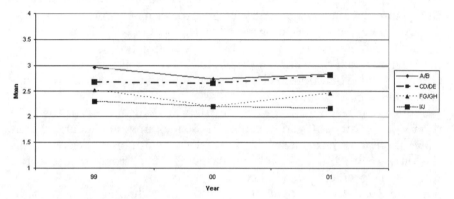

FIG. 3.3. Significant DFG differences in use of commercial test prep materials the month before ESPA.

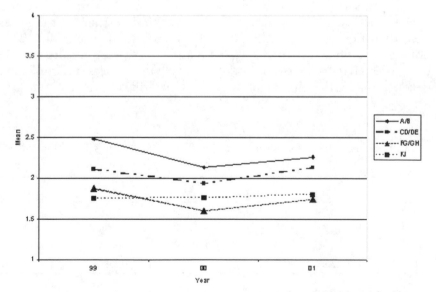

FIG. 3.4. Significant differences in DFG use of commercial test prep materials throughout the year.

implementation of ESPA. In part, this was due to prior interests in such reforms as Whole Language and the use of the NCTM standards in wealthy districts before the state standards were adopted. The difference also reflected the history of more district-supported professional development in wealthier districts.

Additional evidence of the differential impact of ESPA on instructional strategies was provided by statistical analysis (ANOVA) of the 2001 survey questions about instructional response to the previous year's ESPA scores. Teachers in the lowest wealth districts reported more change than their counterparts in the highest wealth districts. These differential changes included introducing new content, changing the order of topics, having students do more writing, requiring more oral explanation, and doing more test preparation in general (such as teaching test-besting skills or holding practice sessions with ESPA-like items); but not increased use of manipulatives and open-ended questions. All statistically significant differences are summarized in Table 3.3.

Notice that teachers in the A/B districts have higher means than the three other wealth categories on all of these measures, and all are statistically different from the means for the highest wealth districts (I/J). Thus, the lower wealth districts change practices more in response to test scores. The extent to which such changes can be attributed to pressure and support from local districts is the subject of the next chapter. Still, it is clear that an intensification of test preparation in the lowest wealth districts is accompanied by changes in content and by increased use of instructional strategies associated with reform such as having students write more and explain their reasoning orally. It is also clear that teachers in the lower wealth districts are increasing direct test preparation in general, a phenomenon observed in other states such as Texas, where pressure to raise test scores led to "activities whose sole purpose is to raise test scores" (i.e., decontextualized test preparation) such that drill on practice items re-

TABLE 3.3

Instructional Changes in Response to Last Year's ESPA Scores That Differed Significantly by DFG

DFG	Content	Order	Writing	Explanation	Test Prep
A/B	3.79**	3.46*	4.31**	4.08*	3.69**
CD/DE	3.55*	3.30	4.01	3.96	3.56*
FG/GH	3.50	3.39*	4.05	3.85	3.45
I/J	2.91	2.57	3.60	3.49	2.89

*significantly different from I/J at $p < .05$.
**significantly different from I/J at $p < .01$.

placed the regular curriculum in the poorest schools (McNeil & Valenzuela, 1999, p. 8).

To explore differences in the instructional impact of test preparation more fully, we examined DFG differences in the pedagogy–test preparation factor scores. A one-way ANOVA by district wealth groups indicated that teachers did not vary significantly on the inquiry-embedded factor, but did vary on the didactic and decontextualized factor in both mathematics ($F = 8.723$, $p < .001$) and science ($F = 5.040$, $p = .002$) (see Table 3.4). Bonferroni multiple comparisons indicated that factor scores of math teachers in the lowest wealth districts (A/B) exceeded teachers in the wealthiest districts (I/J) by .73 of a standard deviation ($p < .001$). In science, factor scores of teachers in the lowest wealth districts (A/B) exceeded those of teachers in the highest wealth districts (I/J) by .64 of a standard deviation ($p = .003$) and those of teachers in the next highest wealth category (FG/GH) by .42 of a standard deviation ($p = .028$). This suggest that teachers in the lowest wealth districts are using more didactic instruction and direct or decontextualized test preparation in both mathematics and science than their counterparts in the higher wealth district.

The interview data also suggest that teachers in the poorest districts respond differently than teachers in the wealthier districts to the state assessment in terms of change in content and test preparation. For example, when asked about subjects that might have been ignored in the past, one teacher stated that her (low-wealth) district did not teach science prior to ESPA. "I think because it wasn't measured on standardized tests. And unfortunately, in an inner-city district, the number one means of deciding what's important in the classroom is what are we gonna [sic] be tested on? Reading and math were it, and that's where the focus is."

Teachers in the special-needs districts spoke about attending professional development workshops "geared toward ESPA training" and how they incorporated what they learn:

TABLE 3.4
Pedagogy–Test Preparation Factor Score Means by DFG

DFG Category	Math Inquiry-Embedded	Math Didactic-Direct	Science Inquiry-Embedded	Science Didactic-Direct
A/B	0.10	0.23[a]	−0.07	0.29[a, b]
CD/DE	−0.13	0.22	−0.03	0.00
FG/GH	−0.01	−0.15	0.03	−0.13
I/J	0.06	−0.50	0.14	−0.35

[a]significantly different from I/J at $p < .01$.

[b]significantly different from FG/GH at $p < .05$.

And I learned that the children need to do the things hands on, because they need to see it, they need to feel it, they need to understand it. And basically everything in my classroom, to the best of my ability, I try to do it hands on. Use the terms that are in the ESPA. I do a lot of research. I read a lot of things that are expected on the ESPA. And I just try to bring it. Unfortunately it sounds like that I'm teaching to the test, but in a way I am. I mean I know you're not supposed to do that, but I believe that you need to, if we need to meet these standards.

At least one special-needs district in our sample supplements the classroom teacher's instruction. Children receive additional whole-class test preparation in the month before ESPA by the in-house basic skills teacher and by an outside consultant, both of whom drill students on ESPA-like problems drawn from a commercial test preparation book.

Although many teachers in the least advantaged districts perceive the test to be a force for improving instruction, some express doubts about fairness. One teacher in a special-needs (low-wealth) district expressed praise for the ESPA, but also talked of the constraints faced by teachers in her district:

And in my classroom the ESPA, and the accountability issues of the ESPA for myself and for my students, have made me a better teacher .... I was very pleased with the fact that I was allowed to include both math and technology aspects in my PIP [Professional Improvement Plan] because I was able to indicate that I wanted to improve student growth in math. Not through text study and worksheet completion but through problem-solving activities that was sometimes not finished in a day.

She told us that her students' scores went up after she stopped teaching exclusively from a math text and started using TERC Investigations (materials developed by the Technology Education Research Center with funding from the National Science Foundation), and some of the activities she learned in her graduate courses and professional development workshops. She pointed out that a shortage of materials had been an ongoing problem in her district, so teachers set up a lending system. Her district offered graduate credit through one of the local colleges, and provided professional development workshops on math or "ESPA math" every 2 to 3 weeks at each grade level. Participating teachers requested to have manipulatives distributed in lieu of stipends.

As an Abbott district[1] adopting a whole school reform model, teachers in this district were under pressure to change their practice to increase test scores. District administrators visited classrooms with checklists of what they wanted to see in terms of materials, instructional approaches such as small-group work, posted standards and rubrics, and displays of student work. This pressure filtered into classroom practice. In her colleague's classroom observed the month before ESPA, students were exhorted to show their work and reminded that under the scoring rubric an explanation was required for full credit:

> Show your work! Show your work! If this was the ESPA test, you'd have to be prepared. This is the type of problem you would see on ESPA. If you just show this [she holds up a four-digit number] that's not enough. It's very important. You have to show how you got that answer. Remember it's graded on a rubric. So you have to show and explain how you were thinking.

This teacher reminded students of the ESPA rubric scoring that she uses in the classroom, and told a student that his journal entry was a 2 (on a 3-point scale) because he hadn't provided enough explanation. Later in the lesson, she admonished, "Someone else is going to grade your test. Remember, every fourth grader is going to take the test, and they get shipped away to be graded. So talk to them, explain your reasoning in writing. They aren't going to call me and ask me what you meant." The frequent mention of ESPA rubric scoring was typical of her lessons. Unfortunately, students were rarely probed for deep understanding, nor challenged to think of alternative solution methods. Instead, despite all of the graduate work and professional development, the focus was on providing a response that would gain full marks on ESPA.

Although crediting ESPA with assessing student thinking and for providing an impetus to improve their practice, teachers from special-needs districts question the fairness of holding their schools and students to the same standard as those in more privileged districts:

> Do they know that they can't compare our kids to kids from Princeton? We have children who were crack babies, whose parents did drugs when they were pregnant. And these kids have learning, severe learning disabilities .... They don't have the support at home. The reinforcement at home. So whatever they get from school, is it.

Another talked of the disconnect between tested content and their students' lives, and the disadvantage they face due to lack of resources:

> I've looked at some of the problems in the ESPA .... I think for me some of it just seems to be not related to—you know, especially in an urban environment just not related to anything I think is useful for them. I just think to some degree it might be isolated as to actually what's happening in the classroom. You know, because in some of these districts, students are challenged. They don't have the materials available. They don't have the resources available to present to these kids. And so the kids, I think, they're gonna [sic] be left behind in that regard. But it's not—it's just due to the lack of resources. You know, so in that regard it's a little unforgiving.

Still another spoke to the achievement gap and wondered if they will ever reach parity: "But what happens when the poorer districts finally catch up? Now what's gonna happen? What's—do we test them more? Do we give them more? Does the standards go up even higher? What—you know?" And teachers from the affluent districts echoed their sentiments as they pondered the challenges facing the less advantaged districts:

> And those that don't have materials to work with are at a distinct disadvantage and unless the state can make sure that all of the schools are provided with the equipment, and not only have the equipment, but the training to use it, I don't know how we can say that we have equity ... Cubes, measuring equipment, and lots of things that the kids can actually use and inquiry approach that a lot of districts probably don't provide for their students.

Use of Test Scores to Inform Instruction

We asked a number of questions about access to and use of ESPA scores. The first question related to whether teachers had access to test results. As seen in Table 3.5, among the 301 teachers participating in the 2001 telephone survey, approximately 229 (76%) stated that they had been given information about school, class, and individual student results from the 2000 administration. Note that whereas 91% received school-level information in the form of school average or proportion passing and 78% received information on individual student math and/or science scores, only 40% received information on their class' math and/or science cluster scores. The cluster scores, which reflect mastery in content subdomains such as number sense, operations and properties, or spatial sense and geometry, are the most important for helping teachers decide what topics to stress in the coming year, whereas school and classroom averages give a sense of how well a school or teacher is doing but not what to do about it. The latter form of feedback may add to a teacher's sense of pressure or well-being, but the former is most likely to help teachers reflect on at least one dimension of instruction—curriculum coverage—and it is the kind of data least often shared with teachers.

Participation in follow-up meetings to discuss test results was reported by 179 teachers (78% of the 229). Meetings with principals and other teachers were the most frequent (68% and 69% respectively), while meetings with supervisors were much less frequent (34%). In the interviews, some teachers mentioned that these meetings included discussions on strategies teachers could use to improve students' test scores. For example, one teacher stated, "We had a grade-level meeting and there were other fourth grade teachers and we had a copy of the published results of the ESPA. And we sat down and we talked a little bit about it and found out that everybody's doing something different trying to help the students to do better on them. And we con-

TABLE 3.5

**Proportion of Teachers Receiving Information About 2000 ESPA Scores
and Having Meetings to Discuss Them**

	# Yes	% of Those Getting Data	% of All Teachers
Did you receive:			
Individual students math or science scores	178	78	59
Class average or proportion passing	159	69	53
School average or proportion passing	208	91	69
Comparison of your school or class to the state average	186	81	62
Math or science cluster scores for your school	141	62	47
Math or science cluster scores for your class	91	40	30
Had follow-up discussion regarding ESPA scores	179	78	59
Met with principal to discuss scores	156	68	52
Met with supervisor to discuss scores	79	34	26
Met with other teachers to discuss scores	158	69	52
Met with anyone else to discuss scores	35	15	12

cluded we really could use some help preparing them. That we all could benefit." Only 20% of the teachers receiving score information felt that ESPA scores were not used to evaluate their teaching effectiveness in math and/or science.

When we asked teachers how they had changed their mathematics and science teaching in response to the 2000 ESPA scores in the survey, teachers gave responses similar to responses to the interviews (see chap. 2). Results are presented in Table 3.6. After combining the two highest rating options, the greatest changes reported were more use of open-ended questions in class and on tests (75%, combined; 36%, a great deal), having students explain their reasoning orally more frequently (73%, combined; 29%, a great deal), and having students do more writing (72%, combined; 42%, a great deal). One teacher included all of these when she stated:

> I've also done a lot of work with writing and rubrics and the kids are quite proficient in knowing what needs to be included in their writing when I give them either an open-ended question or some type of writing assignment that they need to work on. Just things in general like that. And working a lot with [them], making sure that they're able to explain their answers. That's really in all areas, too, whether it's science or math or if they're reading something and they need to give me an answer, tell me why.

TABLE 3.6

Descriptive Statistics of Teachers' Reported Changes in Response
to Last Year's ESPA Scores

Likert Item	N	Mean	SD	Percent Selecting Option	
				4	5
Changed class content, teaching more of some topics and less of others.	229	3.5	1.2	34	21
Changed the order of topics taught.	229	3.3	1.4	27	24
Have students do more writing in math and/or science.	229	4.0	1.1	33	42
Have students explain their reasoning orally more frequently in math/science.	229	3.9	1.0	44	29
Have students use more manipulatives/ experiments/hands-on activities.	229	3.4	1.1	32	18
Use more open-ended questions in class and on tests.	229	4.0	1.1	39	36
Do more test preparation in math and/or science.	229	3.5	1.1	31	19
Use more homogenous grouping for math and/or science instruction.	227	2.3	1.3	13	6.6
Feel ESPA scores used to evaluate teaching effectiveness in math or science.	226	2.9	1.3	18	16

Note. 1 = Not at all, 5 = A great deal.

CONCLUSION

This chapter used a mix of surveys, interviews, and direct observation to address questions about how test preparation affects instruction, and whether test preparation increases or decreases educational inequities. Our findings point to the ambiguity and mixed benefits of test-driven reform. We have seen teachers adjust to the demands placed upon them by becoming more aware of and interested in elements of reform but also by intensifying conventional practice. These divergent responses are both more extreme in the poorest districts. In fact teaching to the test may reinforce the inequities that standards-based reform was intended to counterbalance. When we look at the changes taking place in New Jersey, we see an embedded, reform-oriented approach to test preparation that incorporates test preparation into the regular curriculum by using manipulatives, cooperative groups, and open-ended items as an opportunity for children to explain their reasoning orally and in writing. At the same time, there is an increase in decontextualized test preparation such as drilling students on multiple-choice items and practice tests taken from commercial test preparation materials.

Teachers in disadvantaged districts are responding to the state tests (and their low test scores) more than their colleagues in wealthier districts. But this difference is as ambiguous as the general pattern. Teachers in poor districts are changing content and adopting instructional strategies consistent with some reform strategies (such as having students explain their solutions both orally and in writing). They are also increasing the use of manipulatives and open-ended items at the same rate. Unfortunately, teachers in poor districts are also increasing their decontextualized test preparation through the use of commercial test prep materials, teaching test-besting skills, or holding practice sessions with ESPA-like items more than teachers in wealthier districts, a circumstance decried by many critics of high-stakes accountability (McNeil, 2000).

Beyond issues related to differences in district wealth, it remains to be seen what factors encourage teachers to change their practice. One factor that does not to be of critical importance is analysis of test data itself. Though most teachers see some data, they tend to see the kind of information that creates pressure to change practice—e.g., school averages—rather than the information like cluster scores that can help teachers refine their practice. In fact, the way test data—which could support teachers' decision-making processes—are reported raises the larger issue of what pressures and support teachers experience and how those influence their teaching. That is the subject of the next chapter.

ENDNOTE

1. As a response to ongoing school finance litigation (*Abbott v. Burke*), a 1997 decision (*Abbott IV*) required the state to immediately provide funding for 30 urban school districts that would match the per pupil expenditure in the state's wealthiest districts, substantially increasing the operating budgets of those districts. The next year the court called for the implementation of whole school reform (WSR) programs in all the schools in those urban districts.

4

Pressure and Support

William A. Firestone
Lora F. Monfils
Roberta Y. Schorr
Jennifer E. Hicks
M. Cecilia Martinez

One of the recurring questions about standards-based reform is how to encourage teachers to adopt the practices that such reform suggests. One prominent view is that educational systems are so disjointed and loosely coupled that what teachers do depends heavily on their own beliefs and preferences (Richardson, Anders, Tidwell, & Lloyd, 1991; Weick, 1976). Another view, suggested by Michael Fullan (1991), is that ultimately, change depends on what teachers do and think, but that they are amenable to a mix of pressures and supports. As he said, "Successful change projects always include elements of both pressure and support. Pressure without support leads to resistance and alienation; support without pressure leads to drift or waste of resources" (p. 91). Theories of reform differ, however, in their emphasis on pressures and supports. Advocates of accountability see the problem of reform as a lack of motivation, particularly on the part of teachers. They argue for creating incentives linked to test scores that encourage teachers to reform their practice. Others argue that teachers want to do the best they can but need supports that help them to learn to use new practices in meaningful and effective ways.

New Jersey's education reforms created few formal incentives beyond a general interest in raising test scores and offered limited learning opportunities beyond what came from studying the test and results. However, a mix of factors including school and district responses to the tests and proximity to universities (or other sources of professional development) created some variation in both the pressure and support that teachers experienced. This chapter uses variation in teachers' personal situations to explore how pressure and support influence instructional practice in the context of a state testing program.

Our findings suggest that although often combined in practice, pressure and support are not always as complementary as Fullan (1991) indicated. Publicizing test scores generates weak and unfocused incentives to raise scores that—especially where people do not know quite what to do to achieve that end—create a diffuse sense of dread and pressure to improve. Rather than promoting the extensive changes envisioned by the authors of state and national standards, this pressure reinforces conventional practice as represented by didactic approaches to instruction, as well as short-term strategies for raising test scores. On the other hand, supports for changing practice in ways that are aligned with state and national standards do encourage teachers to explore more inquiry-based practices that are compatible with those standards. These supports take several forms and encourage responses to the state test that are embedded in everyday practice.

To explore the differential effects of pressure and support, we first review the arguments about pressure and support. Then we examine in some detail how teachers describe the pressure and support they face and present further analyses from 3 years of statewide survey on the effects of pressure and support on self-reported practice.

THE PRESSURE AND SUPPORT DEBATE

Here we review the arguments in favor of pressure, support, and other considerations as the major factors influencing teaching practice.

Pressure and Accountability

The argument in favor of pressure comes out of such fields as business, economics, and political science. These fields tend to see teachers—like everyone else—as rational actors who are driven by a form of economic self-interest and respond to the incentives created by the job. However advocates for pressure argue that schools provide neither clear standards of performance nor incentives linked to performance that would motivate workers:

> Lack of proper performance incentives may explain why education appears to lag behind many other sectors in its ability to harness the drive and ingenuity of its workers. There is no clear relationship between the performance of teachers and schools and the incentives and rewards that they are offered. We believe that innovative teachers and principals are the key to student achievement but that the structure of incentives currently works to inhibit and constrain them. (Hanushek, 1994, p. 5)

To these people, lack of incentives is a primary feature of inadequate accountability. Regardless of what their students learn, teachers earn the same salary. Unless they want to leave teaching, there is little or no room for promotion. In fact, until state standards and assessments came along, there was, generally speaking, very little consensus on what teachers were expected to teach and students to learn. Critics such as Hanushek want accountability systems to provide measures that define acceptable performance and stronger incentives linked to those measures to motivate improvement and focus efforts (Adams & Kirst, 1999; Hanushek & Meyer, 1996; National Alliance of Business, 2000). In several states, this has led to experimentation with providing financial rewards to schools where test scores rise to meet certain standards and threats of various forms of takeover where test scores are low and do not increase sufficiently (Editorial Projects in Education, 2001).

Yet strong incentives can have perverse effects. Other literature on teaching to the test identifies the negative effects of linking sanctions to test scores (Clotfelter & Ladd, 1996; Corbett & Wilson, 1991; McNeil, 2000). Under those conditions, some observers find that teachers will essentially let the test drive substantial portions of their curriculum. Subjects on the test will be covered much more intensively than those not on the test. Critics of state testing fear that it will encourage educators to substitute test preparation materials and drill on the test for even conventional curriculum materials and pedagogy. When teachers feel pressured to raise test scores and lack adequate supports, teaching to the test would be expected to promote direct instruction and discourage inquiry-oriented teaching (Corbett & Wilson, 1991; McNeil, 2000).

Though many reformers are critical of teaching to the test, some have tried to use this phenomenon to promote improvement. Especially in the early 1990s, these reformers argued for using various forms of performance assessments and portfolios as part of state assessment systems. They hoped that tests or assessments using tasks requiring students to show their work, justify their answers, and work with a variety of symbol systems would promote inquiry-oriented instructional approaches where students would be more actively engaged in the process of building understanding (Resnick & Resnick, 1992; Rothman, 1995). How likely this is remains to be seen because the available evidence is mixed (Newmann, Bryk, & Nagaoka, 2001; M. L. Smith, 1996).

Whereas most discussions of accountability systems take a rational perspective that emphasizes how formal incentives linked to performance measures generate pressure to meet standards, pressure associated with testing may also result from symbolic and cultural factors. In fact, the same accountability policy is often interpreted quite differently in the same state (Firestone & Mayrowetz, 2000). Principal leadership, messages from the district offices, and extensive time spent on preparation for state tests during professional-development sessions may all signal to teachers that a test is important and generate pressure to respond whether constructively or otherwise.

Support

A variety of sources of support for reform have been identified. The principal's support can be very important for a wide variety of changes in practice (Louis, Toole, & Hargreaves, 1999). Although research on principals has a plethora of models using different normative frameworks, dimensions of leader behavior, and intended effects (Leithwood & Duke, 1999), the bulk of the evidence suggests that principals support improvement indirectly. They are less likely to provide direct training or guidance on how to use specific instructional approaches than to create a context that encourages experimentation and change. They do that by creating conditions where teachers can improve their knowledge and skills. Principals set goals; they build a vision of improved practice and encourage teacher commitment to that vision, with the hope of creating a context for sharing knowledge of practice among teachers (Hallinger & Heck, 1996). Thus, principals are more likely to support change in general than any particular practice, and they may do so by getting teachers to focus on broader ends—such as implementing state standards—rather than narrow means.

Learning opportunities represent another form of support. Some analysts have suggested that accountability theories that focus on incentives are not likely to work well until it is clear that teachers know how to do what is expected of them. For that, they need opportunities to learn the content in the curriculum, how children make sense of that content, and effective ways to teach it (Berman, 1986; Shulman, 1987). There is a growing body of practice-based knowledge on effective professional-development strategies that can provide the learning opportunities that enhance teachers' knowledge about how to help children meet new standards (Loucks-Horsley, Hewson, Love, & Stiles, 1998). A small number of studies show that well-designed programs can have a lasting effect on instructional practice (Schorr & Koellner-Chark, 2003; Schorr & Lesh, 2003). In particular, professional development can promote the adoption of more active approaches to student learning that are in line with national professional standards (Cohen & Hill, 1998; Supovitz, Mayer, & Kahle, 2000). Nevertheless, professional development rarely reaches its potential for promoting change, in part because the duration of most professional-development activities is too short and not designed to help teachers fundamentally change their worldviews or effectively synthesize new ideas into instructional practice (Firestone, Camilli, Yurecko, Monfils, & Mayrowetz, 2000).

Finally, appropriate physical materials would seem to facilitate teaching. It is hard to imagine didactic instruction without at least textbooks, and more active student learning strategies often require a wide variety of materials, equipment, and/or technological tools. Moreover, some approaches to professional development include materials and training so that the one complements the other, as with the professional-development workshops that are associated with the adoption of a new textbook or curricular series (Loucks-Horsley et al., 1998).

Other Factors

Pressure and support operate in the context of teachers' preexisting knowledge and beliefs. It is becoming increasingly clear that teachers need to know a great deal about content, instructional methods, and "pedagogical content knowledge"—the intersection of content knowledge and general understandings about how students learn and how to teach for student learning—to be effective. Moreover, detailed knowledge of content and how children learn it is especially necessary for the more inquiry-oriented approaches to student learning that are embedded in both national and state standards, including New Jersey's (Carpenter, Fennema, Peterson, Chiang, & Loef, 1989; National Commission on Mathematics and Science Teaching for the 21st Century, 2000; Shulman, 1987). This knowledge may also affect the nature and number of teachers teaching to the test.

In addition to their knowledge, teachers' beliefs about their own efficacy may affect their willingness to adopt new practices. Teachers' personal beliefs about mathematics and science strongly influence the ways in which they teach (Ball, 1990). In addition, most teachers have beliefs about the way mathematics and science are learned that precede actual classroom experience and are held through years of teaching (Tabachnick & Zeichner, 1984; Thompson, 1985). In related research using general social psychological models, teachers' sense of efficacy has been studied extensively over the last quarter-century. In this research, teacher efficacy is generally conceptualized as having two dimensions: general teaching efficacy—the belief that teachers can affect what students learn—and personal efficacy, the belief that the individual has the capacity to influence children. These two dimensions are not strongly correlated. Usually, efficacy is measured at a general level, but some subject-specific measures have been developed. Both dimensions of efficacy have been linked to a wide variety of important outcomes including student achievement, teacher commitment, and willingness to implement new innovations (Tschannen-Moran, Woolfolk Hoy, & Hoy, 1998).

The characteristics of children are also likely to influence teachers' willingness to teach to the test or adopt various instructional strategies. The challenges of teaching large numbers of disadvantaged students—especially students for whom English is not their native language—are more severe than is the case with other children. The problem may not be the characteristics of the students, however, so much as the relationship between student and teacher when cultures are too diverse on a number of dimensions (Knapp, 1995). Whether because of low expectations, failure to communicate effectively across cultural barriers, the difficulty of maintaining order which can be more challenging in urban classrooms, or lack of pedagogic and/or content competency, teaching in poor, urban schools is generally more focused on didactic instruction than strategies that provide for more active student learning (Haberman, 1991; Knapp, 1995). It also may be that poor children receive less teaching overall, including both didactic and inquiry-oriented instruction (Hafner, 1993). McNeil (2000) is among those who suggest that teaching to the test is more prevalent among teachers serving poor and minority children, and test preparation may take time away from more subject-based instruction. Given the well-documented differences between rich and poor school districts on so many dimensions from student achievement to governance, it would be surprising if there were not differences in instructional practice that reflected district wealth and student characteristics (Berliner & Biddle, 1995; Hannaway & Talbert, 1993).

METHODS

To explore how pressure and support influenced teaching to the test and various instructional approaches, we conducted a multilevel analysis of 3 years of survey data. We also explored what teachers had to say about the pressures and support they experienced.

The Survey

For the survey analysis, we used the responses we received from teachers in 1999, 2000, and 2001. The measures of teaching to the test and inquiry and didactic instruction were those employed in chapter 3. Here we describe the measures of pressure, support, teacher characteristics, and poverty that we used. The specific questions are included in Appendix B.

To measure pressure to ensure that students score high on the Elementary School Proficiency Assessment (ESPA), we asked teachers to respond to five items on a 4-point Likert scale running from strongly agree to strongly disagree with items like "when I design lessons and activities in math and science, it is understood that an important goal is to raise ESPA scores" (see Tables 4.1 and 4.2). The "principal support" scale focused on the principal's support for standards and the state assessments. It was also a five-item scale that included such items as "my principal understands what good standards-oriented math and science is like."

We examined support through learning opportunities in two ways. First, we asked teachers how much time they spent in professional development on "strategies to help students score high" on the ESPA in math and science, asking about each subject separately. Second, we asked teachers about

TABLE 4.1

Scales and Items

Variable	Number of Items	Sample Item	Alpha (3-year range)
Teaching to the Test: Month Before	7	Teach test-besting skills the month before ESPA	.71 – .78
Teaching to the Test: All Year	7	Use commercial test preparation materials throughout the year	.71 – .74
Inquiry-Oriented Math	8	Have students show or explain a concept in more than one way	.65 – .75
Didactic Math	6	Emphasize the importance of following procedures in solving math problems	.63 – .68
Inquiry-Oriented Science	8	Allow students to design their own science experiment	.63 – .70
Didactic Science	6	Begin each new unit by defining scientific terms	.50 – .57
Pressure	5	March and April are pretty rough in this school because of the time and attention focused on getting ready for ESPA	.47 – .60
Principal Support	5	My principal is making changes to implement the mathematics and science standards successfully	.56 – .61

Note. Likert scale items: 1 = almost never, 2 = once in a while, 3 = most of the time, 4 = almost always.

whether they had participated in a variety of activities, which included: taking college courses in math or science, teaching math or science through serving on a school or district curriculum development committee, working on a textbook selection committee, and/or participating in various federally funded professional-development programs available in the state. We added up all the activities in which each teacher participated. We reasoned that the first kind of professional development would focus more narrowly on preparing for the state test. The second was more diverse but included many activities that focused on mathematics or science content and/or approaches to teaching those subjects.

To find out about material supports, we asked teachers what access they had to textbooks in mathematics and science and to hands-on materials that would be useful for teaching mathematics (e.g., manipulatives and calculators) and science (science kits and measurement and observation tools). Teachers responded on a 4-point scale where zero meant that they had none and 3 meant that they had enough for every child.

TABLE 4.2
Pressure, Support and Other Variables in HLM Math and Science Teaching Analysis

Variable	Description or Item	Mean	SD
Principal Support	Principal support scale score	3.08 3.10	0.53 0.51
Pressure	Pressure scale score	3.16 3.18	0.52 0.51
ESPA (Math) Professional Development	One item: Professional development on helping students score high on ESPA in math (0 = none, 3 = more than 2 days or 16+ hours)	1.44	1.15
ESPA (Science) Professional Development	One item: Professional development on helping students score high on ESPA in science (0 = none, 3 = more than 2 days or 16+ hours)	1.06	1.09
General Professional Development	Sum of 14 dichotomous teacher initiated professional development items for previous year (mentoring, curriculum writing, college course, SSI participation)	2.10 2.20	1.42 1.45
Access to Textbooks (Math)	One item: Access to mathematics textbooks (0 = none, 3 = enough for every child)	2.92	0.46
Access to Textbooks (Science)	One item: Access to science text books (0 = none, 3 = enough for every child)	2.52	1.02
Access to Manipulatives	One item: Access to mathematics manipulatives (0 = none, 3 = enough for every child)	2.35	0.58
Access to Calculators	One item: Access to calculators (0 = none, 3 = enough for every child)	2.94	0.34
Access to Science Kits	One item: Access to science kits (0 = none, 3 = enough for every child)	1.84	0.76
Access to Measurement Tools	One item: Access to measurement and observation tools (0 = none, 3 = enough for every child)	2.05	0.72
Knowledge of Standards (Math)	Sum of 2 items: One item about knowledge of national math standards and one about knowledge of state math standards (1 = awareness only, 5 = expert)	6.30	1.74
Knowledge of Standards (Science)	Sum of 2 items: 1 item about knowledge of national science standards and one about knowledge of state science standards (1 = awareness only, 5 = expert)	5.93	1.66
Personal Efficacy	One item: When I really try I can get through to the most difficult or unmotivated students. (1 = strongly disagree, 5 = strongly agree)	3.24 3.23	0.70 0.70
District Factor Group Year	As calculated by state into eight groups indicating district SES Response is from 1999, 2000, or 2001 sample	— —	— —

Inquiry-oriented Math	Inquiry-oriented math pedagogy scale score	2.84	0.49
Didactic Math	Didactic math pedagogy scale score	3.04	0.47
Inquiry-oriented Science	Inquiry-oriented science pedagogy scale score	2.81	0.43
Didactic Science	Didactic science pedagogy scale score	2.78	0.45
Teaching to Test-Month before	Teaching to the test the month before ESPA scale score	2.90 2.92	0.54 0.55
Test to Test- All year	Teaching to the test throughout the year scale score	2.47 2.49	0.50 0.50

Note. When numbers are stacked, math teacher means and standard deviations are the top number with science teacher means and standard deviations below. These statistics are based on 3 years of data used in the HLM analysis—686 measurements per variable from 392 math teachers, and 632 measurements per variable from 365 science teachers.

We also wanted to learn about teachers' knowledge and beliefs. One set of questions asked teachers about their knowledge about both national math and science standards and the New Jersey Core Curriculum Content Standards. Teachers were asked to rate themselves as having anything from awareness-level knowledge to being an expert who "could lead a workshop." We asked about one dimension of teaching efficacy—personal efficacy—using one Likert item: "When I really try I can get through to the most difficult or unmotivated students."

To measure the proportion of poor and minority children, we used the same state-developed district factor group (DFG) measure used in chapter 3. Finally, in order to assess trends over time, we noted the year from which the response came (1999, 2000, or 2001).

To explore trends over time and to test our hypothesis about pressure and support, we used a two-level hierarchical linear model (HLM) for repeated measures with time-varying covariates. Repeated observations from the 1999, 2000, and 2001 surveys were modeled as a function of time at Level 1, nested within teachers at Level 2, thus combining all 3 years worth of data in a single model.[1] The strength of this approach is that we were able to include all teachers with complete data for each year of participation, including those who participated for fewer than 3 years. Among those who taught mathematics, 392 teachers met this criteria: 80 with complete data for all 3 years, 134 with 2 years of complete data, and 178 with 1 year of complete data. In science, there were 365 teachers with complete data: 71 with 3 years worth, 125 with complete data for 2 years, and 169 with 1 year of complete data.

The basic assumptions of this type of analysis are that teachers vary in how they change or "grow" from year to year, and an individual teacher's response in any given year is a function of his or her own growth trajectory plus random error (Raudenbush & Bryk, 2002). To model change or growth over time, "year" was included as an indicator variable to capture linear change (growth rate at each time point) and "year-squared" was used to capture the curvature or change in growth rate. Because we were interested in capturing change due to the implementation of ESPA, "year" was coded to indicate year since the first administration of ESPA (0 for 1999, 1 for 2000, and 2 for 2001).

Three rounds of analysis took place. Although we were ultimately interested in assessing the effects of the pressure and support variables, we needed to first determine whether a linear growth model or quadratic growth model would best fit the data. To do so, we ran models with only "year" and "year-squared" for each of the math and science instructional scale scores (inquiry-oriented pedagogy, didactic pedagogy, teaching to the test the month before ESPA, and teaching to the test throughout the year).[2]

Next, we introduced district wealth (DFG) as a possible explanatory variable at the teacher level to assess the differential effects of district socioeconomic status (SES) on initial status and growth rates. Though not strictly speaking a teacher variable, all teachers in the analysis taught in the same school (and thus district) for the duration of the study. DFG was a significant predictor of initial status ("true score" for the first year) in some models, but not of growth rate. DFG was retained as a Level 2 predictor of initial status in all models to maintain comparability across disciplines and practice.

Finally, Level 1 predictors were introduced such that each year's measures of teaching practice and test preparation were regressed on the pressure and support variables from the same year. We entered all independent variables simultaneously to explore their joint effects, as we had indications from earlier work that these variables were indicators of the larger school and district context in which instruction occurred. We followed this procedure for all HLM analyses. We also calculated effect sizes, which enabled us to compare the relative contribution of each explanatory variable for math and science pedagogy and test preparation.[3] All analyses were conducted using HLM 5 (Raudenbush, Bryk, Cheong, & Congdon, 2000).

Interviews

All the teachers who were interviewed were asked a number of questions about the pressure and support they received. For instance, teachers were asked such questions about their professional development as "When you want help to improve your teaching or develop new ideas, where do you usually turn?" They were also asked in an open-ended way for their views about the ESPA—"What do you think of the ESPA?"—during which they had the opportunity to comment on any pressure they felt to raise test scores or support they received in dealing with the test. In addition, they were explicitly asked about their interactions with their principals and with district staff in ways that should have elicited comments about any pressure or support they received (see Appendix D).

Once interviews were completed, they were transcribed and entered into a qualitative data management program. Then interviews were reviewed in a semi-inductive manner to develop a coding scheme that reflected both teachers' comments and the original research questions. This coding scheme had several nested layers that permitted identifying, for instance, where teachers discussed pressure stemming from the principal separately from that stemming from the central office as well as a variety of different kinds of supports (see Appendix E). Comments were then organized by codes and examined both to note the frequency of codes among the 75 interviewed teachers (some teachers were interviewed in more than one year) and for the substance of what was discussed with regard to each code.

FINDINGS

We discuss findings separately for the interviews and the survey.

Interviews

Though pressure and support appear to have somewhat different effects—pressure encourages didactic instruction and decontextualized, short-term test preparation whereas support encourages more inquiry-oriented instruction and test preparation integrated into regular teaching—teachers report more support than pressure. When we limited our examination to pressure and support coming from the formal hierarchy—that is, central office and principals—43 out of 75 teachers mentioned experiencing some kind of pressure whereas 56 described some form of support. With numbers like these, many teachers must experience both, but support is more prevalent. Here we explore how teachers experience pressure and support and then some of the combinations that appear in practice.

Pressure. Accountability theories expect the pressure to respond to tests to be a rational reaction to the way incentives are linked to test scores, but this response depends on whether strong or weak accountability systems are in place (Adams & Kirst, 1999). Strong accountability systems are designed so that teachers or students will experience direct consequences, such as a financial incentive or promotion to the next grade, as a result of test scores. With weak accountability systems, publication of test results may lead less directly to incentives or sanctions or at least the risk of them for teachers and students.

The limited pressure from direct incentives reflects a state policy that linked few if any incentives to test scores. Instead, indirect accountability from the negative publicity stemming from low scores threatened to put district and schools at risk politically and reduce the goodwill needed to get financial support for education. In addition, teachers did experience pressure from parents. They also experienced a sense of responsibility for students that tended to counter the pressure coming from the central administration, but not always in a constructive way.

The most frequent source of pressure on teachers came from the formal hierarchy. Twenty teachers mentioned some kind of pressure coming from the district and 25 mentioned it coming from the principal. Such pressure was not uniform. For instance, seven teachers said that their principals did not put great pressure on getting good ESPA results. According to one, "it's nice in a sense. He doesn't make you nuts about it.... You know, he'll give you stuff, but he won't like [sic] keep saying, 'Are you doing this? Are you doing that?' "

Sometimes, administrative pressure took the form of what one teacher called "a domino effect from the hierarchy all the way down to the child, trying to have them [sic] do their best." Another teacher described a similar situation where "the administrators have been on our cases to increase the scores, but not giving us any techniques as to how to do it." This teacher recognized why the administration was "on her case." According to her, the central administration was "feeling the pressure because the scores are published and comparing districts and stuff like that, and Newtown[4] is a very nice town and we've always done well on standardized tests. And here's the ESPA test and we're not doing that well."

In other cases, the pressure was less explicit. Without a great deal of direct communication or threats from administrators, teachers understood the situation that district leaders faced, believed that their interests and those of district administrators were similar, and tried to cooperate. As two teachers explained:

> I think it's important for them because I think just the press that goes along, you know, associated with it. You know, people read the newspapers. And, you know, they are judged by their scores. So they are very sensitive, as is the principal. He is sensitive to that. But you know, not to the extent that ... he's gonna put any undue stress on teachers.

> I mean they'd have to be crazy not to want to focus on it, because today politically, I mean education's a very large political issue. I mean they're publishing scores in newspapers and they're trying to pass budgets in places, where the situation, where, you know, the taxes are high and people are reluctant to spend money.

Whether in its direct or indirect form, pressure related to the need for good publicity for the district was mentioned by at least 11 teachers.

Among the indirect ways to communicate pressure was district provision of workshops, which could be perceived as both pressure to change or support for change. Nine out of 75 teachers perceived districts' efforts in allocating many resources in workshops and pushing teachers to quickly change teaching strategies as illustrative of how important ESPA was for them. A teacher commented: "That's why like we've had all those in-services. So I imagine since they're taking us—there's even times, you know, they've taken us away from instruction. Then I think 'ESPA is very important.' " Workshops were also perceived as pressuring when they drove instruction toward test preparation or when they were mandatory. As one teacher explained:

> I took ESPA English because they made us take that. Every third- and fourth-grade teacher went to that. I hadn't signed up for it ... I didn't feel that I needed to go to this workshop on it. But I went. We were all forced to go. Because I remember getting my paperwork and going, "I didn't sign up for this." "No, everybody did. Everybody's going." I don't—it's there if you want it and if you need it. But that's it.

Four of the nine teachers also viewed district workshops as supportive. In total 14 of the 75 teachers implied that they perceived the district's role in providing workshops as supportive because the district made it easier for teachers to incorporate the changes mandated by the state:

> Oh, they give us a lot of training. I've been to many, many ESPA training [sessions]. As a matter of fact, there was a meeting yesterday on ESPA, and then there will be a meeting next Monday on ESPA. They train us in the writing problems, they train us in the poetry problems, and then they'll say OK. Now take this problem, go back and do it and ... baseline, look at what skills you need to work on and things like that. So they're very, very supportive.

Meetings communicate pressure more directly than workshops do. Fourteen of the 16 teachers who referred to meetings mentioned that they discussed issues about ESPA, such as how to score or how to teach specific test prep strategies. One teacher said, "50% of the meetings are ESPA talk." Another teacher said that "[ESPA scores] are the topic of the day." In one district the meetings were organized for only the fourth-grade teachers. Some teachers mentioned that leaders would show scores and they would "lecture" the teachers about the results.

The type of information that the district presents is also a way to communicate pressure. Some districts give teachers photocopies of the newspaper where the scores were published. In chapter 3, we mentioned that 91% of the teachers who received test results were given the school average. Far from informing about the specific instructional needs of the students, the presentation of school average scores could create more pressure. A teacher told us: "Oh my goodness, and the pressure on for ESPA. We all wanna [sic] do so well. It's very competitive in our district. Every school wants to be better than the other, every classroom wants to be better than the other." Only 5 out of the 22 teachers who discussed their scores talked about the content of the test and only 7 discussed the meaning of the scores. "But my biggest concern is that I really don't know the difference between a proficient or highly proficient answer. You know, how is it rated? That's the thing that frustrates me."

Some teachers also experienced pressure from parents, but this was more inconsistent. One teacher reported that, "in our town, there was a big hoop-de-doo because the parents are up in arms because of—that we didn't do as well as they would have wanted ... And I actually had a parent call me and say, 'Oh, did you see the newspaper? ... Why is that?' " Another teacher reported that "it was interesting what the parents thought. Some said, oh, no, its [sic] your job. You have to get that child to do the best on the test. Some parents said, 'it doesn't mean anything to me.' " Many parents were less concerned with their children's test scores than some broader conception of the child's welfare. As one teacher explained:

> The parents in the fall when we have our open houses one of the biggest questions we get as fourth-grade teachers is "Tell us about the ESPA. What's it like? We hear it's terrible. We hear it's long. What will this do to my child when he goes to middle school? Will he be able to get into a good college." I mean, you get all these concerns.

Moreover, parents did not necessarily understand the kind of changes the state standards were encouraging. According to another teacher, "So many parents don't realize that. It's almost like they need a lesson in why teachers teach the way they might teach." Thus, some teachers found parents very focused on test scores and others not. Some parents seemed to view test scores in the context of some larger vision they had of what their children needed. And when teachers made some kinds of changes in response to the test, especially those that differed most from conventional practice, they had to explain those changes to parents.

Finally, teachers were concerned about the amount of pressure placed on their students to do well on tests. Teachers felt that this pressure was more likely to work against student success. This concern took two forms. The first was sympathy for the pressure that children were under. Teachers explained that:

> By the time our children sit down to take it, they're a mess. They're a basket case because there's been too much press about them, too much from their parents about them.

> I don't like the amount of time that the children are exposed to the test. This is a grueling week for fourth graders. I don't think they are ready for that kind of pressure.

The other theme was a sense of vulnerability because children simply lacked the knowledge or skills to pass the test. These teachers explained that:

> There's nothing a school can do or a parent can do or a teacher can do to speed up that individual's development. That's like trying to make your kid walk when they're a year old because your nieces and nephews are walking, but your kid is not ready to walk until they're [sic] 15 months old. Well, they're not going to do it until they're 15 months old. But if they had to take an ESPA on it at a year old, they'd fail.

> Some kids come to us, they can't write a sentence. They can't write one single sentence. How are we going to get that child prepared for a test that the state expects them to write a paragraph? ... I don't think the people who made up the test really know what fourth graders are all about.

These latter comments can be interpreted in two ways, either as a realistic assessment of the ability of 9-year-olds, which is at odds with the assessment of those writing the state standards, or as the classic low expectations that high standards are intended to overcome. In either case, they are a manifestation of a lack of the personal efficacy that we found associated with both inquiry-oriented instruction and long-term test preparation (see later discussion of survey results). One understands why such teachers are unlikely to respond to incentives (whether direct or indirect) in ways that encourage classroom environments where children have the opportunity to think more deeply about the content introduced in class. Such teachers simply do not think their efforts will be successful. It should be noted that the teachers who thought the test was too difficult for their students were not limited to the poorest districts. They were found in rich and poor districts alike.

Support. Teachers mention three kinds of support: materials, curricular assistance, and learning opportunities. Some of these were more apparent than others, and what existed varied in quality. Materials were mentioned by about a third of the teachers (25). On balance, materials appeared relatively easy to obtain. Most teachers seemed to think they could get what they needed although, in some districts, there was a sense that funding for materials was becoming more scarce. At least one teacher explained that she had bought materials for a science experiment and complained how difficult it was to ask children not to write in what were supposed to be consumable books in reading. Moreover, when resources were limited, it was clearly easier to get materials that supported ESPA directly. As one teacher explained:

> Recently with like all the hands-on science that was coming across, with the test, with the ESPA, we ... mentioned to the principal we need magnifying glasses, ... and he found the money for that. But if I saw, you know a brand-

new program I wanted to try, I don't think that there's anybody I could go to and say, 'Hey, could we buy [that],' not if it was a big, involved thing.

In many districts, teachers received a great deal of materials related to the state test. They said, "We've gotten some, you know, ESPA packets here and there and sample ESPA this and sample ESPA that" or "They've provided us with a lot of the packet information and a lot of answer keys, which has been pretty helpful." It was less common, but certainly not unheard of to get materials that supported active, hands-on learning. Teachers reported getting new, sophisticated learning materials from the Technology Education Research Center (TERC) and other organizations developing and supplying them. Teachers also had access to science kits that were often rented from one of a few nonprofit organizations around the state that made a business of sharing the more expensive and less frequently used materials with a number of districts.

Curricular assistance was mentioned less often, by 14 teachers. Much of this discussion was actually about regular, ongoing curricular revision. In almost all districts, such revision happened on a regular cycle and would continue whether standards were in place or not. However, as teachers noted, and as was much more explicit in some districts, "I think a lot of it would be ESPA driven because [it] really got going when the ESPA tests really started coming along, so I can only assume that that's when it really revved up so to speak" or "I think the curriculum is really changing and [the district] keeps up to date with it. We do have some meetings about ESPA to help keep us informed or if they can come up with any brilliant ideas as far as what we should be doing or how we should be doing it." Thus, ESPA informed this revision process.

In addition, some districts made special efforts to align materials and parts of textbooks with specific state standards. According to one teacher:

> When the standards were introduced, Ridley [a pseudonym for the district] aligned—well math actually was the first one … the math department aligned our curriculum with the standards … And then went through our textbook that we used and said like let's say I wanted to use the standard for set operations. In my book, my big binder that I got from the math department, it says you can use math textbook pages 6, 7 and 8 to teach the standard. So obviously the math department has made it very, very easy for us to align the math curriculum with the standards.

Beyond providing materials and aligning curricula, many districts provided teachers with opportunities to learn about the new content and what were believed to be instructional approaches required or implied by the new standards and assessments. Many of these came through collective events like workshops in or outside the district. Thirty-five teachers described such events, but they differed very much in character. For instance, for some this meant attending conferences targeting the standards. One teacher noted:

> We became very interested in NCTM [National Council of Teachers of Mathematics] standards. They have allowed us to go to regional and national conferences. First of all so that we could embrace the idea of how we were going to write a curriculum, and that wasn't just one person. We sent a whole team of people and it was representative of every grade level and of different schools. When that team came back we began to show the other teachers what we had brought back.

Others were in districts that focused on short-term test preparation. They described people who "come in when we have our workshops that have spoken to us. But really on the ESPA, just different things for us to get better." From teachers' comments, many districts sought to align their professional-development programs with the new standards and tests, but at least one teacher differentiated between her district's ongoing professional development and preparation for ESPA where "it hasn't really been professional development. We've gotten some material … some of the past tests and things that are on ESPA."

The extent to which professional development was linked to ESPA and the state standards also varied. Some programs were largely opportunistic. One teacher, explained with only a little exasperation that "A lot of times it kind of goes in through the back door though. And I love [math specialist] a lot and I think he's working hard in his job. But he'll like [sic] write a grant first and then he'll run around and try to get people to get on board with it. And you know, sometimes it ends up falling to the same people a lot." The workshops in this district often reflected opportunities the math specialist found rather than a more coherent plan for improvement focused on ESPA or anything else.

In addition to opportunities to learn through regularly scheduled workshops and meetings, a good deal of professional development occurred as part of teachers' day-to-day activities. Some of this came as a result of the Abbott decision, which governs funding to the state's poorest, urban districts. These districts receive special state aid as a result of the court order governing their financing. The court order requires that they adopt a "whole school reform plan" such as Success for All, Accelerated Schools, or America's Choice. Teachers in those districts work with trainers from those programs in their schools. The districts also receive special funding to have a variety of whole-school reform facilitators and content coordinators who typically are skilled teachers who have been given nonclassroom assignments to work with their peers. In addition, almost all districts have central-office curriculum staff; those that are large enough may have mathematics or science curriculum coordinators available to work with teachers in their content areas. Additional assistance may come from principals.

Much of the work of these additional staff involves curriculum development, but they often provide other assistance as well. Our study noted that in some districts they observed teachers, and their observations, at least in principle, reflected the intent of state and national standards better than those of principals. One teacher explained that:

> We now have supervisors observing us also. Whereas our principal who is kind of like the general practitioner and has her specialty or his specialty, but you know when the social studies supervisor comes in you know—or the science—they know everything there is to know about science and they know how it should be instructed. So they're looking much more for hands-on. They don't want to see classrooms that are sitting there quiet. They want the kids doing.

Even so, the knowledge represented by those doing the supervising reflected a mix of what is current and what had been more prevalent during previous rounds of reform. Another teacher described a supervisor:

> [He] does a wonderful observation … When he does an observation in my classroom, he's reminding me of all the different … levels that I've hit. And, you know, kind of a little bit of Madeline Hunter too. And it's—he's really good at what he does. And he wants to see that. He wants to see the kids doing hands-on. He wants to see them cooperative. He wants to see them communicating. He wants to see them writing, even in math. So I think he's kind of stuck in the middle.

Beyond their work with special experts, teachers shared information with their colleagues. Almost all teachers—72 out of 75—said they talked with their colleagues, but the quality of that discussion varied. Often discussions were about what one teacher called "Nuts and bolts type things, questions. The other day, for your other science observation, I didn't know the difference between cc's and milliliters. I asked the nurse. She knew." Other teachers mentioned sharing information after someone had come back from an out-of-district workshop. It also appeared to be common to talk about how to keep children motivated and interested. They might also discuss how to get materials. The following comment illustrates how teachers might share about several areas:

> We talk about how we're going to get materials to teach science. In science, that's a particularly hard one. Math we have a lot of manipulatives. We exchange teaching ideas, like if we come across in a journal or something like that, we'll copy it and give it to my other fourth-grade teachers. That sort of

thing. We talk about how to meet the standards, how to best teach to get there. We've talked about grouping, would that help or would that be a deterrent, would that be detrimental. Those kinds of things.

The quality of these discussions depended in important ways on the nature of the social relations between teachers. Classically, teaching is an isolated occupation where teachers have limited opportunity to share information with each other and where norms of privacy constrain sharing even more (Lortie, 1975). Yet, when norms develop that encourage sharing, teachers can be their own best help in learning to improve practice (Louis & Kruse, 1995; Rosenholtz, 1989). To some extent, this bore out among the teachers interviewed. One teacher started out to explain that she used teachers much as she did other resources: "I usually turn to a lot of resources like books and, usually like other teachers and stuff. Like I use the Internet. Get a lot of ideas." However, a little more discussion revealed important differences among teachers in how they approached mathematics teaching in particular:

I just kind of try to get them to see that it needs to be hands-on. There's a big philosophy difference between a lot of teachers as to whether they need to do that computation all the time, or whether they need to be critical thinkers. I guess it's kind of like that, talking about that. And I think there's a lot of teachers that haven't been part of the [professional-development program], so they don't have the resources and the materials so I would assume that it's probably more difficult to teach if you don't. So usually sometimes just sharing materials and stuff.

In two districts in particular, teachers had developed working relationships that encouraged sharing. If the teacher just quoted was separated from her peers by professional-development experiences she had had that others had not, the teachers in these schools shared a number of experiences in common. In one district, a teacher said that:

[She and her colleagues discuss] the sessions that we go through, go to with [professional developer] and people from the district. Many of them I know because I've worked with them before or, I've had their kids or whatever, whatever, ... So lots of times in group, after group is over or even before if I see them around, I'll—one person I've talked to on the Internet occasionally about the fact that I'm doing this and I need some ideas or they're not getting that. And a lot I do that with [name of colleague]. And even with the other two fourth grade teachers in my building. I mean, we're a pretty close knit group the fourth grade teachers in terms of planning with each other. Not as much as we'd like to, but we're beginning to approach that idea.

Another teacher described how she shared with teachers at meetings:

> And generally I go back to teachers who were very supportive of me when I
> first started that are in our building. "What do you think, how should I try to
> do this?" I go to a lower-grade teacher and generally an upper-grade teacher. If
> I find certain kids that are having problems with certain areas, I'll go to their
> previous teacher to find out what they used that worked with them. But first,
> my first stop is usually in our meetings. After that, there's two teachers, three
> teachers that I always go to for advice. Then after that, it's if there's any there
> teachers in the building—oh, in my math class [with the professional devel-
> oper mentioned earlier]. How can I forget that?

However, this more active sharing that focused more intensively on both content and student problems seems to be the exception rather than the rule.

Survey

Although the relationships are not strong and the effects are moderate to
small, results of the HLM analysis indicate that changes in pedagogy and
test preparation since the inception of ESPA vary by discipline, as do the
factors associated with these practices. The survey data suggest a pattern
where teaching to the test is more prominent in poorer districts. Pressure is
associated with short-term responses to the test and, to some extent, with
more didactic instruction; and the more knowledge-based supports are associated with longer-term responses and somewhat more inquiry-oriented
instruction. Moreover, the teachers who report that they are better informed and more confident teachers are more likely to report engaging in
inquiry-oriented instruction. Finally, mathematics teaching is more sensi-
tive to the factors measured in this study than science teaching, perhaps because it has been an integral part of the fourth-grade curriculum in New
Jersey, whereas science was introduced recently in many schools in direct
response to ESPA. Based on what we've learned, we believe that more energy is devoted to improving mathematics instruction than science instruction. It may also be relevant that when science test scores became available,
they were generally higher than scores in mathematics and especially in language arts, so subsequently less attention was given to the science.
       When we examine the regression coefficients (fixed effects) for teaching
to the test the month before the ESPA is given (Table 4.3), three variables
might indicate some sense of compulsion to do more. The most obvious is
pressure, which has one of the largest effects of any of the predictor variables
for both mathematics and science.[5] Another indirect indication of some
sense of special responsibility to get children prepared is DFG, where there is
more teaching to the test in both mathematics and science in the poorer districts, the same ones where children historically score the lowest. The third

TABLE 4.3
HLM Results: Teaching to the Test the Month Before ESPA

Fixed Effects	Math		Science	
	Coefficient	Effect Size	Coefficient	Effect Size
Intercept	1.198***	—	1.774***	—
District Factor Group	−.035**	−.07	−.047***	−.09
Year	−.394***	−.73	.014	.03
Year Squared	.180***	.33	n/a	—
Pressure	.200***	.37	.209***	.38
Principal Support	.120**	.22	.099*	.18
ESPA Professional Development	.068***	.13	.024	.04
General Professional Development	.003	.01	.022	.04
Access to Textbooks	.099*	.18	.018	.03
Access to Manipulatives	.022	.04	n/a	—
Access to Calculators	.071	.13	n/a	—
Access To Science Kits	n/a	—	.038	.07
Access to Measurement Tools	n/a	—	.015	.03
Knowledge of Standards	.037**	.07	.020	.04
Personal Efficacy	.026	.05	.009	.02

$*p < .05$; $**p < .01$; $***p < .001$.

factor, at least for mathematics, is time. When other factors are controlled, teachers' short-term responses to the mathematics test were most prevalent in the first year, declined in the second year, but began to increase again the third year, as indicated by the significant coefficient for year-squared.[6]

Some supports also contribute to short-term preparation for the test. Principal support for standards and assessments, with the second largest effect across all models, is important for both mathematics and science. Two other variables are important for mathematics, but not science: professional development focused on ESPA (which as the interviews indicate has an element of pressure along with support) and access to textbooks. In addition teachers who report knowing more about mathematics (but not science) standards report more short-term preparation for the test.

Pressure does not contribute to teaching to the test throughout the year (Table 4.4), but like teaching to the test the month before the test is given, long-term preparation is more prevalent in poorer districts. In mathematics too, time is a factor. Teaching to the test throughout the year declined from the first to the second year and increased slightly between the second and third years.[7] Test preparation in science did not change significantly in the three years of the study.

Among the supports, principal support for standards contributes to year-long teaching to the test as does professional development focusing on ESPA. Both of these variables influence both math and science. General professional development has a small positive effect on year-long test preparation in science, but not in mathematics. Materials have no discernible influence on year-long test preparation. However, among the teacher characteristics, both knowledge of the standards and personal efficacy contribute to long-term test preparation in mathematics.

Didactic instruction is perhaps the least well explained of all the dependent variables examined here, especially for science (Table 4.5). Pressure encourages teachers to use this approach more in mathematics. Although not affecting didactic instruction to the extent seen in short-term test preparation, pressure has the strongest relationship with this form of instruction. Didactic teaching in mathematics does not vary by district wealth but it does in sci-

TABLE 4.4
HLM Results: Teaching to the Test All Year

Fixed Effects	Math		Science	
	Coefficient	Effect Size	Coefficient	Effect Size
Intercept	1.184***	—	1.688***	—
District Factor Group	−.043***	−.09	−.051***	−.10
Year	−.232**	−.47	−.033	−.06
Year-Squared	.083**	.17	n/a	—
Pressure	.036	.07	.037	.07
Principal Support	.140***	.28	.137**	.27
ESPA Professional Development	.079***	.16	.046**	.09
General Professional Development	.019	.04	.036*	.07
Access to Textbooks	.098**	.20	.030	.06
Access to Manipulatives	.022	.04	n/a	—
Access to Calculators	.048	.10	n/a	—
Access to Science Kits	n/a	—	.019	.04
Access to Measurement Tools	n/a	—	.010	.02
Knowledge of Standards	.034**	.07	.018	.04
Personal Efficacy	.057*	.11	.043	.08

*p < .05; **p < .01; ***p < .001.

TABLE 4.5
HLM Results: Didactic Instruction

Fixed Effects	Math		Science	
	Coefficient	Effect Size	Coefficient	Effect Size
Intercept	2.954***	—	2.813***	—
District Factor Group	−.012	−.03	−.024*	−.05
Year	−.039*	−.08	.018	.04
Pressure	.082*	.17	.015	.03
Principal Support	.035	.07	.027	.06
ESPA Professional Development	.038*	.08	.030	.07
General Professional Development	−.038**	−.08	−.014	−.03
Access to Textbooks	.077*	.16	.047*	.10
Access to Manipulatives	−.072*	−.15	n/a	—
Access to Calculators	−.032	−.07	n/a	—
Access to Science Kits	n/a	—	−.002	.00
Access to Measurement Tools	n/a	—	−.049	−.11
Knowledge of Standards	−.031**	−.07	−.010	−.02
Personal Efficacy	.023	.05	−.012	−.03

*$p < .05$; **$p < .01$; ***$p < .001$.

ence; there is more didactic science instruction in poorer districts. Changes in didactic and inquiry-oriented instruction were linear rather than quadratic. Looking at the coefficient for year, we see that the amount of didactic instruction in mathematics declined somewhat over time, but didactic science instruction did not. Professional development focusing on ESPA encourages didactic instruction, but general professional development has the opposite effect. The former relationship may reflect the element of pressure in ESPA professional development, whereas the latter probably reflects the generally inquiry-oriented approach to professional development offered by most universities and professional-development organizations in the state. Both of these relationships hold for mathematics, but not for science. We think that this is probably because more professional development is offered in the former area. Access to textbooks is positively associated with didactic instruction in mathematics and science, but access to manipulatives would seem to discourage it in mathematics. Finally, teachers who report understanding the standards better also say they engage in less didactic instruction.

Inquiry-oriented instruction (Table 4.6) has some similarities with long-term test preparation. Here too, pressure is not a factor for mathematics or science, nor is DFG, but like didactic instruction, the amount of inquiry-oriented instruction declined slightly with time. Among the supports, principal support for standards and assessments has a strong relationship with inquiry-oriented instruction in both fields. General professional development also contributes to inquiry-oriented instruction, but professional development related to ESPA only contributes to inquiry-oriented instruction in mathematics, not in science. The association of ESPA-oriented professional development to both didactic and inquiry-oriented instruction may reflect the mixed nature of the ESPA and the kind of preparation offered for it. Textbooks have no discernible relationship to inquiry-oriented instruction, but there is a positive association with calculators in mathematics and kits in science. Finally, teachers who report understanding the standards better and higher levels of personal efficacy engage in more inquiry-oriented instruction in both subjects.

CONCLUSION

Test preparation in New Jersey takes place in a variable context of pressure and support. The mix of pressure and support teachers experience influence the kind of teaching to the test in which they engage.

TABLE 4.6
HLM Results: Inquiry-Oriented Instruction

Fixed Effects	Math		Science	
	Coefficient	Effect Size	Coefficient	Effect Size
Intercept	1.622***	—	1.909***	—
District Factor Group	.006	.01	.002	.01
Year	−.075***	−.15	−.049**	−.11
Pressure	−.047	−.10	−.024	−.05
Principal Support	.097**	.20	.079*	.18
ESPA Professional Development	.041**	.08	.025	.06
General Professional Development	.043**	.09	.026*	.06
Access to Textbooks	.023	.05	−.006	−.01
Access to Manipulatives	.028	.06	n/a	—
Access to Calculators	.114*	.23	n/a	—
Access to Science Kits	n/a	—	.042*	.10
Access to Measurement Tools	n/a	—	.039	.09
Knowledge of Standards	.055***	.11	.046***	.11
Personal Efficacy	.052*	.11	.086***	.20

$*p < .05$; $**p < .01$; $***p < .001$.

In spite of weak formal incentives from the state, teachers experience notable pressure from the formal hierarchy, principals, and central-office staff. Sometimes it comes directly through exhortation to do better; sometimes it is indirect. Either way, teachers understand very well that their districts will be better able to obtain necessary funding if test scores go up. Pressure related to publicity and the formal hierarchy is not consistently supported from other directions, however. Some parents do care about their children's test scores, but many have a broader view of their children's welfare. These parents may worry about the stress youngsters are put under or how all of this relates to their future. They will not automatically support a state-testing regime. If the instructional strategies that contribute to high scores are unfamiliar, such parents may well balk unless they are educated about state-mandated testing. Finally, some teachers in rich and poor districts alike simply doubt that their students can do the work. Without some kind of intervention, these teachers are not likely to increase their efforts to meet state-set targets simply because they think such targets aren't feasible.

Most of the support that teachers talk about is very concrete. It consists of materials, changes in curriculum to help them align their teaching with the content on the tests, and learning opportunities. Learning opportunities include special activities like workshops and training sessions, but they also include job-embedded learning opportunities that come from university partners, specialists, superiors, and peers. The kind of learning experiences make a difference with some reinforcing short-term, decontextualized test preparation and others more fundamental changes in practice. It should also be noted that some of the teachers' peers and superiors bring a long history of educational reform with them. Thus, some of the professional-development teachers receive deals with older approaches to improvement that may or may not be well aligned with current ideas about standards-based reform.

Recent literature has placed considerable emphasis on learning opportunities, but access to materials plays an important role in influencing both general instruction and test preparation. Providing equipment and materials that can be used as part of more challenging mathematical and science tasks is important for encouraging that kind of change whereas more traditional textbooks would appear to reinforce didactic instruction and short-term test preparation. This is another indicator of how money can make a difference in educational reform. The issue though is not how much is available but how it is spent.

The evidence from New Jersey suggests that, at least with regard to test preparation, pressure and support as practiced are not as complementary as Fullan indicated. The key to encouraging the kind of instruction envisioned by New Jersey's and national standards is to provide supports in the form of learning opportunities that help teachers understand what they are teaching and how to teach it. Pressure encourages decontextualized approaches to test preparation and—to a lesser extent—conventional didactic practice.

Learning opportunities that focus on new approaches to instruction promote inquiry-oriented instruction. However, even then, such instruction is more likely among teachers who are better informed and whose personal efficacy is high enough so they have firm beliefs that they can successfully teach their children well. Finally, the evidence presented here reinforces the conclusion of chapter 3 that test preparation as an end in itself is more prominent in the state's poorest districts although more general approaches to improving instruction are not clearly related to school demographics.

ENDNOTES

1. Often referred to as growth curve modeling, this type of analysis is premised on two assumptions: (a) the observed status on a variable of interest for an individual at a given time (in particular, an individual teacher's survey response or scale score in the second year of this 3-year study) is a function of a growth trajectory and random error, and (b) there is individual variation in growth trajectories meaning here that teachers vary in how they change or "grow" on the response from year to year (Raudenbush & Bryk, 2002). To capture growth or trends over time, "year" was used as an indicator variable to capture linear growth or change (instantaneous change at each time point) and "year-squared" was used to capture the curvature or acceleration of each growth trajectory (change in growth rate). With the variable "year" specified as time from first ESPA administration, the Level 2 intercept represents the "true" scale score at onset of ESPA (initial status), and the "year" coefficient would indicate rate of change in points per year during the study, whereas the "year-squared" coefficient when included in the model would indicate the rate of acceleration (or change in the rate of change)

2. Identification of significant predictors was based on hypothesis tests for time and other fixed effects, in which the ratio of the estimated effects to their standard errors (Wald statistic) is compared to a t distribution with $J - Q - 1$ degrees of freedom, where J is the number of Level 2 units and Q is the number of Level 2 predictors. Selection of the appropriate error structure (unrestricted, homogeneous or constant variance, heterogeneous or variance that varied as a function of time) was based on chi-square tests of model fit that compare deviance statistics for each pair of models. In all cases, the unrestricted models provided the best fit to the data. Under the unrestricted model, there is no modeling of random variation between persons in the regression coefficients because all variation is absorbed into the covariance matrix for the repeated measurements. Therefore, explanatory variables introduced in Level 1 are treated as fixed effects at Level 2, meaning that their effect is not expected to vary randomly across teachers.

3. Effect sizes were calculated by dividing raw (unstandardized) regression coefficients by the standard deviation of the dependent variable.

4. Newtown and other district names are pseudonyms. Some districts that were studied in more depth were given such pseudonyms. See chapter 6.

5. To help with interpreting these results, consider holding all other factors constant for teaching to the test in mathematics. With an effect size of .37 and regression coefficient of .20, if pressure were increased by 1 scale point per year, there would be an associated increase in teaching to the test the month before ESPA of a

bit more than 1/3 of a standard deviation per year, and almost half a scale point (.40) over the course of 2 years. An effect size of .37 is moderate for this type of research.

6. The growth rate for any year is the first derivative of the growth model evaluated at that time point. Thus, holding all other factors constant, the mean rate of change in short-term test preparation in mathematics is $-.394 + 2 * .180 *$ (year) for a rate of change of $-.394$ scale points in 1999, $-.034$ scale points in 2000 (a much slower decrease), and an average rate of increase of .326 scale points per year in 2001.

7. Growth rates for teaching to the test throughout the year were $-.232$, $-.066$, and 0.1 in 1999, 2000, and 2001, respectively.

5

The Principal,
Test Preparation,
and Educational Reform

William A. Firestone
Lora F. Monfils
Margaret Hayes
Terrie Polovsky
M. Cecilia Martinez
Jennifer E. Hicks

The analyses in chapter 4 suggest that the principal has considerable influence over how and how much teachers teach to the test. Where principals support the state's standards and assessments, teachers spend more time on both short- and long-term test preparation and are more likely to engage in inquiry-oriented instruction in both math and science. That principal support helped to explain teaching practice in more of the analyses in chapter 4 than any other variable illustrates its importance. Yet, these findings suggest some incongruities in the principal's role. Why for instance does principal support for standards and assessments both encourage short-term test preparation, which is associated with more conventional forms of instruction, but also support inquiry-oriented instruction?

Although the findings reported so far point to the importance of principal support for influencing the nature of teaching to the test, they provide little insight into what principal support looks like and how it contributes to the inquiry-oriented responses to the state test (or inquiry-oriented teaching more broadly). Moreover, they provide little insight into the factors that might motivate principals to become more assertive in promoting improved practice.

This chapter addresses three questions about how principals influence teaching:

- What is the division of labor between the principal and district office staff?
- What is the nature of principal support and how do the typical patterns of support in New Jersey compare to general models of principal leadership?
- What factors influence principal leadership?

DISTRICTS, PRINCIPALS, AND TYPES OF LEADERSHIP

To set the context for the analysis of how principal leadership influences teaching to the test, we briefly review past research on the three questions just raised.

Division of Labor

Various claims have been made about the importance of principals and the central office, often focusing on rather different outcomes. For instance, the effective schools literature of the 1970s and 1980s touted the critical role of the principal in promoting high achievement, and more recent and sophisticated quantitative analyses confirm that principals can help raise achievement, albeit indirectly by influencing teaching (Bossert, 1988; Hallinger & Heck, 1996). There is also considerable evidence that principals can be important for facilitating schoolwide change (Fullan, 1991; Louis, Toole, & Hargreaves, 1999). More recently, Spillane (1996) argued that districts matter, at least with regard to enacting state reforms. This new emphasis on the district fits with some of the earliest research on school improvement, which also highlights the key role of district leadership (McLaughlin, 1990; Rosenblum & Louis, 1981).

The issue is not so much whether districts or principals make the more major contribution to change, but whether they make different kinds of contributions. For instance, because education is governed through districts, district offices have budgetary authority and can be a major source of the financial resources needed for changing practice (Heller & Firestone, 1995). Spillane (1996) argued that school districts are in a critical position to define state standards policies, which are often ambiguous. This capacity to define comes in large measure because district offices are often the primary source of content expertise among district administrators, and the larger the district, the more extensive and more specialized will such expertise be (Hannaway & Kimball, 2001). Thus, to the extent that a reform depends on curricular, pedagogic, and content expertise, one would expect the district office to play a major role. This is certainly the case with standards-based reforms where the measured outcome is test results in specific subjects, and where the reform rhetoric emphasizes the importance of deeper knowledge of the content in specific fields (National Council of Teachers of Mathematics [NCTM], 2000). One might expect principals to provide less content-specific leadership in the face of strong central-office professionals, but little is known about how access to expertise is used by principals.

Models of Leadership

At least in theory, principals can make a wider variety of contributions than can districts. These are captured in three frequently discussed models for transactional, transformational, and instructional leadership (Leithwood & Duke, 1999). The first two models are general and have been applied to a wide variety of fields whereas instructional leadership is education specific (B. M. Bass & Avolio, 1994).

Drawing on the work of Burns (1978), B. M. Bass and Avolio (1994), and others, Leithwood and Duke (1999) defined transactional leadership as the conventional approach that leaders use to engage followers and the focus of most past leadership research. Transactional leadership is based on exchange and bargaining where the leader offers valued things in return for compliance on new or ongoing initiatives. It is generally amoral and does not involve any invoking of higher purposes. Nor does it focus on the details of the work process. It is something a generalist can do. Moreover, the emphasis is on increasing positive incentives through contingent rewards, management-by-exception, and a laissez-faire approach to supervision. Transactional leadership has received little attention in the study of the principalship, except for those who examine micropolitics, but principals would seem to have a variety of resources at their disposal that they can use to persuade teachers to change their behavior (Blase, 1993). These certainly include various ways to put pressure on teachers but are less likely to include support.

In the general leadership literature, transformational leadership is seen as the most powerful way to promote change. It goes beyond the neutral, exchange of transactional leadership to embody new purposes and policies with great moral import. Usually, charisma is viewed as central to transformational leadership. Transformational leaders are said to combine the four "i's" of idealized influence, inspirational motivation, intellectual stimulation, and individualized consideration in the service of improvement. Moreover, there is a collective aspect to the work of transformational leaders. They shape not only the willingness of individuals to change what they do but also affect the culture of the organization, such that others can reinforce and support the message of the transformational leader. This may be necessary with larger changes, as leadership from multiple sources may be necessary to enact the substantial institutional makeovers that transformational leadership often aims for (B. M. Bass & Avolio, 1994; Leithwood, Jantzi, & Steinbach, 1999).

Transformational leadership covers two recurring themes in the study of the principalship. One is the focus on goal setting. One key finding of the effective schools literature was that where children achieved at higher levels than predicted by their socioeconomic background, the principal made high achievement for all children the school's top goal. This was more a matter of focusing attention than providing technical expertise, although effective principals did seek to coordinate curriculum, schedules, and resources to focus on teaching and learning (Bossert, 1988). A strong vision is also associated with effective change, although sometimes that vision grows out of the change process rather than being present at the start (Heller & Firestone, 1995; Louis & Miles, 1990). There is a substantial body of research indicating that principals can be instrumental in building a shared vision in a school (Smylie & Hart, 1999).

A related element of transformational leadership is the building of a community where teachers collaborate, share information about teaching and students, and solve professional problems together. Collaboration among teachers builds learning about teaching, and such learning can contribute to improved practice. There is even some evidence linking communities of teachers working together to more inquiry-oriented instruction (Louis & Kruse, 1995; Newmann & Associates, 1996; Rosenholtz, 1989). Principals can be instrumental in building and supporting such professional communities (Louis & Kruse, 1995; Smylie, Conley, & Marks, 2002). Such community building is likely to be interpreted as supportive by principals.

Instructional leadership is specific to schools and includes the work that principals do directly with teachers to improve their teaching (Blase & Blase, 1999; Kleine-Kracht, 1993). Dialogue about instructional leadership has changed with shifting ideas about instruction. Some of the earlier discussions began with formal authority. The principal's license to provide such leadership comes from the basic employment contract, which authorizes principals to come into the classroom and observe teaching as part of normal supervision (Dreeben, 1970). However, such leadership can include a much broader array of activities, including professional development, curriculum development, and action research, among others. The authoritative dimension has been downplayed in recent years in favor of a more participatory, inquiry-based approach to helping teachers reflect on their work in the process of improving it (Blase & Blase, 1999). Moreover, insofar as instructional leadership focuses on the improvement of teaching, it need not come just from the principal.

In addition to shifting instructional leadership from formal authority to joint inquiry processes, there has been a change in the substance of instructional leadership. The instructional leadership coming out of the effective schools research was content free. It had to do with managing the use of time, class size, grouping arrangements, curriculum pacing, and a variety of other resources to facilitate teacher learning, but it did not necessarily require the principal to be a content expert (Bossert, 1988; Leithwood & Duke, 1999). As definitions of expertise in teaching focus more on an understanding of the specific subjects taught (Shulman, 1987), the expectation is growing that instructional leaders should also have a deep understanding of the subjects in the curriculum and ways to help children develop stronger knowledge about those subjects (Stein & D'Amico, 2000). There is a broad concern that, with the possible exception of language arts, most principals lack the necessary understanding of specific subject areas. Programs are now being developed to help principals develop the necessary expertise (Burch & Spillane, 2001; Nelson & Sassi, 2000). This concern about the need for content-specific instructional leadership is another reason for the recent interest in districts as leaders of reform (Spillane, 1996).

Applying these models is difficult because different authors have developed them in somewhat different ways. Some see charisma as central to transformational leadership (Hoy & Miskel, 1996) whereas others exclude charisma from their definition (Leithwood et al., 1999). On the other hand, some aspects of transformational leadership overlap substantially with what some define as instructional leadership (Leithwood & Duke, 1999). Thus, it is sometimes more useful to focus on specific leadership activities than broader models when trying to determine what supportive principals do. Some activities discussed as part of these models—for instance, community building and providing knowledge about instruction—are likely to be interpreted as support. Others, like close formal supervision, might be interpreted as pressure.

Pressure and the Principalship

There has been very little speculation about the conditions that would encourage principal support for implementing standards policy or taking any particular approach to leadership. Yet, the arguments that link such policies to teachers would seem to apply to principals as well. The assumption behind all such policies is that formal accountability systems will draw attention to measured outcomes, but the debate reflects the disagreement about how standards policy will affect teaching. Advocates of such policies believe that the attention will be beneficial whereas opponents believe that the policies will contribute to administrative pressure on principals, which they will pass on to teachers with the kind of negative effects for students already described (Adams & Kirst, 1999; Corbett & Wilson, 1991). It is not clear what advocates of standards expect of principals; opponents would be surprised to see substantial support for teachers and would predict a great deal of transactional leadership increasing the pressure on those working in the classroom.

Similar issues surround the socioeconomic background of students. Some people hope that standards and assessments will draw principals' attention to the education of poor and low-achieving students in ways that will equalize educational outcomes whereas others believe that these policies tend to disequalize, leading to more stigmatization of poor children and more pressure from administrators to raise test scores at any cost, even if it means teaching to the test (McNeil, 2000; O'Day & M. S. Smith, 1993).

A compounding factor is the role the community plays in implementing standards policies. Some research suggests that local communities do not fully understand or support standards and assessment policies. In these instances, strong ties between schools or districts and their communities might undermine the effects of standards policies by making other issues more salient (Fairman & Firestone, 2001). We still know very little about how community perceptions interact with standards policies to influence principals' thinking about their work.

METHODS

To explore the context and nature of principal support, this chapter relies on two data sources: teacher interviews and the principal survey.

Teacher Interviews

Although a number of questions from the teacher interviews provided useful information, we relied primarily on the following:

- How important are the Elementary School Performance Assessment (ESPA) scores to your principal? To your district staff? What does your principal do to help prepare you and your students for the ESPA? (Probe materials, workshops, pressure.) What do your district staff people do to help prepare you/your students for the ESPA? (Probe materials, workshops, pressure.) Do you feel that ESPA results are used in your evaluations? (Probe for pressure and accountability use.)
- What other things has your principal done to encourage you to improve your math and science teaching? (Probe: types of resources provided; i.e., time, materials, money for professional development.) Does your principal come to observe your class and make suggestions, either informally or for formal observations?
- When you want help to improve your teaching or develop new ideas, where do you usually turn? (Probe: professional development, peers, principal, instructional materials.)

Teachers who saw their ESPA scores from the year before were also asked with whom they discussed those scores. If the principal was one of those individuals, the teacher was asked what the discussion was about (see Appendix D).

When interviews were coded, one node in the coding scheme focused on the principal's role with several subnodes including tone or quality (support or pressure), provision of instructional assistance, observation, provision of resources, test pressure, delegation to district, and evidence of principals bringing cohesion.

Principal Survey

The principal survey included a mix of closed- and open-ended items (see Appendix C). From the former, we developed three scales. Whereas there was no direct measure of principal support for standards and assessment, there was a measure of principal ESPA preparation activities. Principals reported how often they did six things:

1. Arrange for professional development related to ESPA and tested subjects.
2. Hold pep rallies, pizza parties, and other social events to motivate students.
3. Tell teachers and students that doing well on ESPA was a high priority.
4. Require teachers to cover ESPA topics before the test was administered.
5. Express disapproval of teachers who were not working hard enough to raise ESPA scores.
6. Focus on core curriculum content standards while supervising and evaluating teachers.

The scale had a reliability that ranged from .71 to .76 across the 3 years.

Two scales assessed aspects of principal accountability. One consisted of two items assessing accountability to the community by asking the extent to which parents and the school board held the principal accountable. The second assessed the importance of ESPA for holding principals accountable to the superintendent, the school board, and parents. These scales had reliabilities that ranged from .57 to .62 and from .74 to .88 respectively.

In addition, principals were asked open-ended questions about the major issues the school faced in the last 2 years, the major issues the district faced in the last 3 years, curriculum changes in math or science in the school in the last 3 years, the criteria principals used to evaluate teachers, the things happening in the school to ensure that students were learning the state core curriculum content standards, and the things happening in the school to prepare students for ESPA. We focused our analysis on the principal responses from year 2000. The number of principals providing at least one codable response to specific items ranged from 97 to 122.

Although these responses were generally quite short, an experienced principal reviewed them all and inductively derived a set of codes for each question. Each question was then coded by the principal and two experienced teachers. Each response was coded by the principal and one of the teachers. Rates of agreement among raters ranged from 78 percent for the principal's criteria for evaluating teachers to 90 percent for the district-level issues. Answers to these questions provide a qualitative description of the situations of principals coping with ESPA.

Analysis Strategies

Different analytic techniques were used with each data source. With the closed-ended questions on the principal survey, we examined basic distributions and correlations among principal variables. We also examined correlations between measures from the principal survey and measures from the teacher survey aggregated to the school level. To learn more about the factors affecting principals' activities, we regressed the principal accountability scales and District Factor Group on principal support and related measures.

With the open-ended principal questions, we began by simply examining frequencies and what principals and teachers actually said about the issue in question. However, we used these responses in conjunction with the information from the teacher interviews.

With the teacher interviews, we looked for specific themes within coded sections of interviews that helped to clarify what the principals did and how those actions were perceived by teachers. We also examined teacher descriptions of how they were supported by their districts. Understanding of these themes was enhanced by both examining the content of teacher statements and counting the frequencies with which themes appeared. We also looked at how teachers described the principals who had received the highest and lowest principal support ratings for standards and assessment in the surveys. In these cases, we compared responses for the top and bottom third. We also examined how principals given the highest and lowest support ratings by teachers differed in their answers to questions.

We now turn to our exploration of the division of labor between principals and the central office, the nature of principal support, and the effects of pressure on the principalship.

THE DIVISION OF LEADERSHIP LABOR

When we compare the contributions of the district office and principals from the perspective of teachers, the differences are not quite what might be expected from the literature. It had as much to do with formality and specificity as with content knowledge. Whereas both the district office and principals engaged with curricular and instructional issues, they did so in different ways. The district office's role was more formal. For instance, the district was the primary source of formal professional-development opportunities. As one teacher said, "It's really more the curriculum developer that does that. He sends out flyers of workshops and professional-development stuff." The interviewed teachers represented 26 districts. In 15 of these, the district organized formal professional-development opportunities. The principal only did so in five districts. One teacher spoke derogatorily of the principal "passing the buck" for playing such a limited role with respect to curriculum and instruction, but others believed that the major responsibility for supporting instruction rested with the central office. The principal's job was to complement and sustain the district's in-service offerings by finding substitutes to free time for teachers to participate and by supporting innovations in the classroom. Teachers explained that the principal has "just been very supportive, allowing us to attend, we've had district meetings where all the fourth-grade teachers have gotten together with our assistant superintendent" or the principal "works in collaboration with district making in-services and resources available to teachers."

The district was also responsible for the formal curriculum. Teachers explicitly said that the districts defined the curriculum in 13 districts. Only in one district did a new principal initiate a new math program. On the other hand, principals in seven districts were reported to have organized extracurricular events to motivate students for the test, such as a pizza party to mark the completion of ESPA testing.

The principal's instructional involvement was more informal. For instance, principals were more likely to make suggestions to help teachers improve their practice. These might include advising a teacher on how to handle a classroom disturbance or discussing other issues relating to classroom management. Principals were mentioned as the source of such day-to-day guidance by teachers from seven districts whereas teachers only mentioned central-office staff in two.

Other tasks were shared by the principals and the district office. For instance, both the district (6 districts) and the principal (7 districts) called meetings with teachers that focused on reaching state standards or doing well on the ESPA. There was even more discussion of getting material resources (including both supplies and time) from both the district (13 districts) and the principals (16 districts).

LEADERSHIP DESCRIBED

Teachers' comments and principals' responses both suggest that only modest instructional leadership was provided by principals. Though most principals provided material support, the most supportive principals provided assistance and information about instruction, either directly or indirectly. They also avoided reliance on formal authority. A few principals also provided individualized consideration. What is striking is how little principals did to focus goals in their schools or to build communities and cultures where teachers work together.

Material Support

Most principals in this sample offered teachers material support. For instance, interviewed teachers reported that their principals gave them time and resources to prepare for ESPA. Many teachers responded that their principals ordered the books they asked for and bought the material they needed. One said that, "The fourth-grade teachers felt that they needed more problem-solving things for the ESPA. She went out and ordered things for us. So she's always encouraging and she's right there with us all the time and believing in us and I think that's very important."

Teachers felt some ambivalence about this financial support. Some indicated that the only help they got from the principals was with money, what one of them described as "instrumental" assistance. As one explained, "In general, there hasn't been a whole lot of methodology help or anything like that, It's really been with the money as far as purchasing ESPA prep material. That's really it." Other teachers said their principals would do smaller things like photocopy articles or download things from the Internet—"I guess basically she photocopies articles that she sees like in the NCTM magazines and journals. She shares things, workshops and whatever." Still, this help was more in the form of providing things rather than interacting with teachers about ideas, content, or instructional methods.

To teachers, this material support was pervasive. Thirty-seven of the 48 principals on whom teachers commented (77%) were said to provide this kind of material support, but this was not something that supportive principals did more than any others.

Principals might have gone beyond making materials available to make more substantial changes in teachers' assignments to focus on ESPA. They could have made more structural changes that would focus resources rather heavily on ESPA. A number of observers have suggested that how time is allocated in schools is important both for student learning and for facilitating change (Elmore, 1995; B. Smith, 2000). Time allocations were changed only in rare instances. Furthermore, only seven principals talked about adding content specialists or staff developers in math or science, changing the roles of teachers to provide support as lead teachers, or adding personnel for curriculum development or to reduce class size. What was more common in the principal interviews was "intensification," which included changing the use of blocks of time or adding time before or after school or during the summer, as well as specific tutoring. When asked what they did specifically to prepare for ESPA, about a quarter of the principals (28) mentioned something of this sort, including, for instance, "Two periods a week to teaching strategies and deficit area from last year's ESPA."

Thus, the kind of material support that was offered appeared marginal. It may have focused attention on ESPA, but it did not change the way the school was organized in any fundamental way.

Eighteen of the 48 principals were reported by teachers to explicitly make ESPA a priority. Those who were reported as supportive were somewhat more likely to be reported as making ESPA a priority (48% of the most supportive principals and 39% of least supportive ones). Making ESPA a priority might have been part of a goal-setting, vision-building, transformational process, but it appeared to have had more to do with emphasizing ESPA when ordering materials. When we asked explicitly how important were the scores to the principals, 20 out of 27 teachers (71%) said that the principals put too much emphasis on ESPA. These teachers reported on 16 different principals so 13 out of 16 were said to overemphasize the state test.

Moreover, teachers reported that principals' concerns about ESPA influenced their budget decisions. In some cases, teachers said that before ESPA, they were given very little money for materials, but now it was easy to get support for things that could be justified in terms of ESPA. According to one, "She will buy us just about anything [if] we say it looks good for ESPA …. For certain things the money is not there. But it gets a little annoying to know that you ask for something for ESPA and all of a sudden, here is $400 to buy it." In addition, principals expressed their concern about ESPA. As one teacher explained, "He's made it a top priority in language and math. He feels it's only fair to the kids to have them well prepared for the test."

Like teachers, principals frequently mentioned providing materials. When they were asked what they did specifically to prepare for ESPA, 36% (50 of 138) said that they used some form of test preparation materials. In response to a more general question about curriculum changes in the last 3 years, 43 principals mentioned buying new math materials or programs, 25 mentioned buying math manipulatives, and 52 discussed moving to new, more activity-based science programs or adding other materials. It seems likely, however, that most of these changes were more initiatives of the central office reported by the principal than the result of the principal's own initiative. As with the teacher reports in most cases, there were no differences between principals reported to be most and least supportive. However, 52% of the most supportive principals mentioned buying new science programs or materials but only 36% of the least supportive principals did.

Assistance With Instruction

Principals also provided assistance with instruction. Much of it, according to teachers, was indirect. Almost two thirds of the principals (31 of 48) were said to arrange training for teachers. This was done by 17 of the 21 principals reported to provide high support and only 6 of the 13 who provided low support. This category does not include principal-provided training. It does cover situations where principals inform teachers about training opportunities and provide substitutes and other resources, enabling them to participate. Thus, it can be viewed as an amalgam of instructional and transactional leadership. Teachers explained:

> [My principal helps] by encouraging us and allowing us to go out and be involved in these staff development programs. I mean, my principal could easily say no, I don't want you out of the class. No problem. You know I just told her that I was invited to go to the teachers, the math convention in Chicago. And I'm going to that in April.

> Our principal is very helpful. He's allowed us to go to some workshops and he's given us the freedom to choose some effective professional development opportunities and he's really been supportive of that in terms of time.

> You know, he says, "If you are interested, would you like to go? Would you like to do this?" So in that respect, (he) guides me in professional development. And whenever I am doing professional development I always look for his expertise to go over it before I ever go out and say what do you think of this ... He professes that everybody really should go and continue becoming learners.

These teachers also commented on the principal's enthusiasm for professional development, as well as the willingness to provide resources.

Principals provided some confirmation for the teachers' views. In an open-ended question about recent math and science curriculum changes in the 2000 teacher survey, 18 out of 97 principals mentioned providing staff development. In a more specific question about preparation for ESPA, two fifths of the principals—58 of 138—said that they provided teacher workshops or time in faculty meetings to focus on that issue. However, the principals reported to be most supportive did not mention these activities more than those said to be less supportive.

Getting directly involved with instruction was less common. Still, according to teachers, just under half the principals—22 out of 48—either provided advice to teachers or offered help in the classroom. This practice was somewhat more common among the principals who supported the state standards and assessments (52% vs. 31%). Advice could take a variety of forms, but usually it came in ways that gave teachers the options of what to accept or how to build on it. According to one teacher:

> He'll come into my classroom and sit in the back of the room if I'm teaching a lesson, and, um, as I'm teaching a lesson I'll pose questions on him. And he'll pose 'em back. And then we'll get the kids involved. Before you know it, we're

in this big discussion about something and then he'll disappear ... he'll add a little something to it that I probably wouldn't have thought of.

Another teacher shared the following:

> The principal brings a lot of things into our building that are not done across the district, and can be applied to any subject area. I had said she had bought us these two books about, one called "Activators," one called "Summarizers." Different kinds of ways to open your lesson and close your lesson. So you have like a little more stuff in the bag of tricks.

Sometimes advice, or at least what the teachers said they got out of it, was general. One teacher described her principal as one who "talked a lot about the way that we need to focus on having children talk about what they think."

Sometimes when principals work in the classroom, they are more focused on the children than on the teacher. Three principals worked with students in a way that motivated them and may have modeled instructional approaches. Teachers said, "He is in and out of the classrooms with the kids investigating so that if the kids are doing some kind of project they'll say 'Can we invite Mr. XXX down to see how well he does this?'" or "She pops in randomly. She usually tends to find her way during math and she takes part in the discussion, which is great. Kids know that she is interested."

Supportive principals also reported directly that they are somewhat more active in curriculum and instruction. In the principal interviews, almost half of the most supportive principals (17 of 38) said they had introduced a new math program recently whereas 11 of the 33 least supportive principals reported such changes. However, in keeping with a kind of behavior that contributes to both didactic and inquiry-oriented instruction, the kinds of programs introduced varied widely from the Connected Math program and the University of Chicago Every Day Math program, which are intended to be conceptually more challenging, to the Saxon program, which tends to focus more heavily on basic mathematical operations. Although the principal interviews did not bear on this point, most of these programs involved curriculum or textbook adoptions that would probably have required central-office approval.

Formal Authority

Principals tended not to rely extensively and overtly on formal authority in their instructional leadership. Moreover, the formal elements they used most were those that could be cast in other ways and fit best with such other activities as offering advice and resources. For instance, almost half the principals (23 of 48) were reported by their teachers to observe for activities related to ESPA and the state's standards during teacher observations. This activity was viewed somewhat ambivalently by teachers. Some saw such observations as supportive and in keeping with the kind of giving advice described earlier: "She's supportive in, you know, visiting the classroom. She'll ask what's going on." Others saw the same activity as relying on positional authority and applying pressure. Another teacher said, "Well, she enforces. She makes sure that it is being done. And she's, as a matter of fact, a lot of observations this year. Surprise observations …. A lot of times, you know, the teachers are all saying, 'She hit me in math, she hit me in …' "

The ambiguous nature of observation created some vagueness in how it was used. For instance, teachers report that the most supportive principals were somewhat more likely to observe in the classroom than the least supportive. More than half of the most supportive principals (12 of 21) were said to conduct observations as opposed to just over a third of the least supportive ones (5 of 13). In the principal interviews, classroom observation is more directly linked to teacher evaluation. Only 15% of the principals report using observation and evaluation to ensure that students are learning the core curriculum content standards, and there is essentially no difference between the principals related as most and least supportive. When asked what was happening to help get teachers and students ready for ESPA, only 2 out of 138 principals mentioned observation and evaluation but both of them were reported by teachers to be among the least supportive of standards.

Other activities that rely on formal authority either were used less extensively or had no relationship to support for standards and assessments. For instance, teachers of only two principals reported that those principals asked teachers to refer to standards in their lesson plans. One teacher explained that "she encourages all the teachers to put [standards] into their, to their lesson plans. How do I say this nicely? It was a while before she truly understood what they were all about but she's a, she's a supporter." Principals thought they relied on lesson plans somewhat more than teachers did to reinforce standards. In their interviews, 28% said they monitored lesson plans as part of their effort to implement the core curriculum content standards and 3% said they did so as part of their program to get ready for ESPA, but there were no differences between more and less supportive principals in these areas.

According to teachers, using meetings to discuss ESPA- and standards-related issues was more common; 12 principals (30%) were said to do so. Four principals organized grade-level meetings. One teacher talked about having weekly grade-level meetings to discuss testing and standards implementation. Another talked about having schoolwide meetings "where we tell her how we feel about ESPA and our frustration, and [she] is trying as much as she can to be a support system for us if we have a problem." A third talked about using meetings to "come up with rubrics for K–4 for the writing process … because we wanted other people to take part in the great experiment." Holding meetings was not done more by the more supportive principals than the less supportive principals.

Other data from the principal survey suggest that the explicit use of formal authority was not central to the repertoire of most supportive principal. Formal authority was heavily represented in the principal ESPA preparation scale. It included such items about the use of authority as questions asking how often the principal "Require(s) teachers to cover ESPA topics before the test was administered," "Express(es) disapproval of teachers who were not working hard enough to raise ESPA scores," and "Focus(es) on core curriculum content standards while supervising and evaluating teachers." There was also a form of transactional leadership with regard to students with the item about providing pizza parties and the like. Only "arranging profession development" fell into the instructional leadership category. This scale was negatively associated with teachers' reports of principal support ($r = -.188, n = 125, p < .05$), suggesting some tendency for supportive principals to avoid relying on formal authority.

Because principal ESPA preparation was negatively correlated with principal support, we explored to see if it was positively correlated with teachers' perceived pressure, but there was no significant correlation.

Though both principals and teachers downplayed the use of formal authority, principals did evaluate teachers. Examination of the criteria they reported using reinforces the view suggested in chapter 4 that principals were eclectic in their approach to instruction. Principals were asked to describe the criteria they used to evaluate teachers, and most provided several. Those identified by a quarter or more of the principals include:

- Class climate: the quality of teacher–student interaction—47%.
- Active engagement: teacher-centered instruction, teacher acts as facilitator or uses learning centers or cooperative learning—42%.
- Effective teaching strategies: students are on task or teacher uses direct instruction—38%.
- Quality and clarity of lesson plans—31%.
- Core curriculum content standards: principal assesses alignment of content with standards—26%.
- Student progress: principal examines student work or improvement but not test scores—29%.

Four of these criteria—class climate, quality of lesson plans, alignment with the core curriculum content standards, and student progress—are neutral with respect to approach to instruction. They could fit with either inquiry-oriented or didactic instruction. Active engagement reflects an orientation more akin to inquiry-oriented instruction. In that regard it is close to both national and state standards of practice. "Effective teaching strategies" reflect the major theme popular in professional development over a decade ago. Effective teaching often overlapped with "direct instruction," which is very close to didactic instruction—that is, it could be useful for raising test scores but did not fit as closely with the new state standards and their implications for instruction. These two approaches were mentioned about equally by principals. Finally, given the growing emphasis on subject knowledge in the literature on both teaching and leadership, it may be significant that only 13% of the principals used content knowledge as an evaluation criterion.

No criteria were mentioned more by principals reported to be more supportive, but two were mentioned at least somewhat more by less supportive ones. One was effective teaching strategies, identified by 53% of the less supportive principals and 40% of the more supportive ones. The other was differentiated instruction where the principal reported that she or he looked for a variety of teaching strategies to meet diverse student needs. It was discussed by 18% of the more supportive principals and 34% of the less supportive ones. Because differentiated instruction can be consistent with the inquiry-oriented approach, it appears that less supportive principals are partial to criteria that fit both approaches to instruction.

Rare Leadership Elements

Some other frequently mentioned themes in the literature on leadership were not evident in data concerning these principals. For instance, we found little evidence of building cohesion among teachers in a school. Only 10 principals were said to work toward that end. In these instances, the principal organized meetings in which teachers were active participants and not passive spectators. They were given the opportunity to undertake projects with their peers and to discuss their ideas. The principal supported this kind of community building by encouraging sharing among teachers, or by creating committees where the teachers could be active participants, as the following example indicates:

> We have a professional-development committee that I served on until two months ago. Part of the focus of the professional development committee is to provide workshops for teachers to address the needs for the ESPA, but not just fourth-grade teachers. Down through the younger grades as well, because fourth-grade teachers in this district have rallied. And we have decided that it's important to make it known in our schools that this is not just our responsibility, but the responsibility of K through 4.

In this example, the principal created a context where teachers could assume leadership around a shared issue, in this case ESPA.

Individualized consideration or caring was also present, but infrequent. Teachers pointed to 10 principals who they thought "cared" about them in some personal sense. This caring always had a personal dimension to it that can come from what the principal says or from being a good listener, as the following teacher comments illustrate:

> The morale in our building is just amazing, and it's because of her. She boosts you up. She says wonderful things about you, about the kids .... And I think just that nurturing, positive feeling from her. You can't help but want to do a good job.

> She's had meetings with us where we actually tell her how we feel about ESPA and our frustration and is trying as much as she can to be a support system for us if we have a problem.

> So she's always encouraging and she's right there with us all the time and believing in us and I think that's very important.

Teachers were more likely to say that their principal cared about them than that their district or people at the district level did. Such comments were only made about one district. It should be noted, however, that not only are these manifestations of transformational leadership rare, but also they are no more frequent among the principals rated as supportive of state standards and assessments than those who are not.

In sum, supportive principals introduce teachers to new ideas and facilitate their access to knowledge from out-of-school sources and may even offer some advice and guidance to teachers. With the exception of direct observation, which is somewhat ambiguous, the supportive principals appear to prefer a less authority-based approach to instructional leadership than their less supportive peers. Generally, teachers and principals agree, principals downplay reliance on formal authority in directing attention to standards and assessments, and supportive principals minimize that authority more than their less supportive peers. The criteria they use to evaluate teachers are eclectic, reflecting about equal emphasis on conventional instruction and newer, more inquiry-oriented strategies, but suggesting relatively little understanding of specific content areas. Some of the most powerful elements of transformational leadership—goal setting, building a community, and even showing consideration (at least as teachers saw it)—were quite rare.

THE CONTEXT FOR PRINCIPAL SUPPORT

Interviews with principals make clear that standards and assessments must compete with a variety of issues for administrators' attention. We asked principals to identify the three most important issues that their school and their district have faced in the last 3 years. Some principals listed more than three issues, and some listed fewer. All in all, 19 issues were identified. Table

5.1 summarizes those that were mentioned by 20% or more of the principals. The most important issues at the district level, in the eyes of principals, were those related to enrollment changes—including rapid increases or decreases, the school redistricting that goes with such change, and high rates of student mobility within and among schools—and funding issues, including reductions in state revenues and the failure to pass budget referenda[1] and bond issues. The next most important issue concerned facilities, including the need for more space or the repair of old buildings. The third most important issue was staffing, including administrative turnover, shortages of teachers, and the need for better qualified staff. After all of these issues came the need to align the district's curriculum with the state's core curriculum content standards, although that need might have been either in any of a number of curricular areas or across several. The need for effective test preparation followed all of these.

Social desirability may have affected principals' responses. For instance, test preparation's lower rating than curriculum alignment may have reflected the stigma attached to an overemphasis on test preparation and the acceptability of aligning curricula. Nevertheless, it is clear that assessments and standards had to compete for district administrators' attention.

Principals thought these same six factors were the most important at the school level, but the order of priority differed. Curriculum alignment and test preparation were both perceived to be more important at the building level than at the district level, but both still fell behind enrollment issues, and test preparation was still listed after funding and just barely ahead of facilities.

Principals rated as most and least supportive by teachers rated different issues most important in their buildings, but these differences were indirectly related to instruction. Twice as many of the least supportive principals worried about staffing issues (27% vs. 13%) whereas more of the supportive

TABLE 5.1
Most Important Issues

	In District (n = 122)		In School (n = 119)	
	Percent	Rank	Percent	Rank
Enrollment change issues	49	1	41	1
Align curriculum with CCCS and/or ESPA (any subject)	28	5	32	2
Facility issues	35	3	29	3
Pressure to improve test scores prepare for tests: ESPA or other	24	6	27	4
Funding: budget issues including referenda	47	2	26	5
Staffing issues	33	4	24	6

principals were concerned about facilities (35% vs. 16%). There were no substantial differences with regard to curriculum or test preparation.

On the other hand, there were numerous differences between principals serving in wealthy and poorer schools. We separated principals into categories representing high-, middle-, and low-DFG (district factor group) districts and compared the differences between those from high and low DFG. More principals from high-DFG districts mentioned enrollment changes (63% vs. 30%), facility issues (41% vs. 26%), and the challenges of aligning curriculum with the standards and ESPA (41% vs. 17%). However, more principals from the lower DFGs mentioned test preparation (36% vs. 19%). Some of these differences are somewhat surprising. The presence of well-publicized facilities problems issues in the Abbott districts that are considerably greater than in the rest of the state would lead one to expect more principals from low-DFG schools to raise that problem (Firestone, Goertz, & Natriello, 1997). It may be that principals from wealthier districts have not given up on so many issues.

Alternatively, aggressive parents in wealthy districts may raise more issues for principals, or the specifics of the problem may be such that principals from wealthy districts are more likely to raise them. For instance, the principals from wealthy schools raise different enrollment issues than those from poorer ones. The principals in poor schools complain about "turnover," changing students during the year. As a result, they argue, the students tested may not be the ones taught, so the school "takes the blame," in a sense for students that could not be helped to do better. Principals in wealthy schools worry very little about turnover, but they are very concerned about enrollment growth and overcrowding. New Jersey's wealthy districts are experiencing more growth than the poor ones. This growth, rather than the decay of existing buildings, is probably the reason that principals from wealthy districts complain about facilities, as well. As another example, principals in wealthy districts may feel that proper alignment of curriculum may be enough to raise test scores whereas those in the poorer districts may feel that stronger measures are needed and focus more directly on test preparation. This orientation of principals may contribute to the stronger emphasis on direct instruction and decontextualized test preparation in poorer schools.

With the competition among issues for administrators' attention in mind, we explored further the connections between accountability concerns and district wealth on the one hand and principal support for standards and assessment on the other using data from the spring 2000 survey.[2] Table 5.2 shows the results of regression analysis of teacher-reported principal support for standards and assessment on three context variables:[3] DFG, the community's interest in holding the principal accountable (community accountability), and the centrality of ESPA to principal accountability. Given past expectations about the potential negative effects of accountability policies,

TABLE 5.2

Regression Analysis of Factors Associated With Principal Support,
Perceived Pressure, and Principal ESPA Preparation

	Principal Support (n = 125)	Pressure (n = 125)	Principal ESPA Preparation (n = 142)
DFG	−.059^{ns}	−.265**	−.510**
Community Accountability	−.056^{ns}	.023^{ns}	.132^{ns}
ESPA Accountability	−.029^{ns}	.050^{ns}	.187**
Adjusted R^2	.000^{ns}	.038***	.332**

Note. Standardized regression coefficients are reported; ns = not significant.

*$p < .05$; **$p < .01$; ***$p < .10$.

we also explored the associations of these factors with teachers' perceptions of pressure and principals' self-reported ESPA behavior.

Two factors are associated with principals' self-reported ESPA behavior. The first is DFG: Principals are much more active (and more likely to rely on formal authority) in poorer districts. They are also more active when ESPA is used to hold them accountable to the superintendent, school board, and parents. This reflects the observation made by some teachers and reported in chapter 4 that principals are sometimes in a position of communicating concern about test scores that is felt most directly at higher levels. As might be expected, teachers in poorer districts report more test-related pressure, but after controlling for district wealth, there is little association with principal accountability. None of the factors explored here are associated with teacher-reported principal support. Although these findings may reflect the limitations of the sample (e.g., some principals had teachers who did not participate), they tend to reinforce the pessimistic expectations that standards and assessment policies alone are not only not likely to help teachers adopt more inquiry-oriented approaches to instruction, but also that they work against those who might create a context for others to support such approaches.

CONCLUSION

This research helps clarify how principals make the significant contribution to test preparation and inquiry-oriented instruction noted in chapter 4 and how they mediate between the classroom and higher levels of the educational system. These findings reinforce the expectation of a division of labor between building leadership and the central office with the latter more directly responsible for responding to state policy and making curricular and professional development decisions and principals often cast in a supporting role. Instructional change seems most pervasive when principals and the central office play complementary roles. Principal support and central-office professional development both have a pervasive effect on teaching although principals tend to be eclectic with regard to approach, favoring neither inquiry-oriented nor direct instruction. This is an important point. The research on principal and district leadership for instructional change rarely intersect. Much of the research on principals almost ignores the district context. Yet, the way district leaders, by which we mean the mid-level district staff who actually work with teachers regularly, and principals interact and the extent of complementarity of their work should have important implications for the reform process. This work suggests that where different levels reinforce each other, teachers will be more likely to change practice in ways suggested by common influence and support.

A more detailed analysis of what principals do suggests that all principals focus resources on raising test scores. These resources tend to be marginal—buying materials or adding programs outside the regular schedule—rather than major investments or restructuring of the school day. The principals that teachers find most supportive provide more assistance related to teaching. Some of this leadership is indirect. Supportive principals make learning opportunities available to teachers and provide some guidance, but their use of formal authority to draw more attention to the standards and the state test is limited. Some of them do roll up their sleeves and provide detailed instructional guidance. The evidence suggests that supportive principals are helpful but instructionally eclectic. Most do not have a strong instructional philosophy. Those that do are as likely to turn to the older direct-instruction approach as the more current emphasis on inquiry-oriented education.

Principal support takes the form of advice more than direction. Supportive principals tend to shy away from relying on their formal authority. Their observations of teaching and accompanying feedback come outside the formal evaluation process, and they tend not to call meetings, rely extensively on lesson plans, or do other things that underline hierarchical distance from teachers. What they offer is the knowledge that they have, which is often practice based without reflecting recent developments in the subject area fields, or resources.

Some leadership activities associated with most definitions of transformational leadership, for example, goal setting and charisma, are almost totally absent in this sample; whereas others, including building community and showing individualized concern, appear but only rarely. This is not surprising. When acting as middle managers, principals may have difficulties projecting a strong vision or working to build community. Moreover, to the extent that transformational leadership requires a vision, principals' own instructional eclecticism may reduce the likelihood that they will take strong views of important issues related to the state's standards and assessments.

The picture that comes through these data is not of principals focusing their efforts to respond to state standards, but rather of individuals who make marginal adjustments to their work—a few more resources, a little more attention to instruction—to help teachers accommodate a new situation. There is a symmetry here with our findings about teachers who also appear to be making marginal adjustments to the new standards and assessments. The principal's marginal adjustment reflects the variety of pressures that go with the job. In most cases, state accountability demands must compete for the principal's attention. With such a range of issues to address, it is not surprising that principals make only modest changes in their work.

What is not clear from this research is what encourages principals to offer more support to teachers. In a complex environment with many competing priorities, we have no evidence that policies increasing accountability enhance principal support for standards and assessments. If anything, such policies encourage principals to rely on their formal authority and engage in behaviors that are negatively correlated with support for standards and assessments. Nor is there evidence that demographic and financial factors promote principal support. Instead, poverty seems to encourage principals to rely on their formal authority and may contribute to teachers' sense of pressure to conform to policymakers' expectations. We need to know a great deal more about how principals decide what response to make to state testing policies, why some of them provide the modest form of instructional support that we have identified, and why more intensive or extensive responses seem so rare.

ENDNOTES

1. All New Jersey school budgets must be approved by popular referenda.

2. We replicated these analyses with the spring 1999 and 2001 survey data and got quite similar results.

3. All variables were entered into the equation simultaneously.

6

The District
and Test Preparation

Katrina Bulkley
Janet Fairman
M. Cecilia Martinez

As standards and particularly testing become increasingly dominant policy tools for reforming education, all levels of the system need to respond
to demands for higher scores. Whereas teachers are affected directly by
state standards and assessment policies, much of the impact of these policies is mediated by the outlook of, and decisions made by, district administrators about how to attempt to alter teacher practice in ways consistent
with reform goals (Spillane, 1996). Literature on the implementation of
reforms has repeatedly shown that local agents' interpretations and responses to policy changes have a profound effect on policy impact
(Berman & McLaughlin, 1977; Fairman & Firestone, 2001; Spillane &
Thompson, 1997).

In order to understand the impact of New Jersey's standards and assessment policies, and the ways in which, and reasons why, teachers "taught to
the test," we explore how district leaders have responded to the state's
standards and the fourth-grade Elementary School Performance Assessment (ESPA), specifically in the area of mathematics. Though we examine
both standards and testing, our focus is on responses to testing, reflecting
the focus of the district administrators in our study.

Cohen and Barnes, among others, have argued that policy is itself an instrument for teaching and learning (Cohen & Barnes, 1993). Thus, district administrators who were responding to New Jersey's standards, and
seeking to influence teacher responses to the ESPA, had to determine
what their "pedagogy" would be for promoting student learning linked

with new state expectations. Specifically, they had to consider how they could enhance teachers' knowledge and skills and help them to alter their instructional practices in ways that would influence test results. Such decisions are made by administrators who themselves vary considerably in terms of their beliefs and knowledge about mathematical reform.

Building on earlier work exploring district responses to testing (Fairman & Firestone, 2001), this chapter explores the relationship between district pedagogy around testing and the will and capacity in particular districts, including the physical capital (resources), human capital, and social capital (Spillane & Thompson, 1997). The use of state assessment as an important tool to drive instructional change relies on multiple levels of the system to respond with substantive—rather than cosmetic—change.

LITERATURE REVIEW
AND CONCEPTUAL FRAMEWORK

District Responses to Testing

There are a variety of ways in which districts can respond to standards and assessments. Cohen and Barnes (1993) explored the "pedagogy of policy," or how policymakers have sought (consciously or not) to "teach" implementers of educational reforms; they concluded that, "the pedagogy of policy has been didactic and inconsistent" (p. 226). Supporters of standards-based accountability argue that the implementation of aligned standards and assessments can promote increased student learning (M. Smith & O'Day, 1991). Districts developing pedagogy in line with such ideals need to emphasize and support teacher learning that is consistent with the student learning sought by the standards and assessment. However, districts can also adopt "quick fixes" through their pedagogy, teaching teachers how to make minor changes that administrators believe will lead to improved test scores without placing as much emphasis on the fundamental learning that the tests are designed to promote. District administrators might opt for such "quick fixes" under pressure from school boards or parents to raise test scores, and they may lack the capacity to orchestrate systemwide change.

Literature on the district role has primarily focused on reform in general (cf. Firestone, 1989; Floden et al., 1988; Spillane, 1998b), whereas literature on the impact of testing has emphasized teachers' interpretations and implementation efforts at the classroom level (Fairman & Firestone, 2001). Districts must develop or utilize instructional guidance instruments or "tools" in order to encourage teacher change in response to testing. In terms of general reform efforts, Spillane (2000) identified four "formal channels" used by district leaders to shape classroom teaching and student learning—curriculum guides, materials, student assessment, and professional development.

The theory underlying standards-based reform suggests that these policy levers should be aligned with one another, and with state standards and assessments (M. Smith & O'Day, 1991), and these tools can also be drawn on specifically in response to testing demands, as well as for more general reform efforts.

Professional development is the most direct way of "teaching" teachers new information and ideas and helping them to develop their instructional skills; however, districts vary in the amount of professional development provided, the depth of content and continuity, and the level of "centralization" of these offerings (Little, 1989). Additional "pedagogical tools" could include using other resources, including altering the role of staff or the use of time, and providing test-specific information to students and parents.

The process that districts choose to use in response to testing reflects another set of pedagogical choices. Spillane (2000) discussed the value of teacher change and learning that builds on and challenges teachers' current thinking, and linked the use of teacher leaders as central agents in the change process to the development of such learning. The role of teachers in reform efforts is reflected in the tools or policy levers used. As Floden and his colleagues (1988) discussed, some districts encourage teacher participation and design policy levers that encourage teacher involvement (i.e., in the district planning process or as teacher leaders), whereas others focus more on the decisions of district administrators with little teacher input.

In terms of responses to testing more specifically, Fairman and Firestone (2000) found that, in Maine and Maryland, the districts and teachers they studied mostly responded to state standards and assessments by doing more test practice activities in the format of the new assessments and adding new topics to the curriculum, rather than focusing on fundamental changes in pedagogy (also see Firestone & Mayrowetz, 2000). It is important to attend not only to what tools are being used in response to testing demands, but whether these tools constitute an overall coherent and consistent strategy, or are merely "piecemeal" changes (Floden et al., 1988; Porter, 1989). In Fairman and Firestone's analysis, the districts' approaches were "piecemeal," altering some policies and practices while leaving many others unchanged, rather than a systemwide approach that incorporated an analysis of all district strategies that were relevant to content-area reform.

Finally, in high-capacity districts, Spillane and Thompson (1997) found that administrators and teacher-leaders, "frequently saw their task as helping their colleagues learn key reform ideas, rather than telling them what the reforms were about and forcing them to change" (p. 192). Thus, there was variation in the process of change (top-down vs. collaborative with teachers). In the more collaborative approach, administrators placed more value on teachers' professional judgment and experience.

Why Do Districts Respond to State Standards and Testing in Different Ways?

Research on districts offers some fairly consistent findings on the reasons behind district responses to reform in general, as well as to testing more specifically. The concepts of district *will* and *capacity* are particularly useful.

District Will.   Several authors have discussed the "will" that is necessary for local agents, including district administrators, to implement change consistent with reform ideas; such motivation is seen in part as the result of the "fit" of district policy with reform ideals (Firestone, 1989; McLaughlin, 1987). Fairman and Firestone (2001) argued that individual will to develop new knowledge is similar to professional commitment, and requires some ability to understand the nature of the change sought by the policy.

According to Fairman and Firestone (2001), state policy interacts with districts' and teachers' will and capacity to influence instructional change. They found that district will depends on some mix of the nature of the state policies (such as stakes or other accountability tools), size of district, governance structure of the districts, and the values of individual administrators. The "will" of district leaders to seek changes consistent with reform more generally is closely tied to their own understandings of reform ideas (Spillane, 1996, 1998a). Fairman and Firestone also found that, whereas some district leaders felt compelled to comply with state mandates, others felt more independent and disagreed with or did not understand the premise of the reforms.

The support of district leaders for reform linked to testing is also likely influenced by other demands on their time and by the level and nature of community pressure to improve test scores. For example, if the district has already committed to implementing certain curricular or testing changes, then administrators may be reluctant to redirect their energy and money when a state policy change comes about (Spillane, 1996). Spillane (1998a) also noted how, in one suburban district he studied, "community interest in test scores was especially influential in the suburban assistant superintendent's efforts to make sense of the reforms" (p. 50; see also Fairman & Firestone, 2001). Fear of embarrassment over public comparisons of district test scores was one reason that some administrators in Maine and Maryland felt compelled to give more attention to math topics tested by the state or teach test-taking skills (Firestone, Mayrowetz, & Fairman, 1997). Though administrators' beliefs about, and understanding of, reform ideas is important, their commitment to change can also be crucial (Spillane & Thompson, 1997).

District Capacity.   The idea of district "capacity" to support reform, whether in general or specifically around standards and assessments, has been raised by a number of researchers (Fairman & Firestone, 2001; Spillane

& Thompson, 1997). Spillane and Thompson focused on three particular aspects of capacity—physical capital and resources, human capital, and social capital—recognizing that these "capitals" are heavily intertwined. Here, we also focus on these three aspects of capacity, but look more specifically at how they are linked to state standards and assessments.

Human capital in the context of district leadership can be defined as "the knowledge and skills that administrators and teacher leaders command ... [along with] the commitment to reform and the disposition to learn" (Spillane & Thompson, 1997, p. 190). Recent research has demonstrated the importance of administrators' beliefs about teacher learning in overall reform efforts. For example, Spillane highlighted how the views of individual administrators on instruction influence their interpretations of state directives (Spillane, 1996; Spillane, 1998a).

These views are particularly important when it comes to the connections between state testing and district leaders' ideas about reform. Spillane (1996) found that some of the districts he studied in Michigan viewed the state assessment as external to their reform efforts. Administrators may value their own locally chosen assessments more than the state's, which may give teachers conflicting messages about what skills to focus on in instruction. It is also important to note that districts do not necessarily have a cohesive district "vision" related to reform efforts; as Spillane (1998b) pointed out, there can be within-district variation in beliefs about reform among key leaders at the district and school levels.

Spillane and Thompson (1997) commented that, in their study, "Invariably we found that the most successful local reformers were knowledgeable about subject matter as well as about current thinking on the teaching and learning of these subjects" (p. 192).

The views that district administrators hold may be linked to convictions about teaching based on their own prior classroom experience and training; their individual convictions may be a more powerful influence on decision making than state policy messages (Spillane, 1996). Spillane (1998b) noted that, "Work in organizations is also shaped by the particular specializations and professional or occupational identities individuals bring to their work. Individuals in these professional communities share norms, knowledge, perspectives, commitments, and often a language or vocabulary" (p. 37).

In terms of social capital, Spillane and Thompson (1997) found, in the districts they studied, that "social capital in the forms of professional networks and trusting—collegial relations—was instrumental to the creation of the human capital necessary to realize the reform ideas" (p. 190). Networks that bring ideas and support from outside a district, including links with universities and professional organizations, can provide an important resource for district administrators trying to understand reform ideas and determine how to approach district change (Spillane, 1998a, 1998b). Spillane (1998b) commented that, "Professional associations are likely to be important in most medium and large district offices where one is likely to find an array of professional specializations, in subject matter or assessment …. Organizational arrangements and professional affiliations help *situate* local policymakers' efforts to understand state policy" (p. 37).

Spillane and Thompson (1997) argued that, "developing social capital involves changing the way people relate with each other in order to enable them to achieve goals that could not be possible in the absence of these relations" (p. 193). They found that links to formal and informal networks— and the use of those networks—were critical in high-capacity districts. This was particularly true in smaller districts, where internal human capital was often more limited (Fairman & Firestone, 2001). In this portion of the study, all of the districts had access to the New Jersey Statewide Systemic Initiative (SSI) as one network for building social capital.

Physical capital (which Spillane and Thompson discussed under the heading of "resources") can include staffing, time, and materials (Spillane & Thompson, 1997). Decisions about the use of these resources are heavily influenced by a district's human capital. As well, district size can have an important impact on capacity, as larger districts have more resources to draw upon and can have district staff that are more specialized (Fairman & Firestone, 2001; see also Hannaway, 1993).

As the preceding literature review demonstrates, district will and capacity can have an important impact on district responses to reform. However, the general emphasis has been on efforts at broad reform, rather than on the more specific issue of responses to state testing, which in many states has become the strongest and most visible aspect of state reform efforts. In this study, we draw on the ideas discussed here to look at the relationships between will and capacity and district responses to state standards and testing. Specifically, we ask:

1. How do districts respond to state standards and testing? What tools and methods do they use to promote change in this context?
2. How does district capacity influence district responses?

STUDY METHODS

Data Collection and Analysis

Data from six districts that represented a variety of contexts (district size, urban/suburban/rural, and district affluence) were utilized in this analysis (see Appendix A for a discussion of the district sample and district characteristics). The study is a comparative case study (Yin, 1994) of six districts, and the primary data used were interviews with district administrators and teachers. In total, 19 administrators and 43 teachers were interviewed. Of the administrators, 11 were interviewed once, and the remaining 8 were interviewed twice. Interviews lasted between 45 minutes and 1½ hours. Following the interviews, tapes were transcribed and district profiles were created, summarizing the key issues raised in each case and important contextual factors.

These district profiles, along with the original interviews, were coded using the Nud*Ist 4 qualitative data software program, based on themes that emerged through the literature and in the process of conducting the study. Key themes used in coding included each district's use of different pedagogical tools to support testing (including professional development, assessment, curriculum, and materials), administrators' beliefs about what teachers need to learn and how they best learn, influences on administrators beliefs, and other influences on district pedagogical choices. Following Miles and Huberman (1994), the coded data were then summarized and placed in data matrices based on the themes utilized in this chapter.

In this chapter, we focus on three districts—Sunset, Ridley and Newtown that demonstrate some of the overall themes and patterns that emerged in the analysis, and the ways in which different tools can be integrated in a variety of ways. In the following two sections, we offer case studies of each of the three focus districts, and then a cross-case analysis that emphasizes these districts but also draws on data from the remaining three districts.

CASE STUDIES

Newtown

Newtown is an outer suburb of a large metropolitan area, and its residents are primarily affluent White families, although the population has become increasingly diverse in recent years. The school system is a focal point in this small community, and parents are active participants in the life of this K–8 district, closely watching indicators, such as test scores. Professional administrative staff is minimal, consisting of the superintendent and one assistant superintendent who covers curriculum and instructional issues across content areas.

Though viewed as an "actively" reforming district by the regional SSI director, Newtown's most extensive efforts have been in science, where strong community support has enabled considerable expansion of the science programs over the past decade and enhanced professional development for teachers in using "kits" that support inquiry-oriented science learning. Prior to the adoption of the state standards and the new state tests, mathematics reform was not a high priority for Newtown administrators.

In response to the state testing system, and especially to scores that were perceived by district leaders and the community as "inadequate," Newtown made a number of changes in mathematics. Traditionally a relatively decentralized district, administrators in Newtown became more controlling in response to pressure to improve test scores. One teacher commented that, "Bottom line, top line, [test scores are] all [the superintendent's] worried about .... Our first meeting with the new superintendent was to go over the test results and compare them to the county, and almost to kind of get a slap on the wrist." The most substantive aspect of Newtown's response was aligning their curriculum to the state standards and test specifications, and then exerting increasing pressure on teachers to follow the district curriculum.

For the most part, however, Newtown's response to state testing focused on more decontextualized and content-based strategies for improving test scores, rather than on developing teacher and student learning through a broad rethinking of mathematical goals and approaches. For example, teachers were required to participate in more specific professional-development activities, including workshops designed to introduce them to content covered on the ESPA and ways to connect that content to their lesson plans. These workshops were taught by outside experts, and teachers were considered the recipients of information.

The district also began using the NJPass, an EPSA "look-alike" standardized assessment, in nontested years, and teachers were expected to take scores and areas of content "weakness" into consideration when designing lesson plans and units. After learning about practices in higher-scoring districts, central-office staff also purchased new materials designed to familiarize students with the format of the test and test questions and encouraged teachers to use them. This set of concrete responses to ESPA was coupled with a general emphasis on raising test scores, and pressure placed on teachers to actively seek to improve scores.

The focus on strategies for improving scores through decontextualized practices reflects a belief that what needed to change was preparation for the process of the test, not student and teacher learning. According to one teacher, "the administrators have been on our cases to increase the scores, but not giving us any techniques as to how to do it." At one point, the curriculum director suggested that teachers had little to learn; in commenting on his frustration with the ESPA, he argued that, for teachers, "It just means pressure and embarrassment and a sense of futility because I think in about 99% cases, they're doing the very best they can ... and it's a bit of an anomaly to me why we would do badly [on test scores]."

From the perspective of teachers, there was more pressure than support for improving scores. This emphasis was not surprising in a district with little expertise in mathematics at the central level, and district administrators who had a relatively basic understanding of the mathematics standards that focused on "hands-on"/active learning.

District will and capacity in Newtown was limited in a number of ways that "fed" upon each other. The motivation of district administrators for making changes in mathematics was primarily external—raising scores—

rather than because of a deeply felt belief in the ideas themselves. Along these lines, there was little human capital available at the district level to promote instructional change in mathematics consistent with state goals, and, as a result, district staff did not build the external networks that can provide valuable social capital. As well, even the SSI Regional Center was limited in its usefulness for building social capital, as this particular center is much more focused on science than mathematics. Such networks might have better enabled the acquisition of additional resources/physical capital (e.g., grants) that could support district change efforts. The more limited and decontextualized response to state standards and testing found in New-town reflects the lack of district capacity to have a more substantive, embedded response to these new challenges. Instead, district staff were left frustrated and confused, uncertain of why their test scores were not improving despite specific efforts to raise them.

Ridley

Ridley is a medium-size, low-income, urban district, with a predominantly minority student population. Across the district, 65% of the students are eligible for free or reduced school lunch, with a higher percentage in some schools. Parental involvement in academic matters within the district is very low; although district administrators have increased their effort to explain the state standards, testing, and curriculum reforms to the public, few people attend these meetings. Ridley's central staff of seven administrators includes a math/science supervisor and a general-curriculum director. Ridley's status as an "Abbott" district is another important layer of district context influencing its ability to respond to the ESPA, although the district was only in the early stages of implementing its school reform plans. Literacy was the most significant focus for reform in Ridley both prior to and during the period of this study, and mathematics did not receive the level of consistent and thorough attention that literacy did.

Ridley revised its math curriculum frameworks after the release of the new state standards, with district administrators leading the process and heavy reliance on help from outside experts. Yet, the district's mathematics and science reform strategy reflected an uneven and piecemeal approach, with more substantive learning opportunities available to only a few teachers, and a lack of training and materials encountered by most teachers. On the one hand, a few teachers participated in the content-rich, after-school workshops and graduate courses that were offered through local universities; these were consistent with a focus on more intellectually challenging practice as a means to improve test scores. Over a period of 5 or 6 years, a professor from a university/SSI center worked with a few teachers from different schools to introduce National Science Foundation (NSF)–supported curriculum materials, to provide feedback as teachers piloted materials, and to model instructional approaches in the teachers' classrooms. The curricu-lum director said: "I think the SSI participation was very good for our schools; although I don't think it directly translated into changed classroom practices, it did raise the awareness of teachers about standards and the need for raising the bar in math and science." District administrators were trying to identify a few teachers who could grow into the role of leaders or re-source staff, and hoped they would motivate other teachers in the district to reflect on their practice. On the other hand, most teachers never engaged in any substantive learning in math topics nor did they have access to the new curriculum materials that the district hoped to implement on a districtwide scale. The district offered only 5 hours of in-service on math topics for ele-mentary school teachers during the 2 years of our study, and had difficulty motivating teachers to attend the after-school workshops. In-service days were devoted to literacy topics and school reform plans, and addressed teachers as passive learners. There were a few after-school workshops on the ESPA, but it was not a major topic of in-service. District administrators tried to entice teachers to attend professional-development activities in the dis-trict by offering incentives such as manipulatives, kits, or stipends.

District administrators acknowledged that changing individual teacher's beliefs and skills required close interaction with more expert educators over a long period of time, but one said it was "a privilege that we don't usually have." The district lacked the financial resources to hire enough substitutes or to pay stipends to all teachers to provide larger chunks of time for teacher learning. By the end of this study, the district planned to begin using outside experts to train a few resource people in the new math curriculum through a "turnkey" process, hoping that these people would help teachers in each school learn how to use the new materials. The "Abbott" funding helped to finance math, technology, and literacy resource staff for each school.

In response to pressure from the school board about test scores, the dis-trict increased its testing activity, to include a district-made test adminis-tered several times per year, a norm-referenced test, a test that more closely resembled the format of the state assessments, and tests administered by the school reform plans. The district also offered summer tutoring and test prac-tice for students, and principals encouraged teachers to use test-besting ma-terials. District leaders used the pressure over test scores as a compelling argument to urge teachers to change practice, though the beliefs of adminis-trators about high-quality education, not testing, was the primary reason ad-ministrators wanted to reform curriculum and instruction.

Besides using a piecemeal approach to change math curriculum and in-struction without providing adequate materials and training, the district di-luted its focus by attempting to reform three subject areas simultaneously, with multiple projects and partnerships with outside consultants and SSI partners. According to one SSI partner, district leaders' high level of ambi-tion to change literacy, math, and science curricula all at once resulted in a lack of focus for district resources and produced mixed messages for teachers about priorities. Ridley's focus on literacy was driven by administrators' beliefs that improving reading and writing skills was key to helping students perform better on the state tests, in any subject area.

According to district leaders, teachers' low motivation to engage in new learning and their low level of professional skill in math and science was the most frustrating barrier for reform. One administrator commented: "We've experienced some push-backs, primarily from our primary teachers, because they've never been asked to do anything with kids beyond simple arithmetic." The curriculum director explained: "We're a bit smarter in terms of what we need to do in order to provide the incentive to pressure, the carrot, the stick if necessary, in order to increase the percentage of transfer from training to practice." Subject supervisors visited classrooms to see if teachers were using instructional strategies they had learned from outside consultants, but were quite disappointed that some projects had no discernable influence on practice.

Overall, Ridley's curriculum supervisors had a high level of will and capacity to support curricular and instructional reforms, not only in response to external pressure from the state test, but more from their individual beliefs about teaching and learning. They held a strong professional background in math education, a good understanding of the pedagogical basis for state and national mathematics standards, and wanted to help teachers move away from textbooks and procedural skills to active student engagement in conceptual learning. Yet, because of the district's larger size, lack of financial resources, lack of focus on math and science reform, and the constraints of school reform requirements, the district was not able to organize in-depth, ongoing training in math for all teachers, to provide sufficient quantities of new curriculum materials, or to create social networks for teachers to share knowledge and skills. The poor climate for professional learning in Ridley's schools and teachers' low motivation and skills were serious challenges to a substantive response to the ESPA, and resulted in more of an emphasis on decontextualized test preparation for many teachers.

Sunset

Sunset is a small K–8 district with a superintendent and one general-curriculum supervisor. Despite an increasing rate of suburban development that doubled school enrollment over a 5-year period, Sunset has retained its strong rural flavor. The changing demographics presented new challenges to district administrators and teachers as they made decisions about curriculum, instruction, and assessment. The predominantly affluent, White community became more diverse socioeconomically, and administrators blamed a slight dip in state test scores on the increased number of special-needs students. Historically, the district has enjoyed strong support and involvement from parents. More recently, a few parents were critical of the district's use of non-textbook-based curricula in math, and others demanded more homework in basic skills, which the district provided through workbooks.

Sunset stands out in our sample of districts because of the high level of professional expertise and commitment of both its administrators and teachers to engage in ongoing, intensive professional learning in math education. The motivation for this effort was internal—from a shared belief in and understanding of the standards-based reforms in math education—but strongly supported externally by a deep-seated and lengthy association with a local university. The impetus for revising math curriculum and instruction came from an elementary school teacher's graduate work at a local university where she learned about NSF-supported mathematics curriculum materials. A school principal and curriculum director who shared a strong professional background in math education supported the efforts of this teacher, and eventually the faculty chose to adopt the new materials along with some Marilyn Burns activities as a basis for rewriting the district curriculum. One teacher said of the principal: "She supports the kind of problem solving, investigative classroom … she understands what's going on in the classroom. It makes a big difference." Sunset's reform activity in math and science predated the administration of the ESPA, and coincided with the release of new state standards and reflected a strong and deep commitment to more intellectually challenging practice. A teacher commented: "I think a lot of what we're doing in this district already was very much in line to the standards even before the ESPA." When a new curriculum director arrived with a strong background in math education and math assessment, she found that, "A lot of the knowledge base with the staff in-house had been developed so … there was a philosophical base that was established." She added: "Some of the work had been begun in terms of mathematics learning. There's a commitment to a philosophy."

The curriculum director provided the necessary resources of time and knowledge to encourage teacher learning. She hired substitute teachers to create release time so teachers could work together by grade level with outside experts. The small size of the district facilitated this approach. Sunset also used a variety of pedagogical tools that included focused, ongoing professional development, curriculum and instructional materials, classroom and district assessment that was consistent with the state tests, and communication with parents to create a coherent message for reform in mathematics education at the elementary school level.

District performance on the state assessments has been an important source of external pressure influencing curriculum and assessment decisions. A few residents phoned administrators to ask why the district's scores were not as high as other affluent districts in the region. The superintendent explained: "It's a wealthy community. In a district like this, we don't have the luxury of not doing well on standardized tests. It's extremely important to our parents how well their children are doing in comparison to like districts." Sunset chose a new commercial test to better reflect the format of the state assessments. They also responded to residents' concerns over test scores by moving away from an inclusion model to self-contained classrooms for special-needs students, hoping that scores on the state assessments would improve. Yet, administrators and teachers were determined not to shift toward test practice or more decontextualized teaching to the state tests. The curriculum director made release items available to teachers, but he did not actively encourage them to use the material. He focused his in-service meetings on explaining the state standards and testing goals, particularly in math, and emphasized that teachers of all grades shared a responsibility for getting students ready for the state tests. The curriculum director also made sure that teachers used the state's core curriculum content standards and testing specifications as a framework for their work on curriculum revision. One teacher commented: "We just got a big, thick binder full of stuff that has sample questions and answers and how the test is given. So they gave us a basic format. But other than that ... the teachers are kind of doing their own [thing] ...."

The district's affluent status meant that it could attract and select teachers who shared its vision for teaching and learning. The curriculum director cultivated a core of teacher leaders from each grade in the elementary school, and supported them with stipends from grant funds. Teachers were heavily involved in choosing math curriculum materials, rewriting curriculum frameworks for math, science, and language arts, developing classroom assessments to use with the math curriculum, choosing and delivering much of the district's in-service on math topics, and leading some meetings with parents. The curriculum director said: "I feel that whatever's been invested in terms of the professional development, it is definitely turnkey in empowering others. I can't do it myself." In its efforts to build and sustain a "new" approach to mathematics, Sunset was able to draw on broad and deep human and social capital (within the district and through their university affiliation), and a high level of resources, to develop a coherent strategy for curriculum reform. Teachers' and administrators' high level of will and capacity created the commitment and focus they needed to implement standards-based reforms in mathematics.

CROSS-CASE ANALYSIS

Strategies for Approaching Standards and Testing

Responses to standards and testing varied from district to district in terms of the "tools" used, how those tools (especially professional development and assessment) were used, and the process of creating and supporting district-wide change. Table 6.1 summarizes the different strategies around tools and process used in the six districts studied.

TABLE 6.1
Types of District Responses to Standards and Testing

Tools Used in Change	The Process of Change	
	District-Driven	Combination of District and Teacher Leadership
Primarily test preparation/ "test besting"	Newtown Willis Creek	
Combination of test prep and systemwide reform	Hillview Ridley	Cedarville
Primarily focused on systemwide reform		Sunset

Tools Used in Change.   Each district used a different combination of tools, including professional development, curriculum change, assessment, and resources, and used these tools in different ways, in response to changing state expectations and specifically the fourth-grade ESPA (see Table 6.2). We were able to identify a continuum of strategies underlying the tools selected. On one end of the continuum, Newtown, the district in our sample that relied most heavily on decontextualized test preparation, focused their decisions on strategies they hoped would be "quick fixes" for lower-than-expected scores. On the other end, Sunset, the most reformed-oriented district, focused most of their resources on in-depth strategies designed to develop teachers' content and pedagogical knowledge and increase intellectually challenging instruction.

Though each district relied on professional development in responding to the ESPA, the amount, type and purpose of these efforts varied. In Newtown, administrators organized teachers' meetings to explain the test format and the strategies to raise the scores. These activities prescribed a set of directions or steps designed to increase success on the test, and reflected a focus on exposing teachers to information about the test, rather than new learning to support changed instruction. Most of the professional-development activities were "one shot" and provided by outside experts and district staff. We found a similar pattern in Willis Creek, another district that emphasized decontextualized test preparation, where most of the professional-development activities were designed around ESPA but included some supplemental workshops with limited classroom follow-up.

Unlike Newtown or Willis Creek, Sunset focused their overall efforts on teaching the teachers the new math program they had adopted. University professors worked with teacher leaders to provide systematic professional development for the district, contributing to teachers' capacity/expertise. In order to encourage a "turnkey process" the district has paired teacher leaders with new teachers. The response to the ESPA combined some profes-

TABLE 6.2
Tools Used in District Responses to Testing

District	Overall Use of Tools	Professional Development	Assessment	Curriculum and Materials	Staffing and time changes	Other Tools	Family/Community Involvement
Newtown	Test-prep oriented.	One-time workshops focused on ESPA content and connecting content with curriculum.	ESPA "look-alike" given in pre-ESPA years. Scores analyzed for areas of content weakness.	Curriculum aligned, centralized. New textbooks purchased aligned with standards, ESPA "test prep" materials.	None.	Before-school program for students identified as likely to score low on ESPA.	Minimal.
Ridley	Mixed.	Intensive ongoing professional development for a few teachers; short workshops for all teachers. Teachers required to demonstrate new practices in classroom.	Multiple standard-ized tests and district assessments given every year. Tests used to diagnose and evaluate.	Curriculum aligned with standards. Purchase of non-textbook-based math curriculum.	Efforts to develop "teacher-leaders."	District requirements used in teacher evaluations.	Sessions offered to parents on standards and ESPA, but poorly attended.
Sunset	Systemwide reform.	Focus on professional development linked to NSF-approved, non-textbook-based math curriculum, with some additional workshops on standards/ESPA and testing strategies.	Standardized assessment in non-ESPA years. Focus on developing alternative classroom assessments.	Curriculum aligned with standards. Purchase of non-textbook-based math curriculum.	Extended time for mathematics lessons. Regular after-school time for teacher collaboration.	More "pull-out" work with students in special-education programs.	Sessions offered to parents on "reform" approach to mathematics.

(continued on next page)

TABLE 6.2 (continued)

District	Overall Use of Tools	Professional Development	Assessment	Curriculum and Materials	Staffing and time changes	Other Tools	Family/Community Involvement
Willis Creek	Test-prep oriented.	Workshops on ESPA focused on content areas to cover prior to test. Some classroom follow-up by district staff and external experts.	Standardized tests analyzed to determine content areas to be covered in more depth prior to the ESPA.	Minor adaptations made for state standards from NCTM-aligned curriculum. New textbooks and some "test prep" materials.	Central office reorganized to focus more on content areas. Time immediately before ESPA focused on test preparation.	After-school program for students identified as likely to score low on ESPA.	Web site with curriculum available to community.
Hillview	Mixed.	Extended ESPA workshops, focused on both substance and "test prep" activities. Intensive math courses available in-district, and math supervisor offers demonstration lessons for teachers.	Standardized tests analyzed to determine content areas to be covered in more depth prior to ESPA.	Curriculum aligned with standards— topics emphasized in ESPA specifically covered in fourth grade. District moving away from textbooks in mathematics.	Teacher placed on "special assignment" to assist in standards/ testing-related work across content areas.	After-school program for students identified as likely to score low on ESPA.	Multiple forms of parental outreach, including workshops and homework help.
Cedarville	Mixed.	Mandatory ongoing workshops focused on content knowledge in tested areas. In-class support/modeling/follow-up provided by teacher coordinators. Teacher study groups around reform effort.	Standardized tests analyzed to determine content areas to be covered in more depth prior to the ESPA. ESPA-based district assessments given monthly in Grades 3 and 4 and tracked by district office.	Curriculum regularly adapted in response to standards, testing, and analysis of test scores. New textbooks and manipulatives purchased, along with test prep materials.	Three teachers hired as "teacher coordinators" in mathematics to provide professional development and in-class support.	After-school program for students identified as likely to score low on ESPA.	Some parental outreach.

sional development specifically on the assessment with "folding in" the test expectations to the ongoing district reform effort in mathematics. The emphasis on teacher learning is reflected not only in formal professional-development activities, but also in their provision of regular after-school time devoted to teacher collaboration. Similarly, the district restructured time during the school day so as to allow for longer mathematics lessons, which they argued was helpful when using a more constructivist approach.

Ridley chose a more mixed response to the ESPA. The district used professional development with a mixture of goals, some aimed to enhance teachers' knowledge and understanding (such as university courses), and others designed to prepare teachers to respond to specific issues of content and test-taking strategies. We identified two other districts in our sample that combined test prep and reform-oriented activities, Hillview and Cedarville. As turnkey teachers were trained at a local university on a math program, each district built internal expertise. Interestingly, Cedarville created a systematic staff development process and used teacher coordinators (teachers on "special assignment") to model lessons for their peers. Administrators also encouraged the formation of teacher study groups where they did research, collaborative planning, and critiquing. These more substantive activities were complemented with workshops on test-taking skills; one teacher expressed that these were useful "in terms of what the kids are expected to do."

Curriculum changes and the acquisition of new materials was a part of the strategy in every district studied. We found that the districts that were more concerned with test scores not only aligned their curriculum with the standards but also supplemented the curriculum with practical activities that teachers could implement right away. These districts were the same ones that did not put a lot of effort into providing teachers with a deep understanding of reform. As discussed later, for these administrators, the reforms were not about changing ideas of knowledge but about altering specific content coverage and introducing new activities. Specifically, Newtown adopted test prep materials and a new math series aligned to the standards, but selected a more traditional textbook series because of a belief that the community would not support a more progressive one. In providing teachers guidance for the newly aligned curriculum, the district operationalized the standards into, as one administrator said, "practical things that you actually do in a math class, like multiply two-digit numbers or whatever." In some cases, their "translation" minimized the mathematical thinking underlying the standards. Using these strategies, the district made sure the content was covered, but did not emphasize a changed approach to the teaching of mathematics. Willis Creek also took this approach as it changed the curriculum into "user-friendly materials" but unlike Newtown, this district put some efforts into teaching the teachers how to implement it. Sunset, Ridley, Willis Creek and Hillview also aligned their curriculum to the standards and worked to move away from a textbook-bound approach to mathematics.

In preparing for the state assessment, all six districts increased the use of mandatory assessment in general. Newtown's use of an ESPA "look-alike" reflected its desire to increase the comfort level of students and teachers with the assessment, and their concern with the issue of "content to be covered." The role of this new standardized assessment was solely to identify areas of weakness or topics inadequately covered. As in Newtown, Sunset adopted a commercial test; however, they used this test in conjunction with additional assessment strategies, including new teacher-developed classroom assessments that were linked with their overall reform strategy. Testing as a pedagogical tool was most heavily used in the two Abbot districts in our sample and in Willis Creek, one of the most test prep-oriented districts. In Ridley, they implemented four different tests with the purpose of tracking student progress and placing the children in summer tutoring programs as necessary. Cedarville used commercial and district-created assessments to track student growth and to determine where to "recover" skills in weak areas.

Alongside student assessment, both Newtown and Ridley also increased their use of teacher assessment, largely through the preexisting evaluation process. In Newtown, teachers commented that scores were used as part of the evaluation process, despite the relatively minimal support for altering instruction in substantive ways designed to improve scores. Ridley was determined to increase pressure on teachers in a variety of ways. The curriculum director argued that, "It is really about pushing ... Because I think we had it first too much support in this district and not enough pressure ... and there are a lot of arbitrary things and we say you must do this. If you are not out there inspecting it, it is not going to happen." Thus, district administrators conducted classroom visits, incorporating a checklist to evaluate if teachers were implementing the programs required. This pressure pushed teachers to change practices rapidly and to attend the district in-services. We found the same pattern in Hillview, where principals and supervisors used regular observations to ensure that lessons were aligned with the standards; these observations were then used in teacher evaluation.

In Sunset and Ridley, but noticeably absent in Newtown, was a concerted effort to engage the community (especially parents) in reform efforts. Such efforts met with additional attention in the more affluent Sunset, but in both cases, district administrators saw the changing approach to mathematics as sufficiently different to warrant "teaching" parents about reform ideas. This pattern is repeated in all districts in our sample that presented a combination of test prep with systematic changes. The strategies were aimed to train parents along with the children in more progressive math, as well as to "sell" parents on these more progressive approaches. In the two districts where there were no efforts to teach the reform to parents, administrators complained that it was the community who pushed for a more traditional approach.

Process of Change.   As the case studies demonstrate, the process of responding to the ESPA also varied in substantial ways across these districts (see Table 6.3). Newtown had the most top-down approach, with little teacher input or use of existing teacher capacity. The other district in our sample in the same category also relied mostly on external experts. On the other hand, Sunset combined district-driven change with a heavier reliance on teachers and teacher leaders. The other district in our sample that also had a combined response used, for example, former classroom teachers acting as mathematics coordinators to help the classroom teachers with the reform. For Ridley, a predominantly top-down approach was combined with an attempt to build teacher leadership. For example, the district has included some teachers in the reform process by identifying teachers' leaders that are part of three district teams. The curriculum director's explanation for this was that, "these two or three people that are each team are responsible for that group of schools in terms of going there in [on] a regular basis providing assistance to teachers." Among the staffing changes, the district is pushing the principal to have a supervisor and coach role.

The districts in this study used a range of tools to respond to new state expectations around standards and the ESPA. Despite a shared state context, district leaders varied considerably in their desire to "teach" the teachers to simply raise test scores or to work with them to provide opportunities for more in-depth teacher learning consistent with reform ideals.

Linking District Will and Capacity and Responses to State Standards and Testing

To better understand the strategies used by districts to respond to the New Jersey Core Curriculum Standards and the ESPA, we examined district will, or motivation to change, district capacity (including human capital, social capital, and resources/physical capital), and barriers or perceived barriers to change (see Table 6.4). Consistent with work by Spillane and Thompson, among others, we found that these different pieces were highly interrelated. Though we separate them for analytic purposes, it should be apparent throughout that different aspects of will and capacity are interwoven.

District Will.   District will, or motivation to seek change in response to state standards and the ESPA, was connected with both internal and external pressures. Externally, will was largely linked to pressure from the community (especially through the school board) and parents to improve test scores.

Among the three focus districts presented here, external pressure was a more salient factor in Newtown than in either Sunset or Ridley. Teachers in

TABLE 6.3

Process of Change in District Responses to Testing

District	Overall Process of Change	Description of Process of Change
Newtown	District-driven	Centralized effort by district staff, using external experts, to change content taught to be more consistent with the ESPA and to improve students' test-taking skills. Teachers relatively uninvolved in decision making.
Willis Creek	District-driven	Teachers involved in curriculum and staff development committees, but process orchestrated and operated by district staff. Heavy reliance on external experts.
Hillview	District-driven	District staff have driven change efforts, but have sought to have some teacher involvement through participation in curricular revision. Primary reliance on district staff and outside experts as "teachers" of standards and test-linked changes.
Ridley	District-driven	Strong district pressure on teachers from district staff, and primary reliance on district staff and outside experts. Use of multiple university and corporate partnerships for funding, curriculum materials, and professional development. Some effort to develop teacher-leaders.
Cedarville	Combination of district and teacher leadership	District initiated, but teachers actively involved in curriculum revision (committee meets frequently with external expert). Teacher coordinators an important aspect of response to standards and testing. External experts used, but conscious effort to develop internal expertise.
Sunset	Combination of district and teacher leadership	District staff and teachers all heavily involved in reform efforts that are consistent with ESPA and standards, but preceded the implementation of state standards and the ESPA. Move to non-textbook-based curriculum originated through teacher initiative. Some use of external experts and university partnership, but most of the work initiated and carried out by teachers with administrator support.

TABLE 6.4
Districts' Approach to Reform and Will and Capacity

District	Will	Capacity				
	Motivation	Human Capital—Availability	Human Capital—Beliefs About How Teaching Needs to Change	Human Capital—Beliefs about How Teachers Learn and What They Need to Learn	Social Capital	Resources
Newtown	Parent and community pressure for improved test scores.	One district curriculum coordinator who covers all subject areas (background not in mathematics).	Focus on need for more active learning.	Little mention of need for teachers to gain content knowledge—more emphasis on using alternative teaching "strategies" and understanding the specifics of the standards and tests.	Working with other districts in consortia to provide professional development and minor connections with New Jersey SSI.	Almost complete reliance on internal district funds.
Willis Creek	Pressure to raise scores from within district and community.	One content supervisor who covers math, science, music, etc. (background not in mathematics).	Emphasis from multiple district staff on teaching strategies and real-life examples and a shift away from "rote memorization."	Little mention of need for teachers to gain content knowledge—more emphasis on using alternative teaching "strategies" and understanding how tests work.	Some connections with other local districts and minor connections with New Jersey SSI.	Almost complete reliance on internal district funds.
Hillview	Strong pressure from parents and school board. Pressure for more general reform from expectations in mathematics community.	Math coordinator active in state associations. Teacher on "special assignment" to help prepare teachers for state testing in all areas.	Math coordinator describes desirable teaching as focusing on problem solving and manipulative use, as well as lessons that include more traditional approaches.	Little mention of need for teachers to gain content knowledge—emphasis on using reformlike strategies.	Connected with local university through New Jersey SSI.	External funds through SSI and other government support.

(continued on next page)

133

TABLE 6.4   (continued)

	Will	Capacity				
Cedarville	District superintendent very focused on raising scores. Pressure for more general reform from expectations in mathematics community.	Well-trained math supervisor combined with math teacher coordinators who provide classroom support.	Math supervisor emphasizes need for active learning and learning linked to real-life applications.	Emphasis on increasing teachers' content knowledge because of belief that lack of knowledge is a barrier to improvement.	Math supervisor active in state math organizations. Multiple teachers and district-level staff have been actively engaged with local university through New Jersey SSI.	Significant additional funding through state litigation, but then cut due to budget shortfall. Some grant support.
Sunset	Pressure to maintain high scores in context of changing district demographics. Strong reform effort in mathematics has supported those aspects of ESPA that are consistent with district effort.	Curriculum director highly trained in mathematics and strong connections with state. Some teachers very highly trained in mathematics.	Learning that may use manipulatives, etc., but focuses on developing students' understanding of conceptual ideas and ability to reason mathematically.	Curriculum director believes teachers need to learn more content and different ways of teaching. Teachers need intensive training, opportunities to collaborate on "real work" with other teachers.	Strong connections with university faculty in mathematics education through New Jersey SSI. Teachers included in building of social capital through links with outside providers and time for internal networking/support.	District staff and teachers have received multiple foundation and government grants to support their reform efforts. District also has strong financial base.
Ridley	Pressure to raise scores from community and superintendent. Pressure for more general reform from expectations in mathematics community.	Multiple administrators with strong mathematics backgrounds. Limited teacher capacity (according to district staff).	For reform, director of curriculum says, "teachers should be looking to have the students construct their own under-standing of what is going on."	District administrators have strong concerns about teachers' content knowledge in mathematics and see need for long-term, intensive professional development.	District and some teachers have made significant efforts to link with outside partners. Multiple partners that schools and teachers can (and do) call upon.	District has actively sought external funding from business, foundation, and government sources.

Newtown emphasized that administrators exert considerable pressure to increase test scores. In districts like Sunset, changing demographics that effectively make the district less affluent and more diverse are adding an additional pressure, and administrators must explain why test scores have dropped or have failed to increase at the expected rate. In the districts of Newtown and Sunset, both affluent, there was considerable concern over the potential for embarrassment if test scores were low in comparison to like districts. Willis Creek also experienced pressure through fear of embarrassment; the superintendent said: "it's a more political response than it is an educational one .... The world out there wants to know, well, how did our kids do vis-à-vis any other school district in the area? So we're constantly being compared ... we suffer from comparison ...."

In the low-income district of Ridley, concern about the public image conveyed by low test scores was raised more directly by teachers than administrators. This is consistent with our findings in the two other low-income districts in our sample. For example, a teacher from Hillview told us, "people say, oh, it's not [test scores] but then you sit there and if it is in the newspaper, you know you are not doing what you are supposed to do."

Internal pressures/expectations can also influence the level of response to state standards and testing. District administrators spoke of using the test and standards to convince other district officials, teachers, and parents of the need to move in more "reform-oriented" directions. However, administrators' understandings of these reforms varied, and reflected their particular professional backgrounds and expertise. Administrators in both Ridley and Sunset shared a strong professional background in math education, and experience working at the state level. These administrators deftly articulated what best practice in math teaching and learning should look like, and were very familiar with state and national standards in mathematics and state testing. Accordingly, administrators in Ridley and Sunset appreciated the significant amount of learning that teachers would have to engage in to fully meet the state standards, and they worked to organize internal and external resources to support that goal, although Sunset did so more successfully. The curriculum coordinator in Newtown did not acknowledge that the state standards implied deeper changes in classroom practice and learning, and he felt no need to offer teachers more substantive learning opportunities in mathematics. We found the same pattern in Hillview where district administrators did not have a clear vision of where they wanted to go with classroom practices. As a result, in this district the scores, as opposed to standards, have driven changes in curriculum, resource allocation, and program implementation.

The pressure to raise test scores and the desire to move toward content and pedagogy consistent with the standards were somewhat divorced in all of the districts in this study. Thus, all districts used at least some test preparation or test-besting materials, even though administrators questioned their educational value. The will to avoid possible embarrassment over test scores was high. Ridley and Sunset administrators and some teachers embarked on reform efforts largely as a result of their individual beliefs and internal will to improve mathematics teaching and learning. Much of this work, including teacher learning activities with SSI support, preceded (in Sunset) or coincided with (in Ridley) the new state standards.

District Capacity

District capacity, such as human and social capital, appear to be somewhat dependent on district will, but not entirely. For example, district leaders in Ridley had high levels of will to reform their curriculum and improve teacher and student learning, but complained that teachers were difficult to motivate and held poor understandings of the reform ideas, and that the district lacked financial and human resources to train the large teaching staff.

Human Capital.   The availability of individuals who can support change efforts in response to state standards and testing involves people who both are able to devote time and effort and have the knowledge and understanding necessary to use their energies to move the district in the directions envisioned by state leaders and supporters of standards-based reform. Districts like Sunset and Ridley, which had more "sophisticated" responses to state standards and testing, also had more human capital. The most reform-oriented district, Sunset, had an unusually high level of human capital at the level of teaching staff, and had administrators at both district and building levels with strong math education backgrounds. Sunset had developed a strong core of teacher leaders who delivered much of the district's in-service on mathematics. In the same line, Cedarville was an Abbott district in our sample with strong internal capacity. The fact that administrators were knowledgeable about the reform contributed to the creation of alternative instances for teacher learning linked with the reform, such as study groups and teacher coordinators.

Newtown, which responded to state standards and testing primarily with efforts to increase scores through content changes and test prep activities, had only one district person who was spread across multiple content areas. In this district, neither the superintendent nor the administrator had a strong background in math education.

District administrators' beliefs about what (if anything) teachers need to learn in order to improve test scores and how they believe teachers are best supported in this learning were related to their reform approach. In Newtown, the most test prep–oriented district, the curriculum director believed that teachers had little to learn.

The main changes he thought were needed involved learning new teaching strategies—more hands-on work, more use of manipulatives, and more "active learning"—that he did not connect with broader ideas of promoting students' conceptual understandings. Interestingly, the other district in our sample, Willis Creek, that carried the most test prep–oriented reform, presented a similar pattern. Administrators in this district thought that teachers needed to learn more about how the test works as opposed to the substance of standards. This was inconsistent with some of the preferences of the teachers in the district, who commented that they would have liked to have workshops on such pedagogical challenges as how to pose open-ended questions in specific areas of mathematics and how to stimulate students to explain their answers.

By contrast, administrators in Sunset and Ridley felt teachers must focus on learning math content and pedagogy at a deeper level, and that teachers should use multiple strategies to support students' conceptual learning. In Cedarville, administrators also recognized that "teachers don't have the content knowledge ... and they really have to have control [of the content]." Acknowledging what teachers needed to learn was an important step in planning professional development in these districts.

In most of the districts, administrators saw a need to "coax" or require teachers to take more responsibility or to get more actively involved in district professional-development or curriculum efforts. This was particularly true in districts like Ridley where administrators had a perception of low human capital and motivation among teachers. In both Newtown and Ridley, administrators were increasing the amount of control they exerted to put pressure on teachers to begin implementing the new curriculum materials and instructional approaches advocated by the district.

Social Capital. As in Spillane and Thompson's (1997) study, social capital—both internal and external—was strongly influenced by human capital. Overall, in these districts, social capital was necessary to support change efforts, but was insufficient without human and internal social capital in the district that was also supportive of such change. Ridley is a good example of this problem: The district provided many projects with outside consultants and SSI partners who worked with a few teachers at a time on obtaining deeper understanding and greater skill in teaching mathematics. Yet, schools in this district lacked the "climate" of commitment to professional learning and collaboration that might be necessary to support teacher learning and implementation of standards-based approaches (Little, 1982).

On the opposite side of the spectrum, teachers in Sunset often took the lead to develop internal networks for sharing ideas and learning how to use new materials. Their administrators supported this effort by providing time for teachers to collaborate and fine-tune their instructional approaches. Though Sunset did not have the number of external partners found in some of the other districts like Ridley, the connections between the district and a local university were very rich and deep. For example, a number of people in the district had done graduate-level work at the university and continued to work with the same faculty as an SSI partner. We identified the same process in Cedarville, where multiple teachers were engaged with a local university and where administrator support was critical in providing the teachers the time and opportunity to meet. In each of these districts, internal social capital provided a "starting point" for building external networks—especially with universities and funders—that could support and enhance internal efforts.

In Newtown, limited internal social capital did not seem to provide the necessary basis for building strong internal and external networks, and the lack of an easily available external partner with a strong mathematics focus did not facilitate the growth of internal social capital. In these districts, internal social capital—generally supported externally—seemed necessary to build human capital that went beyond individual teachers' skills.

Physical Capital/Resources. The availability of resources other than people to support change efforts also varied across the districts in this study, but the availability of financial resources did not predict how aggressively a district pursued reform. Newtown, like Sunset, had greater financial resources than most districts. Yet they did little to change the mathematics curriculum or support teacher learning in that subject. Another wealthy district in our sample, Willis Creek, followed the same process where the resources were placed mainly in test preparation activities, such as after-school programs for low-scoring students or teacher workshops about the test rather than in substantive learning of the reform. Sunset and Ridley were more successful in obtaining outside grants and funding, perhaps due to the greater expertise of their administrators and connections they held with the state and professional organizations. The Abbott funding was an important asset for Ridley, but was viewed by administrators as a mixed blessing because of the additional state demands that came along with the new resources. Ridley hired resource staff to work with teachers at the school level, but district leaders were unsure how the state's mandate for school-based budgeting would affect district control over reform priorities and professional-development activities for teachers. In Cedarville, a poor district with a generally substantive response to state expectations, cuts in funding during the second year of the study resulted in the district returning all of the teacher coordinators to the classroom, depriving teachers of the classroom support the district had provided previously.

Though other studies have suggested that small district size can create more challenges for reform (Fairman & Firestone, 2001), it is interesting that the most systemwide response to standards and the ESPA came from one of the smallest districts. In this case, the limitations of a small district staff were overcome by substantial and deep capacity among the teaching staff in an affluent district.

Administrator-Identified Barriers to Reform. Across all six districts in this study, the three most commonly mentioned barriers to pursuing change consistent with the standards and state testing involved teachers, the community, and resources. Issues around staffing were mostly raised in the lower-income districts, like Ridley. These districts had problems with staff quality, teacher turnover, and the lack of available qualified substitute teachers. Teacher beliefs and resistance to change were also identified as barriers to reform. One administrator in Ridley explained that:

> We have problems with our belief system in terms of many of the staff members not having a sense of efficacy about their ability to influence the development of all children towards high standards and the standards-based curriculum. Teachers do not look at our children and, this is a generalization, but it's a large enough generalization to be an issue in our district, teachers do not look at themselves as having the "Right Stuff" ... to overcome the social pathology that they attach to the kids and the kids' learning capacity.

In Hillview, another district with a working-class population, teachers were more resistant to change. An administrator told us: "The teachers that have been around for 20, 25 years find it very hard to let go of the textbook."

In Sunset, the effort to implement a non-textbook-based curriculum was met with some resistance by parents, and as the community became more diverse, the district had to expend more effort and time defending their and teachers' choice of curriculum materials and overall approach. Administrators in Newtown said that they were not pursuing more reform-oriented approaches in mathematics because of anticipated community resistance, and they had no strategy to build parental and community support.

Financial or physical resources did not always follow where administrators held more rich understandings of the standards-based reform ideas. In Ridley, the district engaged in many partnerships, but each activity typically involved only a few teachers, and did not include the larger teaching staff. Because of Sunset's small size, affluence, and high level of individual capacity, administrators and teachers were able to organize training for all regular teachers and special education staff. Financial capacity was high in Newtown, but administrators did not feel that teachers needed to learn anything different from their traditional approach.

DISCUSSION

The rhetoric behind using assessment to drive instructional change focuses on the nature of the state testing policy and accountability. However, this chapter shows how six districts operating within the same set of state policies responded quite differently. Our conclusions are consistent with research on district reform (cf. Fairman & Firestone, 2001; Spillane & Thompson, 1997), in finding that districts have varying capacity for reform, but they enhance that literature by focusing on strategies used in responding specifically to state standards and testing.

Overall, we found that districts' responses to standards and testing were heavily influenced by their capacity to support more general reform efforts. In the one district where responses were most consistent with the expectations of state reform advocates, and focused on increasing intellectually challenging teacher practice, a combination of factors was involved. The overall capacity and will were very high in Sunset, along with some growing pressure from parents about test scores, and the combination of factors led them to pursue change that was both systemic and deep. The primary catalyst was teachers' and administrators' own beliefs and understandings of the reform ideas, which were lacking in a district like Newtown.

If district administrators do not have a strong interest in reform and a reasonable understanding of the purpose of the assessment and the types of changes in teachers' pedagogical content knowledge, then they are unlikely to respond to state expectations in substantial and sustained ways. Instead, they will turn to the "quick fix" of decontextualized test preparation. They must have the financial resources and the social networks and tools necessary for such change, as well. Administrators need not only to understand reform ideas, but also to believe that teachers need to engage in substantial learning in order to implement them. Though some argue that "teaching to the test" (Resnick & Resnick, 1992) can be a beneficial strategy if the tests themselves are good, the kinds of district strategies consistent with teaching to the test found in this study varied considerably. In keeping with this theme, the will for reform needs to be linked in part to internal "buy-in" or support for state-supported changes, not just external pressures linked with test scores, even if the test has the potential to encourage positive changes in instruction.

Thus, in any income category, the variation in administrators' will and capacity (knowledge and understanding of the reform) and teachers' will and capacity are key to the problem of driving change through testing and standards.

In a few cases, a small number of teachers helped to move their district toward change by bringing back ideas from professional-development experiences. But, in most cases, district leaders needed to communicate a clear goal for moving in this direction and to use a combination of pressure and support to move the more reluctant (and usually older, veteran teachers) to make an effort to learn new content and change practice. In the absence of this leadership or understanding, change efforts are really just superficial, where they match up the topics and lingo of the standards to their curriculum documents, but don't really change what and how teachers are learning and the materials they have to use, or provide ongoing support.

If state policymakers wish to use assessment as a tool to promote instructional change and, ultimately, enhanced student learning, they need to recognize that how districts interpret and respond to new state policies is an important intervening factor in their efforts. It is critical that administrators know *that* teachers need to learn, that they have good ideas of *what* teachers need to learn, and have an understanding of *how* they learn that goes beyond the didactic approach to policy learning so commonly used (Cohen & Barnes, 1993). Though individual teachers may, through their own independent learning, develop the pedagogical content knowledge promoted by reformers, the support of districts in this area could be a significant asset for policymakers. Building district capacity in all its forms may be a critical (although likely not sufficient) mechanism for using state assessments as an effective policy tool for supporting test-preparation efforts that require improving the quality of teacher instruction.

7

Test Scores and Equity

Gregory Camilli
Lora F. Monfils

The primary goal of the standards movement is for all children to learn challenging content, and standards advocates recognize that teachers must be encouraged to teach in ways that are consistent with this goal. States have traditionally used a variety of sanctions and rewards for these twin purposes—improving learning and teaching—but in recent years testing has become an essential ingredient, if not the centerpiece of accountability. Opponents of greatly expanded testing programs worry that in the process of preparing children for assessments, teaching will become more repetitive and, ironically, less challenging. However, if tests scores reflect the unequal conditions of education more than teaching, all of these concerns may be ultimately misplaced. There is a long history of research going back to the first Coleman Report (Coleman, Campbell, Hobson, McPartland, & Mood, 1966) but continuing to the present day (Heubert & Hauser, 1998), suggesting that test scores reflect differences in family background, and "opportunity to learn" (McDonnell, 1995). State accountability systems, to be effective, must address both of these issues.

One argument for state testing is that by holding schools accountable for their students' achievement, the well-documented inequities between rich and poor students and among ethnic groups will decline. Yet, some critics argue that the negative effects of teaching to the test fall most heavily on those children who are already disadvantaged by the American educational system. If accountability policies work as their advocates hope then, there should be some evidence of declines in test score gaps between rich and poor, Black and White, and advantaged and disadvantaged groups more generally. Our data on teaching practice in New Jersey hold out little hope for dramatic reduction in achievement gaps. We found little if any difference in teaching practices between the richer and poorer schools in the state, but teachers serving poor students spent somewhat more time on decontextualized test preparation than did their colleagues serving wealthier students. Nevertheless, to complete our picture of teaching to the test and its consequences, it seemed important to explore trends in test scores to determine if inequities were declining as testing advocates hoped or increasing as predicted by the opponents of testing.

To do so, we focus on an analysis of 3 years of data (spring 1999 to spring 2001) for the New Jersey Elementary School Proficiency Assessment (ESPA). To round out the picture, we also look at the third year's data from the Grade Eight Proficiency Assessment (GEPA) administered in spring 2001, and the High School Proficiency Test (HSPT) administered in fall 2000. It is our goal to understand what state contextual factors drive achievement on the New Jersey assessments, and to reflect on how state reform efforts may have altered preexisting inequities.

EQUITY AND TESTING

Since the Equality of Educational Opportunity Survey (Coleman et al., 1966; Jencks et al., 1972), the relationship between test scores and educational resources has been a topic of considerable interest and importance. The Coleman Report, as it has become commonly known, found that schools had very little effect on student achievement. It was somewhat surprising to find that differences among students' scores *within* a school are larger than those *between* schools once factors such as poverty and mobility are taken into account. Similar findings were obtained in the evaluation of Head Start, Follow Through, and Title I programs (House, Glass, McClean, & Walker, 1978; Picariello, 1968; Westinghouse and Ohio University, 1969). Moreover, achievement gaps between economically disadvantaged and more privileged students continue to be documented to this day (Barton, 2001; Camara & A. E. Schmidt, 1999; Jencks & Phillips, 1998; Kober, 2001; National Center for Education Statistics [NCES], 2000a).

By the time the *Nation at Risk* (National Commission on Excellence in Education, 1983) report was published, test scores of the Scholastic Achievement Test (SAT) and other major test batteries were in notable decline (Koretz, 1986, 1987). Although the consensus was that American schools were performing poorly, there was no evidence clearly documenting *how* schools may have contributed to the decline (see Berliner & Biddle, 1995, for a review of the evidence). Nonetheless, the Commission recommended, in addition to increased school funding, a more challenging curriculum accompanied by standardized testing in order to certify student credentials, identify appropriate instructional interventions, and identify the opportunity for advanced work.

Even before *A Nation at Risk*, advocates of student certification had been working for some time with measurement specialists to establish performance standards for students (e.g., Kane, 2001; Zieky, 2001). Though student certification tests in the United States assessing "minimum basic skills" became popular in the 1960s and 1970s, fulfilling the requirement that all students meet high expectations (e.g., National Council of Teachers of Mathematics, 2000) would require a more challenging curriculum, which in turn would require a more challenging test. In this way, new standards in conjunction with quality instruction and uniformly high expectations could help provide all children the opportunity to learn at a high level (O'Day & M. S. Smith, 1993).

Despite a decade of standards-based reform and cognitively challenging tests, however, most states have generally failed to narrow the achievement gap, not only between minority and majority students, but also between the lowest and highest performing students (Barton, 2001). An inspection of long-term trends from the National Assessment of Educational Progress (NAEP) indicates that although every racial/ethnic subgroup has made significant gains in achievement when compared to students of 30 years ago, the racial/ethnic score gap remains and in some cases has increased, despite initial gains toward closing the achievement gap made in the 1970s and 1980s.

In the 1978 administration of the NAEP math assessment, the African American–White score difference for 13-year-olds was 42 points on a 500-point scale. In 1999, this gap had declined to about 30 points (or approximately three grade levels). During the same time period, the gap in science scores at age 9 decreased from about 55 to 40 points for African Americans and 40 to 35 points for Hispanics in comparison to Whites (NCES, 2000a). By 1999, the African American–White score gap in reading had decreased from 50 to 30 points for 17-year-olds. Yet despite the gap reduction, the average reading score of African American 17-year-olds remained substantially lower than that of their White counterparts by 3–4 years of schooling. Though we have made some progress, it is strikingly clear that most of the work is ahead of us.

NAEP data show national trends but provide little insight into the role of state accountability systems in reducing achievement gaps, except insofar as accountability systems were becoming more prevalent while the achievement gap was shrinking. A more careful analysis of recent state test scores may help clarify the contribution of accountability systems. In practice, however, findings have been mixed and controversial. Though Texas showed considerable narrowing of racial/ethnic score differences on its state assessment (Texas Assessment of Academic Skills [TAAS]) between 1994 and 1998, these results were subject to question because they were inconsistent with corresponding gap increases on NAEP in Texas during the same years (Klein, Hamilton, McCaffrey, & Stecher, 2000). In Delaware, the achievement gap remained consistent across statewide assessments from 1993 to 1995 and 1998 to 2000, with African American students lagging behind White students in all subjects, especially in the top quartile (Zhang, 2002). In North Carolina, a state that provides incentive awards for improving student performance, results comparing actual and expected growth in 1998–1999 and 2000–2001 indicate that inequities were relatively unchanged. Although preliminary analysis of student accountability measures suggests a reduction in inequities between economically disadvantaged and advantaged students, there is some indication that school accountability measures may have increased the differences between racial/ethnic groups (Kaase, 2002). These findings raise questions about how likely one is to find declines in the score gap on state tests with the advent of new accountability systems.

METHODS

To explore the correlates of test scores and the potential effects of reform efforts, we obtained school-level information (e.g., test scores, attendance, proportion of teachers with master's degree) publicly available on the New Jersey Department of Education's Web site. School-level free- and reduced-lunch data for the state of New Jersey were obtained from the Common Core Data Web site of the NCES. Data files were merged based on unique school identifiers.

Unit of Analysis.   Individual-level information is not typically available in New Jersey. However, "school" provides an important conceptual unit of analysis because it is the smallest "unit" at which many education accountability policies are applied. For example, test scores are reported in the local papers at the school level (a weak accountability provision). Moreover, schools in New Jersey span an extremely wide range of demographic variables: There are more than 1,300 schools in 500 school districts with a fourth-grade classroom. This makes New Jersey an ideal context in which to study the "natural" variation in school-level test scores. Although typically the results of test scores are reported in the proportions of students achieving three levels of achievement (partially proficient, proficient, and advanced proficient), average scale scores for schools are usually available and preferable for statistical analysis. We used the latter for all analyses in this chapter.[1]

It is important to keep in mind in the following analyses that the regression coefficients reported herein describe school-level effects. With a degree of caution, however, they can also be interpreted as rough measures of student effects.[2]

Independent Variables.   The variables used for predicting test scores in this study were:

1. year (1999, 2000, 2001 = 1, 2, 3) TIME

2. proportion free lunch PFREE
3. attendance ATTEND
4. student–faculty ratio STFA
5. mobility MOB
6. proportion of teachers with master's degree MA
7. proportion female PFEM
8. proportion African American PAFRAM
9. proportion Asian PASIAN
10. proportion Hispanic PHISP
11. log school size LGSIZE
12. number of suspensions SUSPEND

Dependent Variables. Scale scores from three annual tests for regular education students were used. These include ESPA scores for Language Arts Literacy, Mathematics, and Science for the years spring 1998–1999, 1999–2000, and 2000–2001. On each of these three tests, three levels of proficiency were set (Partially Proficient, Proficient, and Advanced Proficient), and the interval between the Partially and Advanced Proficient cut scores was 50 scale points. For the ESPA tests in 1999, the *achievement score gap* between the wealthiest (district factor group [DFG] J) and poorest (DFG A) school districts was about 40 points for both Language Arts Literacy and Science, and 50 scale points for Mathematics, respectively.[3] Because this score gap between rich and poor schools is a very substantial spread in terms of student achievement (usually about 1 standard deviation at the student level), this quantitative definition of score gap is used herein to provide some help in determining the practical significance of group differences. Though our main focus is on the fourth grade, we also analyzed GEPA scores from spring 2001 and HSPT scores from fall 2000 to provide context. We note that at the time of this analysis, GEPA and HSPT scores were not available for the 3-year period 1999–2001.

Regression Models for GEPA and HSPT Scores. Weighted least-squares regression was used, with the number of students taking the test serving as the weight.

Multilevel Models for ESPA Scores. A two-level hierarchical linear model for repeated measures with time-varying covariates was used. Models with and without student weights gave similar results; and for this reason, the analyses reported herein are unweighted. Repeated observations (test scores and other school variables) from 1999, 2000, and 2001 were modeled as a function of time at Level 1, nested within schools at Level 2, thus combining all 3 years worth of data in a single model.

RESULTS

In this section the results are first given for individual year analyses, followed by a multilevel analysis in which 3 years of ESPA test data (1999–2001) were combined. Only single years are given for the GEPA and HSPT; these show that the results are similar to those in the multilevel analysis of ESPA scores. Frequencies for race/ethnicity were available for the years 1999–2001 whereas gender was available only for 2000–2001; for this reason we could not obtain 3-year trend data for gender. The racial/ethnic categories reported were Native American, African American, Hispanic, and White.[4] There were too few schools with students designated Native American to estimate effects for this group.

GEPA and HSPT Results

GEPA results are given in Table 7.1 for spring 2001 Mathematics only, because the results for the GEPA Language Arts Literacy and Science tests were highly similar. The independent variables for Mathematics with the highest level of impact are free lunch, proportion African American, attendance, and proportion Hispanic. Additional significant factors included attendance, mobility, proportion of teachers with a master's degree, proportion Asian, and number of suspensions. (Note that the beta coefficients in Table 7.1 generally run on a scale from -1 to $+1$, and can be compared with each other. For example, the coefficient $\beta = .107$ for MA can be compared $\beta = .214$ for ATTEND; the effect for attendance is about twice

TABLE 7.1

**Regression Coefficients for the Grade Eight Proficiency Assessment (GEPA)
in Mathematics**

Variable	Slope B	Standard Error	Beta	t Value	Prob
INTERCEPT	−8.357	31.517		−.265	.791
PFREE	−14.913	3.920	−.206	−3.804	.000
ATTEND	2.453	.317	.214	7.737	.000
STFA	−.237	.185	−.025	−1.284	.200
MOB	−.269	.062	−.130	−4.304	.000
MA	.154	.030	.107	5.133	.000
PFEM	7.120	14.126	.009	.504	.614
PAFRAM	−21.467	2.623	−.284	−8.184	.000
PASIAN	17.712	4.934	.074	3.589	.000
PHISP	−11.368	3.285	−.124	−3.461	.001
LGSIZE	.157	.746	.004	.211	.833
SUSPEND	−.209	.043	−.106	−4.889	.000

as large as that of master's degree.) The proportion of predictable variance in school means was $R^2 = .794$ (i.e., 79% out of 100% of the variance in school performance can be predicted by the multiple regression equation), and *the demographic variables account for most of this predictability.*

This is similar to what was found in the Coleman Report, but we do note the importance of variables that may be more amenable to policy decisions such as attendance and proportion of teachers with master's degrees. However, variables such as attendance have limited ranges. For example, attendance typically falls in the neighborhood of 95%–98% in New Jersey. In other words, attendance can be improved only a relatively small amount, and this improvement is wholly inadequate for closing the achievement gap. Percentage master's is clearly an area of interest. But increased levels for this variable depend, among other things, on how schools attract such teachers, the reasons why certain teachers choose to pursue master's degrees, as well as access to educational institutions offering quality master's degrees, and teacher demographics.

For the HSPT, the fall 2000 Mathematics results differ from those of the spring 2001 eighth-grade test (2000 was the last year for which HSPT school files were posted on the Web while this chapter was in preparation). In Table 7.2, it can be seen that the standardized coefficient for proportion free lunch is significant, but much smaller than that for the GEPA. At the same time, the coefficients for the proportion of African American students and Hispanic students are much larger. Attendance is again a strong predictor of school mathematics achievement, and to a lesser degree mobility, proportion of teachers with master's degree, and proportion Asian. Thus, it again appears to be the case that at the high school level, *test scores are driven mainly by demographics* even though schooling factors such as percentage of teachers with a master's degree continue to play a role. The main result derived from these data is that Hispanic and African American students in New Jersey are at significant educational risk in the years spanning 8th to 11th grades.[5]

Multilevel Analysis of Fourth-Grade Scores (ESPA)

For Language Arts Literacy, Mathematics, and Science, the results for the three academic years 1998–1999, 1999–2000, and 2000–2001 were combined into a multilevel analysis at the fourth-grade level. In particular, the information for each year was nested within school. A set of fixed regression coefficients was estimated that can be compared to those in Tables 7.1 and 7.2 (with one exception in Language Arts Literacy, explained later).

What *multilevel* means in this context is that most schools have 3 years of data, and the yearly data are "nested" within schools. Another way of saying this is that the statistical model for the data has a two-level structure with "school" at the top or second level, and "year" at the lowest or first level. Note

TABLE 7.2

Regression Coefficients for the High School Proficiency Test (HSPT) in Mathematics

Variable	Slope B	Standard Error	Beta	t Value	Prob
INTERCEPT	110.731	45.993		2.408	.017
PFREE	−20.862	9.314	−.092	−2.240	.026
ATTEND	3.192	.421	.242	7.589	.000
STFA	−.524	.634	−.020	−.827	.409
MOB	−.770	.143	−.163	−5.368	.000
MA	.318	.077	.100	4.112	.000
PFEM	47.216	26.457	.042	1.785	.075
PAFRAM	−65.786	5.727	−.367	−11.487	.000
PASIAN	47.357	11.251	.097	4.209	.000
PHISP	−52.340	7.016	−.242	−7.460	.000
LGSIZE	−2.439	1.944	−.031	−1.255	.210
SUSPEND	−.178	.087	−.048	−2.062	.040

that similar to the earlier regression analyses, all results are at the school level, and must be extrapolated to student-level effects with some caution.

Two additional predictor variables were included in this analysis to look for test score trends over time for all schools, and for schools with high proportions of racial/ethnic minority students. The TIME variable is *constructed for estimating an overall trend* across the 3 years 1999–2001. A positive regression slope reflects an upward trend. In contrast, the variables TIME*PAFRAM and TIME*PHISP are interaction terms *constructed for estimating the specific trends for African American and Hispanic students*, respectively, during the same time period. As seen in Tables 7.1 and 7.2 from the previous analysis, schools with high proportions of Hispanic and African American students score lower than other schools on the HSPT and GEPA, a New Jersey instantiation of the racial/ethnic score gap found nationally. We would hope, however, that an effective educational accountability policy in New Jersey would begin to close that gap over time.

The other variables in the multilevel analysis are identical to those given in Tables 7.1 and 7.2. An additional variable TDUM (2001 = 1; 1999 & 2000 = 0) was used to designate the academic year 2000–2001 versus the previous two academic years for the Language Arts Literacy component of ESPA because the test changed during this time. Gender was not reported until 2000. Also, school size and number of suspensions did not result in significant estimates. For these reasons, gender, school size, and suspensions were excluded from the multilevel analysis.

Multilevel analyses in addition to estimating regression coefficients or slopes (also referred to as fixed effects in Tables 7.3 through 7.8), can also estimate how much the slopes vary from school to school. Quantification of the variation in slopes can be used to explore the following questions:

1. Does the relationship of free lunch to achievement vary across schools? Because each school varies year to year in its student demographics and test scores, average test scores can be plotted against free lunch for each of the years 1999–2001. In some schools, a high degree of relationship may be present. For a typical school, this means that in the years in which more students were eligible for free lunch, test scores were lower. But this may not be true for all schools. That is, the trend may vary across schools. Another way of thinking about this is to ask the question "Do some schools address the problems that poverty creates for learning better than others?"

2. Does the trend across years (1999–2001) for African American or Hispanic students vary across schools?[6] Some schools may have more positive trends than others whereas others may have more negative trends, and this will cause the slope for trend to have variance across schools. In the interest of equity, it is important to find schools that have upward trends to examine how their programming may be facilitating achievement for African American or Hispanic students. The question here is "Do some schools have a more positive trend than others for African American or Hispanic students over the years 1999–2001?"

Mathematics

In Table 7.3 (fixed effects), it can be seen that all of the aforementioned variables exert an effect on achievement except for TIME*PASIAN and TIME*PHISP. With 1999 as a baseline, there was an upward trend in ESPA Mathematics of about 2.9 points per year. Over a 2-year period, this is equivalent to about 12% of the achievement gap as defined earlier (50 scale points difference between wealthiest and poorest schools in 1999). In addition to an *overall* positive trend for Mathematics, there is a *specific* trend across 1999–2001 for African American students of about –2.75 points per year. Over the course of 2 years, African American students *lost* about 5.5 points, which translates into an *achievement gap* equivalent of 11%. Because the overall gain was canceled by the specific loss, scores were stagnant over the 3-year period for African American students. This trend is large enough to worry about given that it represents New Jersey's best effort to date at educational reform. The current policy levers—though having an overall positive effect—have not been even moderately successful for some, most notably the bulk of African American students.

There are some additional signals from the data that may have positive implications. In Table 7.4 (random effects), it can be seen that the variance components for PFREE, TIME*PAFRAM, and TIME*PHISP are signifi-

TABLE 7.3

Regression Coefficients (Fixed Effects) for Multilevel Analysis ESPA
Fourth-Grade Mathematics

Variable	Slope B	Standard Error	t Value	Prob
INTERCEPT	113.801	18.647	6.103	0.000
TIME	2.946	0.245	12.026	0.000
TIME*PAFRAM	−2.547	0.614	−4.147	0.000
TIME*PASIAN	−1.127	1.913	−0.589	0.556
TIME*PHISP	0.077	0.829	0.093	0.926
PFREE	−29.230	2.373	−12.318	0.000
ATT	1.151	0.194	5.945	0.000
STFA	−0.280	0.071	−3.924	0.000
MOB	−0.075	0.023	−3.333	0.001
MA	0.142	0.017	8.234	0.000
PAFRAM	−15.142	2.160	−7.011	0.000
PASIAN	15.837	5.127	3.089	0.002
PHISP	−10.613	2.761	−3.843	0.000

TABLE 7.4

Variance Components (Random Effects) for Multilevel Analysis of ESPA
Fourth-Grade Mathematics

Variance Component	Estimate	Standard Error	t Value	Prob
INTERCEPT	48.730	3.449	14.127	0.000
PFREE	113.483	24.334	4.664	0.000
TIME*PAFRAM	8.421	3.198	2.633	0.004
TIME*PHISP	32.902	7.458	4.412	0.000
RESIDUAL	49.638	1.559	31.835	0.000

cantly greater than zero, meaning that there is detectable variation of these effects across schools. This may mean that some schools are addressing poverty, as measured by the proportion of students receiving free lunch, better than others. Moreover, for African American and Hispanic students, there is evidence that some schools have a more positive trend than others in mathematics achievement over the years 1999–2001.

Language Arts Literacy

In Table 7.5 (Solution for Fixed Effects), it can be seen that all of the aforementioned variables exert an effect on achievement except for TIME*PHISP. The TIME variable does not appear in this analysis because the scale of ESPA

TABLE 7.5

Regression Coefficients (Fixed Effects) for Multilevel Analysis ESPA
Fourth-Grade Language Arts Literacy

Variable	Slope B	Standard Error	t Value	Prob
INTERCEPT	119.388	14.157	8.433	0.000
TDUM	19.757	0.286	69.107	0.000
TIME*PAFRAM	−1.243	0.460	−2.703	0.007
TIME*PASIAN	−6.008	1.419	−4.233	0.000
TIME*PHISP	0.598	0.557	1.073	0.283
PFREE	−22.650	1.704	−13.289	0.000
ATT	0.744	0.147	5.058	0.000
STFA	−0.080	0.052	−1.528	0.127
MOB	−0.088	0.017	5.087	0.000
MA	0.107	0.013	8.563	0.000
PAFRAM	−11.707	1.583	−7.394	0.000
PASIAN	22.476	3.773	5.957	0.000
PHISP	−4.795	2.013	−2.383	0.017

Language Arts Literacy test was changed in 2000. Differences in testing conditions and scoring led to an increase of about 19.9 points; thus, the 3-year *overall* trend for Language Arts Literacy cannot be estimated. We see that there is a small, but significant, *negative* trend for African American students of about 1.2 points per year. Moreover, Asian American students have *lost* about 6 points per year, which is a loss equivalent of about 30% of the 1999 *achievement gap*. This trend is unsettling news for New Jersey's efforts at educational reform with Asian American students. We note that there may be several explanations for this result, including recent immigration trends.

Despite these declines, there are some positive signals from the data. Similar to the variance component analysis for Mathematics (Table 7.4), the variance components for PFREE and TIME*PAFRAM shown in Table 7.6 are again significantly greater than zero. This suggests that some schools are addressing the negative effects of poverty (as measured by proportion free lunch) on academic achievement in Language Arts Literacy better than others, and some schools have more positive trends over time for African American students.

Science

In Table 7.7 (fixed effects), it can be seen that all of the aforementioned variables exert an effect on ESPA science achievement except for PASIAN, TIME*PASIAN, and TIME*PHISP. In addition, the TIME variable has a

TABLE 7.6

Variance Components (Random Effects) for Multilevel Analysis of ESPA
Fourth-Grade Language Arts Literacy

Variance Component	Estimate	Standard Error	t Value	Prob
INTERCEPT	21.895	1.706	12.835	0.000
PFREE	46.226	10.616	4.354	0.000
TIME*PAFRAM	5.011	1.765	2.839	0.002
TIME*PHISP	2.077	2.215	0.938	0.174
RESIDUAL	33.251	1.005	33.099	0.000

TABLE 7.7

Regression Coefficients (Fixed Effects) for Multilevel Analysis ESPA
Fourth-Grade Science

Variable	Slope B	Standard Error	t Value	Prob
INTERCEPT	186.258	12.811	14.539	0.000
TIME	0.899	0.174	5.168	0.000
TIME*PAFRAM	−0.971	0.490	−1.983	0.047
TIME*PASIAN	1.609	1.362	1.181	0.238
TIME*PHISP	0.977	0.610	1.601	0.110
PFREE	−28.810	1.636	−17.614	0.000
ATT	0.652	0.133	4.896	0.000
STFA	−0.208	0.044	−4.685	0.000
MOB	−0.076	0.016	−4.915	0.000
MA	0.047	0.010	4.689	0.000
PAFRAM	−15.676	1.454	−10.784	0.000
PASIAN	−1.478	3.301	−0.448	0.655
PHISP	−11.055	1.879	−5.884	0.000

significant slope of about .9 points, indicating a weak upward trend in Science scores from 1999 to 2001, although this gain is canceled by a weak downward trend of about 1.0 point per year for African American students. Over the course of 2 years, New Jersey students have shown a 1.8-point increase in science scores. These trends are weak, much like those in mathematics, but provide a mixed evaluation of New Jersey's efforts at educational reform in science. Similar to the variance component analysis for Mathematics and Language Arts Literacy, the variance components for PFREE, TIME*PAFRAM and TIME*PHISP given in Table 7.8 are again significantly greater than zero.

TABLE 7.8

Variance Components (Random Effects) for Multilevel Analysis of ESPA
Fourth-Grade Science

Variance Component	Estimate	Standard Error	t Value	Prob
INTERCEPT	8.604	1.017	8.463	0.000
PFREE	96.330	13.633	7.066	0.000
TIME*PAFRAM	13.366	2.709	4.933	0.000
TIME*PHISP	19.553	4.418	4.425	0.000
RESIDUAL	25.127	0.801	31.369	0.000

In Tables 7.3 and 7.5 it can be seen that relative to White students, both African American and Hispanic students score lower in Mathematics and Language Arts Literacy, whereas Asian American students score higher. However, in Science, as shown in Table 7.7, this trend does not hold; Asian American and White students score about the same. We have no explanation for this apparent inconsistency.

CONCLUSION

For ESPA mathematics, a moderate upward trend over 1999–2001 was estimated, suggesting that test scores actually increased in New Jersey for the first 3 years after the test was introduced. This may represent a real effect of improved mathematics instruction in the state.[7] So much for the good news. The bad news is that there has been little change on variables associated with inequality of educational conditions such as poverty, race, and mobility. These effects remain strong, and there is some evidence to suggest racial/ethnic gaps are changing slightly—and increasing, if anything, for African American students.

The achievement gap based on wealth is essentially the same as that based on race/ethnicity because the richest school districts are predominantly White whereas the poorest school districts are predominantly non-White. Therefore, the achievement gap, which we defined as the average score difference between rich and poor school districts, provides a benchmark or conceptual handle for understanding the practical significance of these results. Although the overall upward trend (all students) was equivalent to about 12% of the gap, the loss for African Americans was almost the same at 11%. Thus, scores for African American students stayed about the same, but the gap increased. Note that at decreases of 10 percentage points of the initial gap per year, 10 years would required to close the achievement gap.[8] Yet, if anything the gap is growing, not shrinking, in New Jersey so the prospects for achieving equity in the generation appear quite bleak.

Taken as a whole, the evidence from this analysis confirms that the bulk of the variation in test scores can be attributed to background, resource, and demographic variables. This is not surprising. It suggests that to date New Jersey's accountability system has not helped to reduce inequities among wealth and ethnic groups, yet this is exactly what needs to occur if test score increases are to be taken as a measure of quality or efficiency of services. Given New Jersey's weak accountability model, some might argue that this finding was inevitable. Other evidence presented in this book suggests that the source of the problem is not so much a poorly designed accountability model as the lack of an educational and social infrastructure necessary to support reform.

Standards, when combined with aligned professional development and effective assessment can lead to change, but the data presented here suggest that these factors have had very little influence on student achievement in New Jersey to date. Despite the general "buy-in" of teachers and the invest-ment of districts across the state as reported earlier, New Jersey's racial/eth-nic score gap remains and, in some cases, has increased. Moreover, the effect of race/ethnicity appears to be above and beyond that of poverty. Though it is not possible with our data to connect this finding to a specific cause, it does seem plausible that the race/ethnicity effect is the result of "many gen-erations of undereducation," that is, "the concentration effects of poverty and racial isolation in urban ghettoes—the many generations of inadequate education and employment opportunities, and a long-term lack of resources for healthy and productive living for adults" (Anyon, 1997, pp. 159–160). Sadly and inexcusably, such results are the norm in America.

In many public discussions of assessment results, the distinction between opportunity to learn and quality of instruction is unintentionally hazy, and in some cases, purposefully blurred. As we have argued in this book, test preparation leads to ambiguous interpretations of test scores. Given the ad-ditional ambiguity in test scores attributable to demographic and geographic influences, it seems unlikely that the early stages of reform will be sustained by accountability strategies in which test scores are assumed to accurately reflect transferable learning that can be attributed to schooling.[9]

Though schooling influences such as attendance and proportion of teachers with a master's degree are demonstrably important, and support the claim that resources (and money by implication) can make a difference, they are not sufficient for improving educational outcomes for all students. As Madaus and Clarke (2001) wrote:

> The task remains of identifying strategies to achieve efficiently and effectively the desirable reform objectives—without having a negative impact on any subpopulation of students. Those strategies will, among other things, need to address the issue of restructuring the academic experiences of students in ways that will help them appreciate the value of academic achievement, in-

crease their expectations and aspirations, and enhance their sense of academic efficacy. (p. 106)

We would add that federal and state policies for the improvement of schools must go well beyond instructional and curricular efforts—and especially testing—by seeking to address the social and economic inequities that impact the lives of so many of America's students.

ENDNOTES

1. Scale scores are more likely to have interval properties and are therefore more consistent with the assumptions of ordinary and weighted least-squares analysis (WLS and OLS).

2. In simple regression models, the raw race/ethnicity coefficients at the school and student levels are similar. In more complex models, different units of analysis may result in different estimates.

3. See chapter 3, p. 40, for a description of district factor groups (DFG).

4. Because we did not include an indicator for the proportion of White students in a school, coefficients for on the proportions of African American and Hispanic students in the regression analysis were always estimated relative to the White students.

5. This conclusion actually applies to Hispanic and African American students who attend schools with large Hispanic and African American populations. By logical inference this result can be extrapolated to individual students.

6. Variation in the trend across schools for Asian American students was also examined. In every analysis, the random effect for TIME*PASIAN was small and nonsignificant, indicating little variation.

7. Though we cannot rule out scale drift from technical testing anomalies, there is no current reason to suspect this is the case.

8. Though this is an extremely optimistic assumption for the pace at which educational reform can be carried out, it is not unprecedented. In the No Child Left Behind Act of 2001, for example, it is required that all students in each major reporting category meet or exceed proficient levels of academic achievement by 2014—that is, in about 12 years.

9. Although states are just now moving to accountability models that take into account the unequal conditions of education, such as value-added models, this approach doesn't take into account the effects of test preparation. Moreover, important work remains to be done to show how such statistical models interact with measurement models.

8

Conclusion

Roberta Y. Schorr
William A. Firestone

The ambiguity of test preparation comes partly from the rhetoric surrounding testing and partly from the range of activities it denotes. Whereas critics see testing as a disease that plagues our educational system, advocates see it as central to the current panacea—standards-based reform—that is expected to save the American educational system. The ambiguity of practice is that test preparation turns out to have elements of both. Some test preparation is decontextualized drill, a short-term response to raise test scores regardless of what students actually learn. But in response to certain types of tests, some teachers are encouraged to explore more intellectually challenging practices and integrate them into their classrooms throughout the year. Which response predominates depends partly on the state test, partly on other policies, and partly on how schools and districts interpret and enact those policies. Taken as a package, however, nothing suggests that the kind of state and local policies and practices observed are likely to overcome the achievement gap between New Jersey's rich and poor children.

In this chapter, we summarize our main conclusions about how tests influence instruction, how local interpretations mediate the effects of state policies, how effective testing is in reducing educational equity, and where educators and policymakers need to go from here.

STATE TESTS AND TEACHING

One tends to think of test scores as the medium through which tests influence practice. In accountability systems, test scores are seen as a prod for low performers to work harder. Moreover, test scores are assumed to provide diagnostic information on how great an improvement is needed, which children need what kind of assistance, and which subjects need more or less attention. Though test scores did contribute to the motivational impact of the state's accountability system, the limited diagnostic use of such data is striking. A quarter of the teachers surveyed never saw test scores, and those who did usually got results back in formats that did not encourage analysis of curricular areas needing improvement. Moreover, because the data came back after children had already moved on to the next grade, it would be hard to use them to analyze student needs.

What really influenced practice is the format of the test items. Here we find a striking paradox. The actual test items were not open to public scrutiny. It was technically illegal to see real test items. As a result, educators and the public had access only to released items selected by the state department of education to be representative of the format and content of the test. Still, the open-ended problems, whether actual or invented by people with access to the actual tests, positively influenced the teachers that we talked to. Teachers reported that as a result of the open-ended problems on the test, they became more motivated to provide students with opportunities to solve more challenging problem activities, and to communicate their reasoning, thinking, and solutions, both orally and in writing. They also said that these types of problems made them realize the importance of having students know, understand, and connect multiple strategies and representations (including symbolic, concrete, and pictorial) for solving problems. This clearly represents a step in the right direction.

Though teachers reported important and substantial changes in their teaching and were genuinely trying to reform according to standards developed by professional organizations (cf. American Association for the Advancement of Science, 1993; National Council of Teachers of Mathematics, 2000; National Research Council, 1996) and governmental entities (cf. National Commission on Mathematics and Science Teaching for the 21st Century, 2000), observation data suggest that instructional practice fell far short of what these standards called for. The New Jersey teachers we visited adopted the surface characteristics of state and national standards, without fundamentally changing their approaches to teaching mathematics and science. The characteristics or strategies that they adopted included, but were not limited to: small-group instruction; use of manipulatives or other hands-on objects; and a focus on what was termed "problem solving," especially problems involving real-world situations or applications. However, these new strategies were modified to fit within older, more didactic patterns of practice. Teachers did not substantively refine, revise, or extend practices to create more challenging learning opportunities for children. Thus, we saw small groups of children seated near each other with little or no mathematical or scientific communication taking place among them. We also saw children using manipulatives or science kits with little or no opportunity to explore mathematical or scientific ideas. And, we saw children working on problem activities, with little or no chance to build, represent, test, defend, or justify solutions. Although the test sensitized teachers to these new strategies and methods, and oftentimes motivated them to start changing their style of teaching, it alone did not get teachers to change the more fundamental aspects of their classroom practice. How, for example, can tests alone get teachers to understand more fully the notion of division of fractions or subtraction with "regrouping"? These are just two examples of the many topics that American teachers tend not to know in a way that goes beyond the execution of rote procedures, and therefore do not understand in meaningful ways (Ma, 1999). When teachers' understanding is limited to surface aspects of the mathematics or science, how can they promote conceptual learning for students?

What was striking was how often teachers, principals, and supervisors equated the surface aspects of these new strategies—for example, the presence of manipulatives, and putting students into groups—with the reforms themselves. We repeatedly found that many of the people that we surveyed and interviewed *believed* that the strategies cited previously and in chapter 2, were what the standards are all about.

Although the teaching practices that we observed were not focused on the more conceptually oriented aspects of instruction, teachers were, at least in principle, moving closer to understanding that students need more than the seat work on procedures and algorithms that had been used so often in the past. Teachers said that the open-ended problems on the test provided them with an impetus for considering different forms of instruction. The teachers repeatedly emphasized that these types of problems encouraged them to rethink their teaching. The modest, surface changes in instruction that we documented may be part of a process that can lead to more substantial improvement. In the meantime, the current instructional changes seem unlikely to help students to develop a deeper understanding of mathematical and scientific ideas. On the bright side, however, many teachers noted that these new strategies did help to make the classroom atmosphere more interesting and appealing. The risk is that by making these changes without fully implementing the intent of such practices, teachers, administrators, and supervisors may be deluded into believing that the standards are "being implemented" and so "mission accomplished."

Whereas the general pattern of instruction observed was the introduction of new strategies without using them in ways that fully carried out the larger intent of those practices—that is, to have children think more deeply about mathematical and scientific ideas—the specific responses to the state tests were mixed. We found a great deal of "teaching to the test," but it took two forms. One was essentially what critics of high-stakes testing would expect. In this form, teachers adopted strategies like "test besting," drilling students on test mechanics, multiple-choice items and practice tests taken from commercial test preparation materials, and emphasizing a procedural approach to solving problems that match to known test items. Teaching test mechanics and setting aside time to practice on commercial test materials and examples from the state Web site was more closely related with conventional didactic teaching—that is, providing students with routines to follow and plenty of opportunity to practice. Such teaching to the test is troubling. It tends to invalidate the test data itself, because any increases may reflect the preparation activity rather than changes in the underlying concept that is supposed to be measured—students' understanding of mathematics and science. More important, it tends to lead to classroom instructional practices that are focused on having children repeat, often with little or no understanding, procedures, rules, or routines most likely to appear on the test. This type of teaching can be quite disheartening for both children and their teachers.

A second form of teaching to the test was identified by teachers who incorporated strategies that challenged children to think more deeply about mathematics and science as part of everyday instruction. This was done in several ways: through the use of tasks that teachers believe to be consistent with the newer and more challenging parts of the test that resemble the open-ended items; by using different types of instructional designs (like small-group instruction where students can talk about their solutions); and through the use of manipulatives or other hands-on materials and equipment. Teachers also told us that they felt that the test prompted them to have their students explain their reasoning more often. Though teachers using this second form of teaching to the test may not have moved as far in this direction as they reported to us, our observations suggest that they were at least trying to ask more probing questions. Perhaps with appropriate support, they will learn how to better facilitate this type of discourse.

In the districts serving the least advantaged students, we did not find strong evidence that teachers used more of one or another form of instruction. We did find more of their attention directed to the test, however. This included both short-term, focused test preparation, and the longer term more intellectually challenging forms. Whatever else was going on in districts serving poor students and the greatest concentration of minority students, educators in those locations were clearly focusing on the state test.

THE CONTEXT FOR CHANGING PRACTICE

Testing is only part of the reform context that teachers face. Though other state policies—most notably in New Jersey, the reforms associated with the Abbott decision in poor urban schools—contribute to that context, much of it is defined by the actions of principals and district staff. If teachers responses varied, so did the context in which they responded. These contexts can be characterized by the pressure and support teachers experienced. In many locations, teachers experienced increased pressure to work harder so their students could attain higher test scores. This pressure was not experienced as a rational calculation about how to respond to changing incentives as suggested by accountability theorists. Rather it was a response to publicizing test scores. These scores had political implications that were most apparent to superintendents and those who dealt with the public. Sometimes pressure came from exhortation from those dealing with actual or anticipated public response to bad test scores. The communication of pressure came in a variety of venues: direct discussions; meetings; and during some professional development sessions. Sometimes, even without administrative intervention, teachers understood and internalized this pressure.

Yet, teachers also reported varying degrees of support in coping with the tests. The support came in the form of access to materials, equipment, and other concrete types of resources, time for interactions with peers, and a variety of learning experiences, including professional-development sessions with consultants or college partners, principals, and other district experts. Although the psychic dimension of support was uniformly helpful, the professional-development "experts" varied greatly in how well they understood the standards and the kinds of instruction suggested by those standards, the content and how children learn the content, and how to help teachers integrate new practices and content knowledge into their classroom instruction.

Overall, however, the professional-development teachers described featured short-term learning opportunities that touched on issues related to mathematics and science education but rarely provided the depth and follow-through needed to help teachers change their practice. In some settings, principals proved to be a key source of support. Supportive principals preferred a less authority-based approach to instructional leadership than their less supportive peers. In all cases, however, their understanding of new standards and the more challenging approaches to instruction that could be triggered by the tests was uneven. When they observed teachers, the criteria they used to evaluate teachers often emphasized both traditional instruction and more inquiry-oriented strategies, with markedly less emphasis on actual content. Moreover, in comparison to suggestions from the literature on leadership, there was very little evidence of the kind of internal community building that can be critical in helping teachers work together to improve their practice. Many principals did not get personally involved in the promotion and/or implementation of the state standards. Rather, they provided teachers access to resources that would expose them to these standards, and it became the teachers' responsibility to implement the standards in their classrooms.

Principals responded to pressure in somewhat the same way that teachers did. When faced with policies that increased accountability, principals emphasized more formalistic authority-based responses that appeared to do little to encourage more engaging teaching. Such formal responses were most prevalent in the poorest districts. What encouraged principals to provide the support that was most useful for helping teachers learn more about how to engage students more actively in learning mathematics and science, remains a mystery in our work.

The six districts we studied responded differently to the state tests. To some extent these differences reflected access to resources. However, there were dramatic differences in the approaches taken among districts having similar access to funding. These differences were reflected in the knowledge, understanding, and access to external sources of support of district administrators. That is, districts had varying capacity for reform, and their responses to tests reflected that variation. In the district where responses were most consistent with the expectations of state reform advocates, a combination of factors were involved. Even in the case where parents seemed to focus on test scores and advocated the use of more conventional textbooks and drill on basic skills, district leaders generally persisted in the direction of a more conceptually oriented approach to instruction. The primary catalyst for this approach was teachers' and administrators' own beliefs about the efficacy of the reform ideas, and this direction for improvement preceded introduction of the new tests. Again, not surprisingly, in districts where administrators lacked either a strong interest in reform and/or a reasonable understanding of the nature of the standards and assessments to which they are being held accountable, they rarely addressed the reforms in deep and long-term ways. External pressures tied to test scores were simply not enough to effect deep change.

TEST PREPARATION AND EQUITY

One of the claims for accountability systems is that they will increase equity of educational outcomes and reduce the persistent achievement gap between rich and poor, majority and minority groups. The assumption is that the publication of state test data will create pressure on urban districts to improve their practice—pressure that we saw in the increased attention to state tests in those very districts—which will in turn help poor and minority children achieve at levels comparable to most American students. Yet, much of the variation in test scores in New Jersey is still attributable to background, resources, and demographic variables. Though variables such as attendance and proportion of teachers with a master's degree influence achievement, their impact is not nearly as great. The achievement gap based on wealth is essentially the same as that based on race/ethnicity. It is critically important to note that whereas there was an overall upward trend for many students, African American students are losing ground in comparison to White students. Thus, in spite of the state's accountability program and special measures taken by the state in response to State Supreme Court decisions, the achievement gap is actually widening.

These results suggest that New Jersey's new accountability system, even in conjunction with the State Supreme Court decision (generally referred to as the *Abbott v. Burke* decision, or simply the "Abbott" decision) has not yet made even modest steps to reduce inequity in educational achievement. The Abbott decision, which directly impacts 30 districts, or 300,000 students (approximately 25% of the student population), is intended to ensure an equal and excellent education for all students. Abbott districts face the many educational challenges that poverty and underfunding produce. The Abbott decision has many components intending to reduce educational inequities. These include, but are not limited to, the use of Whole School Reform models in each of the Abbott schools and the establishment of preschool education for all Abbott children. Because the most recent Abbott measures were decided recently and implementation has been difficult, it may be too soon to expect such programs to produce results that will manifest themselves in increased test scores at the fourth-grade level. Furthermore, these programs need better coordination with other types of supports (such as long-term, research-based professional development) to effect changes that will be reflected on measures such as test scores.

RECOMMENDATIONS FOR REFORM

Though research on a single state must be supplemented with other information when suggesting modifications of the current focus on accountability policies, the New Jersey experience does suggest some directions for future action. In many ways our conclusions contradict the prevailing wisdom on accountability as represented by the recent growth in state accountability policies that is likely to be accelerated by the federal "No Child Left Behind" legislation. Our recommendations cover the format of assessments, access to test information, pressure, and support, including learning opportunities.

The major impetus for change that is related to New Jersey's testing policy, teachers said, came from the introduction of open-ended items into the state's testing system. They noted that they used them as a basis for considering what they felt were more intellectually challenging approaches to instruction. Unfortunately, the tide seems to be turning against the use of such items. Open-ended items were the exception to the rule in state testing programs until about the 1990s. Then a few states—Vermont, Maryland, and Kentucky among others—began experimenting with even more radical breaks from conventional practice in the form of portfolios and performance-based assessment tasks. Practical experience from those states suggests that they too helped to challenge conventional practice and encourage teachers to use more engaging instructional strategies. However, they also proved expensive to use and of insufficient reliability for high-stakes testing systems. Moreover, they were not always well understood by the public. With new regulations requiring that elementary students be tested in almost every grade, and with increasing stakes linked to those tests, the costs and accountability requirements work against more complex performance tasks. The New Jersey experience, and that of several other states, suggests however, that some kind of open-ended assessment items must play a prominent part in state accountability systems if state testing is to contribute to higher intellectual standards.

However, as with other elements of testing policy, test format—that is, the use of open-ended items—is only part of what makes it a good stimulus for educational improvement. For example, an item that is "open-ended" may not be mathematically or scientifically significant, or one that requires students to use their sense-making abilities. For example, many of the typical textbook and test problem activities may refer to real objects and events, but would never actually occur in "real life." The result is that students cannot make sense of the situation using extensions of their own knowledge or experiences. In some cases, students may simply do better if they "turn off" their knowledge and experience in order to give the response that conforms to the teacher or tests notion of the "correct" solution process. This is not the intention of the standards, and should not be the focus of the questions on the test. Open-ended and multiple-choice items need to meet at least two criteria to stimulate more intellectually engaging, inquiry-oriented instruction. First, they must be aligned with the content that we expect students to know and represent the critical ideas in the field. Second, they must provide opportunities for children to actively organize information, consider alternatives, reach decisions, and justify and communicate them using the methodologies of the discipline in question (Newmann, 1996). Items incorporating these criteria will help demonstrate to educators the kind of content that children should learn and illustrate the kinds of activities that will help children develop those capacities.

What of access to information about the tests? Actual test items must be available for scrutiny and test results provided in a timely manner. New Jersey is among the states in which the actual test items are kept confidential even after the test is administered. This is done to reduce the cost of test production. Instead, selected items intended to be representative of the test are available on the department of education's Web site. The test specifications are also available. Together, these supply some level of information relating to the nature and type of questions on the test. We maintain that this is not enough.

We recommend that all states practicing accountability testing make test items (multiple-choice and open-ended) available for public scrutiny so educators and parents can more closely examine what the state considers to be a good, standards-based type of problem activity. Providing stakeholders with the actual items used will encourage a fair and honest debate about the types of problems that are on the test, their alignment with the standards, and whether or not the items elicit responses that provide useful and productive information. It seems unlikely that direct access to test items encourage more "teaching to the test" in the negative sense than already exists, given the extensive availability of commercial test preparation materials.

At the same time, it is important for educators to receive better and more useful information about test results in a timely manner. State departments of education should work with local educators to identify the most helpful formats in which to provide information to teachers, schools, and districts. Doing so is recommended by the National Research Council in its report on high-stakes tests (Heubert & Hauser, 1999). Without such feedback, the diagnostic value of state testing is lost as is its legitimacy.

Beyond the test itself, both state policymakers and administrators need to consider how to balance pressure and support to achieve effective improvement of practice. We disagree somewhat with Fullan (1991) about the importance of mixing pressure and support. Logically, it makes sense that some combination would be more effective than either one alone. Moreover, some pressure may be necessary to get educators to attend to state testing and accountability systems at all. However, even in a relatively low-stakes state like New Jersey, the evidence suggests that the danger is more likely to come from too much pressure than too little. Our work supports that of the numerous critics of high-stakes testing. That is, too much pressure breeds compliance, not thoughtful, challenging teaching.

More attention needs to be given to providing teachers with a variety of effective supports. Some aspects of support would seem to be fairly straightforward. In a state like New Jersey that has adopted intellectually challenging standards and is trying to align its test with them, teachers need the materials to support challenging instruction. Textbooks that reinforce didactic teaching strategies and leave students in a passive role need to be updated with standards-based curriculum and other types of materials such as science kits, calculators, and manipulatives.

Other aspects of support are challenging to create. Teachers need to understand the subjects they teach and effective and meaningful ways to teach those subjects. Because many teachers now on the job lack the requisite knowledge, opportunities for teachers to learn must be part of the normal environment of schools. That is, teachers need to learn more if students are to learn more. Yet, creating those opportunities is quite difficult. On the positive side, there has been a great deal of research on effective models for professional development for teachers and others involved in the teaching and learning process. For example, we now have a better understanding of the role that content knowledge plays in mathematics instruction. More specifically, Ball and Bass (2000) talked about helping teachers learn to know and use content knowledge. They stated that we must be attentive to "what teachers need to know, how they have to know it, and helping them learn to use it—by grounding the problem of teachers' content preparation in problems and sites of practice"(p. 101). This, they added, could help to "close the gaps that have plagued progress in teacher education" (p. 101). Others, such as Loucks-Horsley, Hewson, Love, and Stiles (1998), suggest concrete approaches that can be used in science.

Creating such experiences and opportunities is a substantial undertaking. Often the people charged with designing and/or implementing professional development lack understanding of the ways in which to help teachers and may not be versed themselves in the necessary content knowledge or understanding of how children make sense of ideas in the curriculum. And, as if that were not enough, there are constraints on time for learning and on teachers' opportunities to work together to test, share, refine, revise, and extend what they know through ongoing practice and reflection. Moreover, principals and central-office staff play complementary roles with the more technical knowledge often coming from the latter and critical facilitation coming from the former. In addition, what is intended as support and learning opportunities can easily turn into or be perceived as another manifestation of pressure, as we have seen with many district professional-development programs.

The state, district leadership, principals, and teachers all need to think more about how to create schools that are learning organizations for everyone in them if substantial improvement of student achievement and substantial increases in educational equity are to take place. They will also need to work much harder to create career-long learning opportunities for all educators, for as Dewey noted, "I believe finally, that education must be conceived as a continuing reconstruction of experience; that the process and the goal of education are one and the same thing" (quoted in Dworkin, 1959, p. 27).

Appendix A

Methods

In the spring of 1999, we began a statewide study to examine teachers' responses to New Jersey's fourth grade testing program, the Elementary School Performance Assessment (ESPA), in the areas of mathematics and science. The kinds of teaching promoted by the National Council of Teachers of Mathematics (NCTM; 2000), the National Research Council (1996), and the state of New Jersey (New Jersey State Department of Education, 1996) are quite different from conventional teaching practice (Stigler & Hiebert, 1999), and we sought to determine the extent to which measurement-driven reform operationalized by ESPA would facilitate (or hinder) the implementation of NCTM-type instruction among fourth-grade teachers in New Jersey.

The central dilemma that this research task generated was to reconcile the demands for precision of measurement and representativeness (McGrath, 1982). Teaching is complex work that has been studied with both qualitative and quantitative methods. For example, a variety of observational methods are often used to document such practices, including both direct observation and videotapes. The strength of these methods lie in the precision and richness of description that derive from observing teachers in their natural context. However, due to the time- and labor-intensiveness of such in-depth methods, such methods usually involve relatively small samples, thus limiting the generalizability of results with respect to a larger population. Stigler and Hiebert (1999), for instance, attempted to generalize to all American mathematics teaching from a sample of less than 100 teachers.

To increase generalizability, an alternate approach involves large-scale surveys of random samples of teachers drawn from a known population. The cost of collecting data from so many cases often means that it is possible to ask questions of respondents but not to observe (McGrath, 1982). Yet, self-report data on teaching practice is often suspect because of the fear either that teachers will give the socially acceptable response rather than describing what they really do, or that they will not have a shared understanding of distinctions made by the researchers, and will give inaccurate responses as a result.

Because past work by one of the authors had provided reasonable description of teaching practice, but with a small sample that precluded generalizing to a larger population (Firestone, Mayrowetz, & Fairman, 1998), we placed a premium on getting a large, representative sample that would enable us to generalize our results. We planned to use a survey to obtain that sample. However, recognizing the limitations of surveys, we sought to triangulate with additional data. Although some teachers filled out a rather extensive log of their day-to-day teaching activities and sent us samples of instructional materials, the response rate for this material was very low. However, we also observed and interviewed a sample of teachers and principals. This information was triangulated with the survey data whenever possible. This appendix describes how we drew our samples, and the instrumentation we used.

SAMPLES

The study used four main samples: teachers who were surveyed, principals of the surveyed teachers, districts included in case studies—several district administrators were interviewed in each district—and teachers who were interviewed following the observed lessons. In most cases, we repeated the surveying process for 2 or 3 years.

Teachers for the Survey

In order to characterize statewide responses to New Jersey's testing program, we needed data from a sample of teachers who represented the geographic and economic diversity of the state. Because we thought that professional development might play a critical role in how teachers responded to the tests, we wanted to ensure that some teachers had access to high-quality professional development. Thus, our sample had to be stratified by socioeconomic status and to include a subsample of teachers in districts that were actively providing professional development to teachers. We met the first requirement by using the state's classification of districts into district factor groups (DFG), using such measures as employment, family income, percentage of families in poverty, and the like. For the second requirement, we turned to the New Jersey Statewide Systemic Initiative (SSI), who provided us a list of districts that were actively participating in a variety of professional development initiatives in science and mathematics, including their own and those coming from other organizations. Using this list, we identified districts participating in five or more high-quality initiatives.

Our target sample size was 300 teachers. We began a recruitment process whereby we approached superintendents in a stratified (by DFG and professional development participation) random sample of districts and asked their permission to approach teachers in particular schools in their districts. When permission was received from the superintendent, we then approached the principals of the selected schools in order to get both permission and names of fourth grade teachers. Teachers were then approached directly and invited to participate in the study. Finally, we approached each teacher's principal to conduct an interview on background factors that might affect changing teacher practice.

In Years 2 and 3 of the study, teachers who had participated the previous year were contacted. Naturally, there was attrition due to teachers moving out of grade, school, or district. In the second year, replacement teachers were acquired using the sampling procedure outlined earlier. In the third year, after implementing this replacement procedure, the pool was supplemented with 55 teachers acquired through snowball sampling.

After contacting approximately 600 teachers in Year 1 of the study, data were collected in the form of telephone surveys from 247 teachers, written surveys from 177 teachers, and portfolios of instructional materials from 110 teachers. The response rates were 41%, 30%, and 18%, respectively.

During the second year of the study, all items were combined into a telephone survey to improve response rates, and logs and instructional materials were not collected. In the spring of 2000, 287 teachers, including 160 from the first year, responded to the telephone survey. Of the 358 teachers contacted, 71 declined to participate.

In the spring of 2001, the third and final year of the study, a total of 301 of 332 eligible teachers contacted responded to the telephone survey for a response rate of 92%. Of these teachers, 206 had participated in the 2000 survey, and a subset of 119 had participated in the 1999 survey, as well. Thus, a sample of 119 teachers who participated in the survey all 3 years was available for longitudinal analysis. Samples in all three years were highly representative of the state with regard to geographic, district wealth, and demographic characteristics. Table A.1 shows that the samples recruited reflected the distribution of students in the state across DFGs fairly well.

Principals

Principals were interviewed following their teachers' surveys. In 1999, 83 of 86 principals contacted completed the survey for a response rate of 97%. In 2000 and 2001, surveys were completed by 139 of 166 and 134 of 155, with response rates of 84% and 86% respectively.

We also obtained information on principals from the teacher survey. Because we sampled teachers, not schools, the number of teachers per principal varied by school and study year. For example, in 1999, 41% of the principals

TABLE A.1

Socioeconomic Representativeness of Teacher Samples

	District Factor Group			
	A-B			I-J
Percentage of:	Poorest	C-E	F-H	Wealthiest
Observed Teachers	22	27	16	35
Surveyed Teachers 2001	28	28	28	16
Surveyed Teachers 2000	34	22	23	21
Surveyed Teachers 1999	29	25	24	22
Students	30	24	26	19

had only one teacher completing the survey and questionnaire instruments, whereas the highest participation was among the 7% of principals with four to eight teachers. In 2000, 44% of the principals had only one teacher participating in the study and reporting on her or his response whereas 17% had from four to six teachers reporting. In 2001, 49% of the principals had only one teacher participating in the study, and 20% had four to seven teachers who participated in the survey.

Case Study Districts

In selecting districts, we did not so much seek a representative sample, as one where there was likely to be a strong effort to use available professional development resources to respond to the state's standards and assessments. During the study period, New Jersey had a National Science Foundation (NSF)–funded SSI. The SSI used regional centers to connect school districts with what NSF and the SSI considered to be among the best professional development resources in mathematics and science education. Some districts were much more active in working with regional centers than others. The research team asked three regional centers that concentrated on elementary education to nominate districts that used their services aggressively and had a reputation for providing strong professional development in mathematics or science. Through these nominations, the research team recruited seven districts that varied in size and wealth but were among the most active users of the regional center services and were willing to participate in the study. Data were collected from these districts in the second year of the study. Repeat visits were made to six districts in the third year. One district was not included that year because there was so much turnover in its small district office that the district was essentially reformulating its approach to mathematics and science education. Table A.2 provides demographic information on the six districts that participated in both years of the study.

TABLE A.2
District Characteristics

District	DFG	Size	Grades	Rural/ Suburban/ Urban	District Administrators Interviewed
Ridley[a]	B	5,000–10,000	K–12	Urban	3
Cedarville	B	8,000–12,000	PreK–12	Rural/ Suburban	5
Hillview	CD	5,000–10,000	PreK–12	Urban	4
Sunset	I	1,000–2,000	K–8	Rural	2
Newtown	I	1,500–2,500	K–8	Suburban	2
Willis Creek	I	2,000–4,000	K–8	Suburban	3

[a]All district names are pseudonyms.

Observed Teachers

The observation study focuses on 78 teachers drawn from two samples. The first sample came from the first statewide survey conducted in the spring of 1999. These teachers had responded to two survey scales intended to broadly assess whether the teachers tended toward direct or more inquiry-oriented instructional practices. The direct instruction scale consisted of 11 items and had a reliability of .66. These items asked teachers how often they did things like "emphasize the importance of following procedures in solving math problems" or "supply detailed procedures in order to keep students focused in mathematics lessons." The inquiry-oriented instruction scale had 19 items and a reliability of .80. Teachers were asked, for example, how often they "have students show or explain a concept in more than one way" (Monfils, Camilli, Firestone, Yurecko, & Mayrowetz, 2000).

We then looked for teachers who scored at extremes on both scales, reflecting four self-reported approaches to teaching. Ultimately, 22 of 54 teachers thus identified agreed to participate and were observed during the spring of 2000. Three of the 22 teachers were selected for scoring high on both the inquiry-oriented and direct-instruction scales, six for scoring high on inquiry-oriented instruction but low on direct instruction, seven for scoring low in inquiry-oriented instruction but high on direct instruction, and six for being low on both. Using the same scale-based selection criteria, we also included observation and interview data from 10 additional teachers from the survey sample who had participated in a preliminary observational study in the spring of 1999 to help validate the survey scales. Thus, the combined distribution of self-reported approaches to teaching among the selected teachers from our representative sample was 5 high inquiry-high direct, 12 high inquiry-low direct, 8 low inquiry-high direct, and 7 low in-quiry-low direct.

The second sample came from the seven case study districts. The districts varied in adequacy of funding and in geographic region of the state. Within each district, math coordinators chose teachers who participated actively in the professional development programs. Initially 32 teachers were selected from these districts, of which 31 were observed during their mathematics lessons. In the second year of the observation study, 13 of the first year's teachers returned to the study, and 15 new teachers were added.

Although the sample of teachers is not, strictly speaking, random and not large enough to use the conventional tools of survey sampling, this is a sample that ought to provide evidence of higher than normal practices that represent more change from past descriptions of American teaching in general (Cuban, 1993) and in mathematics (Stigler & Hiebert, 1999) in the direction recommended by the NCTM and other reform groups. First, the sample overrepresents wealthy districts compared to both the distribution of students and of teachers in the survey samples. Second, the fact that almost half the teachers report that they regularly use inquiry-oriented approaches appears unusually high. Finally, the second sample was chosen from districts that were actively involved in professional development aligned with both state and NCTM standards. The low rates of such practices in the observation data (see chap. 2) is in the opposite direction from what one might expect from the biases in the sample.

INSTRUMENTATION

Here we describe the instrumentation for the teacher and principal surveys and the teacher observations and interviews separately. Information on the case studies is provided in chapter 6.

The Surveys

In the first year, we spent a great deal of time developing survey measures of instruction (inquiry-oriented and didactic), teaching to the test, and curricular topics covered in mathematics and science. We also borrowed or developed measures of a variety of factors expected to influence instruction, including access to various kinds of professional development and materials, school climate, principal support, pressure to raise test scores, understanding of state and national standards, and teacher efficacy.

Our first task was to return to the literature and review our initial conceptualization for completeness. This exercise led to the development of a conceptual framework that focuses on teachers' work. It locates that work in three successive contexts: the individual's skills and beliefs, the local (school and district) organizational context, and the larger policy context, including but not limited to state standards and assessments. Because our goal was to get data from a large number of teachers, our challenge was to develop measures for the most important concepts yet minimize the time demands on teachers.

At the same time we reviewed a variety of instruments, including the work of Leigh Burstein and Lorraine McDonnell, then at RAND; John Supovitz and colleagues, Horizon, Inc.; Andy Porter, University of Wisconsin; Henry Becker, University of California, Irvine; Brian Stecher at Rand; and National Assessment of Educational Progress (NAEP) teacher survey among others. We also consulted with content experts available in New Jersey who were familiar with the state standards and with efforts to assess teacher learning as part of the evaluation of the New Jersey SSI evaluation. From this information we developed:

- A telephone survey instrument so teachers could report on their instructional practice.
- A mail-out questionnaire so teachers could report on their content coverage and a variety of factors that might influence their instructional package.
- A format for collecting examples of teachers' mathematics and science assignments.
- A protocol for recording information from direct observation of teachers' practice by the research team.
- A telephone survey so principals could report on factors that might influence teachers' practice in mathematics and science.

These instruments were pilot-tested for clarity and length of time to administer on 16 teachers in five districts. The telephone interview had information on instructional processes used by teachers and the extent to which they report teaching to the test. The mail-out questionnaire had information on curriculum coverage in math and science and a number of the personal and local organizational context variables likely to influence teaching practices. The lesson logs provided examples of teacher assignments with more detailed reports on how those assignments were used by teachers. In the second year, we sought to increase our response rates by decreasing the demand on teacher time, and thus, incorporated the mail questionnaire into the telephone survey, and dropped the collection of lesson logs. Appendix B presents the teacher interview guide used in the last 2 years of the study. Appendix C has the principal interview guide.

Interviews and Observations

Data from the smaller sample included both observations and interviews. Generally, each teacher was observed in two mathematics and one science lesson for each year he or she was in the study. The observers were a mix of mathematics or science education or policy researchers, including Rutgers professors and graduate students. Most had been teachers, and all had some experience with classroom observation for research purposes. During observations, each researcher kept a running record of the events in the classroom, focusing on the activities of the teacher as well as capturing the activities of students. The field notes recorded all problem activities and explorations, the materials used, the questions that were posed, the responses that were given—whether by students or teachers—the overall atmosphere of the classroom environment, and any other aspects of the class that the researchers were able to gather. The coding scheme developed to analyze these observations is described in chapter 2.

We also believed it important to interview these teachers for two reasons. First, we wanted to get their perceptions of the lessons we observed. Second, we thought it would be useful to get teachers to describe their perceptions of the state tests and the contexts they worked in as another way to triangulate the information obtained from the surveys. Appendix D includes the interview guide used for the observations, beginning in the spring of 2001. All post-observation interview data were reviewed, and codes were developed based on emergent themes. Appendix E presents the interview coding scheme.

Appendix B

Teacher Questionnaire

A-1. Which of the following best describes your teaching position? Are you:

a. A self-contained classroom teacher who does NOT teach math OR science to a regular class?

b. A self-contained classroom teachers who teaches
a. Science	1. Yes	2. No	9. Don't know/refused
b. Math	1. Yes	2. No	9. Don't know/refused

c. A specialist who teaches fourth graders:
a. Science	1. Yes	2. No	9. Don't know/refused
b. Math	1. Yes	2. No	9. Don't know/refused

A-2. How many students are currently in your self-contained class?

_____

A-3. How many of the students you teach are of limited- or non-English-speaking ability? _____

A-4. And, how many of the students you teach are classified (with IEPs—Individual Education Plans) as being perceptually impaired (PI) or learning disabled? _____

FOR MATH SPECIALISTS

qa2m "What is the average number of students in the MATH classes you currently teach?"

qa3m "In these classes, what is the average number of students who are of limited- or non-English-speaking ability?"

qa4m "In these classes, what is the average number of students who are classified (with IEPs) as being perceptually impaired (PI) or learning disabled?"

FOR SCIENCE SPECIALISTS

qa2s "What is the average number of students in the SCIENCE classes you currently teach?"

qa3s "In these classes, what is the average number of students who are of limited- or non-English-speaking ability?"

qa4s "In these classes, what is the average number of students who are classified (with IEPs) as being perceptually impaired (PI) or learning disabled?"

A-5. Which of the following best describes the ability level of (the students in your class/the students you teach) compared with the average student in this school?

1. They are primarily of higher ability.

2. They are primarily of about the same average ability.

3. They are primarily of lower ability.

4. All ability levels are represented in my class.

9. Don't know/refused

A-6a. Are the students (within your class/among the students you teach) grouped for MATHEMATICS instruction on the basis of ability?

1. Yes   2. No   9. Don't know/refused

A-6b. Are the students (within your class/among the students you teach) grouped for SCIENCE instruction on the basis of ability?

1. Yes   2. No   9. Don't know/refused

A-7a. Overall, how many of *all* of your students leave class for MATHE-MATICS instruction? _____

A-7b. Overall, how many of *all* of your students leave class for SCIENCE instruction? _____

* * * * *

B. TEACHER'S BACKGROUND

B-1a. How many *undergraduate*-level COURSES (note: not credit hours) did you take in mathematics or mathematics education? _____

B-1b. And, how many *graduate*-level COURSES (note: not credit hours) did you take in mathematics or mathematics education? _____

B-2a. How many *undergraduate*-level COURSES (note: not credit hours) did you take in science or science education? _____

B-2b. And, how many *graduate*-level COURSES (note: not credit hours) did you take in science or science education? _____

B-3a. Overall, how many years have you been teaching? _____ years

B-3b. How many years of teaching experience do you have in third, fourth, and fifth grade? _____

B-3c. How many years have you taught in this school? _____ years

* * * * *

C. SUBJECT MATTER

C-1. In a typical week, how many HOURS do your fourth graders spend on (subject)?

C-2. And, has that amount of time decreased, stayed the same, or increased since last year?

	Hours per week:	Decreased	Stayed the Same	Increased	Don't Know/ Refused
ROTATE CHOICES					
a. Language Arts— Reading and Writing	_____	1	2	3	9
b. Mathematics	_____	1	2	3	9
c. Science	_____	1	2	3	9
d. Social Studies	_____	1	2	3	9
e. Art and Music	_____	1	2	3	9
f. Physical Education	_____	1	2	3	9
g. Foreign Language	_____	1	2	3	9

C-3 & C-4. How often do you use each teaching technique?

    1 = Almost always

    2 = Most of the time

    3 = Once in a while

    4 = Almost never (includes never)

    9 = Don't know/refused

C-3. SCIENCE

ROTATE ITEMS

a. Have students complete science worksheets on their own?

    1   2   3   4   9

b. Have students show or explain a scientific concept in more than one way?

    1   2   3   4   9

c. Have students predict what they expect to happen in a science experiment?

    1   2   3   4   9

d. Have students explain their ideas to each other in pairs or triplets?

    1   2   3   4   9

e. Use a rubric to grade written work or student projects?

    1   2   3   4   9

f. Use small groups for at least half of the lesson?

    1   2   3   4   9

g. Begin each new unit by defining scientific terms?

    1   2   3   4   9

h. Give a short-answer or a multiple-choice test?

    1   2   3   4   9

i. Use scientific models or realistic demonstrations to explain new ideas?

    1   2   3   4   9

j. Use lecturing as the main method of instruction?

    1   2   3   4   9

k. Allow students to design their own science experiment?

    1   2   3   4   9

l. Step back and let students discuss or argue their own ideas?

    1   2   3   4   9

m. Give model problems for which there is a clear easiest approach?

    1   2   3   4   9

n. Emphasize the importance of following procedures in science investigations?

    1   2   3   4   9

o. Have students explain conclusions or solutions in writing?

    1   2   3   4   9

p. Review student portfolios or journals to identify misunderstandings?

    1   2   3   4   9

q. Have students explain the reasoning behind an idea?

    1   2   3   4   9

C-4. MATHEMATICS

ROTATE ITEMS

a. Have students complete mathematics worksheets on their own?

    1   2   3   4   9

b. Have students show or explain a concept in more than one way?

    1   2   3   4   9

c. Have students predict answers before obtaining a mathematical solution?

    1   2   3   4   9

d. Have students explain their ideas to each other in pairs or triplets?

       1   2   3   4   9

e. Use a rubric to grade written work or student projects?

       1   2   3   4   9

f. Use small groups for at least half of the lesson?

       1   2   3   4   9

g. Begin each new unit by having students practice skills necessary for the understanding the concepts?

       1   2   3   4   9

h. Supply detailed procedures in order to keep students focused in mathematics lessons?

       1   2   3   4   9

i. Use manipulatives to explain new mathematical ideas?

       1   2   3   4   9

j. Use lecturing as the main method of instruction?

       1   2   3   4   9

k. Allow students to invent their own procedures for solving a math problem?

       1   2   3   4   9

l. Step back and let students discuss or argue their own ideas?

       1   2   3   4   9

m. Give model problems for which there is a clear easiest approach?

       1   2   3   4   9

n. Emphasize the importance of following procedures in solving math problems?

       1   2   3   4   9

o. Have students explain conclusions or solutions in writing?

       1   2   3   4   9

p. Review student portfolios or math journals to identify misunderstandings?

       1   2   3   4   9

q. Have students explain the reasoning behind an idea?

       1   2   3   4   9

r. Have students work on problems for which there is no immediately obvious method of solution?

       1   2   3   4   9

s. Have students practice computational skills?

       1   2   3   4   9

* * * * *

D. MATHEMATICS AND SCIENCE CONTENT

Mathematics Content

Did you teach fourth grade mathematics 3 years ago?

I'm going to read you some mathematical content areas and skills that you may or may not cover in a typical school year.

For each, I'd like to know:

D-1. How many lessons per year do you and your students spend or plan to spend engaging each topic?

    1 = Zero to two lessons a year to this topic or skill.

    2 = Three to five lessons a year to this topic or skill.

    3 = Six to 10 lessons a year to this topic or skill.

    4 = Eleven to 20 lessons a year to this topic or skill (approximately 2 to 4 weeks).

    5 = Twenty-one lessons or more a year to this topic or skill (approximately more than 4 weeks).

    0 = This topic or skill is not in my curriculum so I do not address it.

D-2. And, if you taught fourth grade 3 years ago, indicate if the number of lessons you spend or intend to spend this year on each topic has decreased, stayed the same, or increased?

Topic	Lessons per Year	Decreased	Stayed the Same	Increased	DK/ REF
a. Paper-and-pencil mathematical operations with whole numbers (adding, subtracting, multiplying, and dividing).	_____	1	2	3	9
b. Doing mental math operations (adding, subtracting, multiplying, and dividing). Note that "mental" in this case means "doing the math in your head."	_____	1	2	3	9
c. Estimation (magnitude, results of computation, and measurement).	_____	1	2	3	9
d. Place value relationships (whole numbers and decimals).	_____	1	2	3	9
e. Adding and subtracting decimals via paper and pencil.	_____	1	2	3	9
f. Identification of geometric figures.	_____	1	2	3	9
g. Area and perimeter.	_____	1	2	3	9
h. Fractions concepts (fractions as parts of a whole, equivalency).	_____	1	2	3	9
j. Measurement (customary, metric).	_____	1	2	3	9
k. Probability.	_____	1	2	3	9
l. "Dealing with data" collecting, organizing, analyzing, and displaying data.	_____	1	2	3	9
m. Statistics.	_____	1	2	3	9
n. Graphing.	_____	1	2	3	9
o. Patterns, functions.	_____	1	2	3	9
p. Open sentences, use of variables.	_____	1	2	3	9
q. "Discrete math" (Combinations, puzzles, optimization, classification, algorithms, networks, and tree diagrams).	_____	1	2	3	9

Science Content

Did you teach fourth grade science 3 years ago?

I'm going to read you some science content areas and skills that you may or may not cover in a typical school year.

For each, I'd like to know:

D-3. How many lessons per year do you and your students spend or plan to spend engaging each topic?

  1 = Zero to two lessons a year to this topic or skill.

  2 = Three to five lessons a year to this topic or skill.

  3 = Six to 10 lessons a year to this topic or skill.

  4 = Eleven to 20 lessons a year to this topic or skill (approximately 2 to 4 weeks).

  5 = Twenty-one lessons or more a year to this topic or skill (approximately more than 4 weeks).

  0 = This topic or skill is not in my curriculum so I do not address it.

D-4. And, if you taught fourth grade 3 years ago, indicate if the number of lessons you spend or intend to spend this year on each topic has decreased, stayed the same or increased?

Topic	Lessons per Year	Decreased	Stayed the Same	Increased	DK/ REF
a. Understanding natural and man-made systems (recognizing systems, identifying parts).	_____	1	2	3	9
b. Investigative skills (observing, classifying, and dealing with data).	_____	1	2	3	9
c. Using mathematics (measurement, estimating, counting).	_____	1	2	3	9
d. Nature and history of science and scientists.	_____	1	2	3	9
e. Selecting and using tools.	_____	1	2	3	9
f. Needs of living things/Life systems.	_____	1	2	3	9
g. Habitats, ecosystems, and adaptation.	_____	1	2	3	9

Topic	Lessons per Year	Decreased	Stayed the Same	Increased	DK/ REF
h. Features and classifications of plants and animals.	_____	1	2	3	9
i. Structure and physical properties of matter.	_____	1	2	3	9
j. States of matter: solid, liquid, gas (heating and cooling).	_____	1	2	3	9
k. Forces, motion, and energy.	_____	1	2	3	9
l. Invisible forces (gravity, electricity, and magnetism).	_____	1	2	3	9
m. Earth materials: rocks, soil, and fossils.	_____	1	2	3	9
n. Weather and climate.	_____	1	2	3	9
o. Earth, moon, and sun systems.	_____	1	2	3	9
p. Stars and galaxies.	_____	1	2	3	9
q. Humans and the environment.	_____	1	2	3	9

* * * * *

E. Professional Development

E-1. In the last year, has any time in your district's in-service or professional development days been devoted to the teaching of mathematics and science?

  1. Yes   2. No   3. Not applicable; no in-service days   9. DK/REF

E-2. Please tell me if you have or have not done each of the following in the last year:

  In the past year have you (READ ITEM)?

	Yes Have done	No Haven't	Don't Know/ Ref
a. Taken any college courses in math or science or teaching math or science.	1	2	9
b. Helped other teachers learn how to teach mathematics or science by serving as a mentor teacher or cooperating teacher with a student teacher or first-year teacher.	1	2	9
c. Helped other teachers learn how to teach mathematics or science by serving as a lead teacher or specialist teacher working with other teachers in your district.	1	2	9
d. Served on a school or district curriculum development or textbook selection committee.	1	2	9

E-3. These are some professional development programs for math and/or science available in the state. Have you participated in (READ ITEM)?

Professional-Development Programs in New Jersey	Yes Participated	No Did Not Participate	Don't Know/ Refused
a. RST^2 from Ramapo College	1	2	9
b. New Jersey State Systemic Initiative Program	1	2	9
c. Local Systemic Change Program	1	2	9
d. Rutgers Eisenhower Project	1	2	9
e. Fairleigh Dickinson University Eisenhower Project	1	2	9
f. Princeton University Eisenhower Project	1	2	9
g. Rowan University Eisenhower Project	1	2	9
h. Stevens University Eisenhower Project	1	2	9
i. Have you participated in any other professional-development programs in the state?	1	2	9

If YES: What are they?

* * * * *

E-4. How much do the following individuals influence the professional development you receive?

Individual(s)	Not At All				A Great Deal	Don't Know/ Refused
a. District officials	1	2	3	4	5	9
b. The principal	1	2	3	4	5	9
c. All the teachers in the school	1	2	3	4	5	9
d. A committee of teachers in the school	1	2	3	4	5	9
e. You, with a personal decision	1	2	3	4	5	9

The following questions are about your professional development in the *last year*.

E-5. How much time did you spend on professional development for (READ ITEM)?

0 = None

1 = Less than 1 day (8 hrs.)

2 = 1–2 days (8–16 hrs.)

3 = More than 2 days (16+ hrs.)

E-6. Was there any follow-up to this professional development by the original providers?

1 = Yes   2 = No   9 = Don't Know/Refused

E-7. Was there any follow-up to this professional development by your
principal or supervisor?

1 = Yes   2 = No   9 = Don't Know/Refused

E-8. How useful was this professional development to you (not at all useful,
somewhat useful, or very useful)?

1 = Not at All

2 = Somewhat

3 = Very

9 = Don't Know/Refused

	QE5 Amount of Time-	QE6 Follow-Up by Provider	QE7 Follow-Up by Principal or Supervisor	QE8 Usefulness
a. Content and/or instructional strategies in science	_____	_____	_____	_____
b. Content and/or instructional strategies in mathematics	_____	_____	_____	_____
c. Strategies for using assessment results	_____	_____	_____	_____
d. Strategies to help students score high on ESPA math	_____	_____	_____	_____
e. Strategies to help students score high on ESPA	_____	_____	_____	_____

E-9. *Knowledge* of several types of standards. For the (READ ITEM), are
you only aware of them, have you read them through once or twice,
understand them somewhat (that is, you can implement parts in
class), understand them well (that is you can implement them fully in
class), or are you an expert (that is, you could lead a workshop)?

1 = Only aware of them

2 = Read through once or twice

3 = Understand somewhat (can implement parts in class)

4 = Understand well (can implement fully in class)

5 = Expert (could lead workshop)

9 = Don't Know/Refused

a. National science standards (e.g., NRC
National Science Education Standards or
Project 2061 Benchmarks) for fourth grade   1   2   3   4   5   9

b. The New Jersey Core Curriculum Content
Standards and Frameworks for Science   1   2   3   4   5   9

c. National mathematics standards (e.g.,
NCTM)   1   2   3   4   5   9

d. The New Jersey Core Curriculum Content
Standards and Frameworks for
Mathematics   1   2   3   4   5   9

E-10. Of the following, which best describes the availability of computers
in school for use by your math and science students?

    1 = None available

    2 = One to three within the classroom

    3 = Four or more within the classroom

    9 = Don't Know/Refused

E-11. How often do you have access to multiple computers available in a
computer lab?

    1 = Almost always

    2 = Most of the time

    3 = Once in a while

    4 = Almost never

    5 = Not available/no lab

    9 = Don't Know/Refused

* * * * *

F. Teaching Materials

F-1. How much access did you have to (READ ITEM)?

    0 = None

    1 = One or two to demonstrate in class

    2 = Enough for children to share

    3 = Enough for every child to have one

    9 = Don't Know/Refused

F-2. In the last year, did this degree of access decrease, stay the same, or in-
      crease?

      1 = Decrease

      2 = Stay the same

      3 = Increase

      9 = Don't Know/Refused

F-3. How often did you use (READ ITEM)? (Note: Semester is defined as a
      half year.)

      1 = Almost every day

      2 = Once or twice a week

      3 = Once or twice a month

      4 = Once or twice a semester

      5 = Never

      9 = Don't Know/Refused

FOR MATH TEACHERS ONLY:	*Access*	*Change in Access*	*Use*
a. Mathematics textbooks	_____	_____	_____
b. Manipulatives for teaching math (e.g., base 10 blocks)	_____	_____	_____
c. Calculators	_____	_____	_____
FOR SCIENCE TEACHERS ONLY:			
d. Science textbooks	_____	_____	_____
e. Science kits (i.e., sets of materials for use in several lessons)	_____	_____	_____
f. Measurement and observation tools (thermometer, hand-lens)	_____	_____	_____

* * * * *

G. Preparation for the ESPA

G-1. The first set of questions is about how often you **do** or **plan to do** the
      following things *in the month before the ESPA*.

      In the month before ESPA, how often do you or plan to do
          (READ ITEM)?

G-2. Now, how often do you do these same things *throughout the entire
      school year*? We're going to use the same 1 to 4 scale with 1 being al-
      most always and 4 being almost never.

FOLLOWING EACH ITEM THAT'S ASKED FOR THE MONTH BE-
FORE ASK: And, how often do you do this *throughout the entire school year?*

a. Teach test-taking mechanics like filling in bubbles, how to put your name
   on the test, or how to pace yourself during the test

G-1. Month:	1	2	3	4	9
G-2. Year:	1	2	3	4	9

b. Motivate students to make their best effort on the ESPA, like suggesting
   they prepare by getting a good night's sleep or encouraging them to
   try hard

G-1. Month:	1	2	3	4	9
G-2. Year:	1	2	3	4	9

c. Have students use rubrics to grade each other's work

G-1. Month:	1	2	3	4	9
G-2. Year:	1	2	3	4	9

d. Teach the regular curriculum using performance-based exercises similar
   to the ESPA

G-1. Month:	1	2	3	4	9
G-2. Year:	1	2	3	4	9

e. Teach test-besting skills like methods for turning story problems into
   arithmetic calculations or how much to write after an open-ended
   math item

G-1. Month:	1	2	3	4	9
G-2. Year:	1	2	3	4	9

f. Use commercial test preparation materials like "Scoring High" and "Measuring Up on the ESPA"

G-1. Month:	1	2	3	4	9
G-2. Year:	1	2	3	4	9

g. Have practice sessions with ESPA-like items

G-1. Month:	1	2	3	4	9
G-2. Year:	1	2	3	4	9

The time period we are focusing on is since the ESPA began.

	Not At All	Small Amount	Moderate Amount	Great Deal	Don't Know/ Refused
G-3. How much have you increased the match between the content of your instruction and the content of the ESPA?	1	2	3	4	9
G-4. How much have you increased the use of open-ended/performance-based exercises in regular instruction?	1	2	3	4	9

G-5. Did you administer the ESPA in:

	Yes	No	Don't Know/Refused
a. 1996	1	2	9
b. 1997	1	2	9
c. 1998	1	2	9
d. 1999	1	2	9
e. 2000	1	2	9

(added 1/2/01)

G-6. Do you Strongly Agree, Moderately Agree,
Moderately Disagree, or Strongly Disagree that (READ ITEM)?

	Strongly Agree	Moderately Agree	Moderately Disagree	Strongly Disagree	Don't Know/ Refused
a. Score differences between schools often reflect students' characteristics more than the work of the staff.	1	2	3	4	9
b. If changes made to teach to the mathematics and science standards are criticized by parents, my principal will defend those changes.	1	2	3	4	9
c. When I really try, I can get through to the most difficult or unmotivated students.	1	2	3	4	9
d. Most of my colleagues have a good understanding of the science standards.	1	2	3	4	9

	Strongly Agree	Moderately Agree	Moderately Disagree	Strongly Disagree	Don't Know/ Refused
e. A teacher is very limited in what he or she can achieve because a student's home environment is a large influence on his or her achievement.	1	2	3	4	9
f. My principal believes that ESPA measures important aspects of student learning.	1	2	3	4	9
g. I regularly share teaching ideas or materials with other teachers.	1	2	3	4	9
h. The core curriculum content standards in math and science have provided helpful guidance for instruction.	1	2	3	4	9
i. My principal indicates that doing well on ESPA is a top priority.	1	2	3	4	9
j. My colleagues agree that the core curriculum content standards in mathematics and science identify important content that our children should learn.	1	2	3	4	9
k. When I design lessons and activities in math and science, it is understood that an important goal is to raise ESPA scores.	1	2	3	4	9
l. My colleagues engage in innovative instructional practices in math and science.	1	2	3	4	9
m. I feel that I am familiar enough with ESPA to adequately prepare my students for the test.	1	2	3	4	9
n. Most of the other teachers in this school don't know what I do in my classroom or what my teaching goals are.	1	2	3	4	9
o. My principal is making changes to implement the mathematics and science standards successfully.	1	2	3	4	9
p. Most of my colleagues have a good understanding of the math standards.	1	2	3	4	9

	Strongly Agree	Moderately Agree	Moderately Disagree	Strongly Disagree	Don't Know/ Refused
q. March and April are pretty tough in this school because of the time and attention focused on getting ready for ESPA.	1	2	3	4	9
r. My colleagues and I work together to develop ways to help children learn the content specified by the math and science standards better.	1	2	3	4	9
s. Too much time is diverted from instruction to raising scores on ESPA.	1	2	3	4	9
t. My principal provides time for teachers to meet and share ideas.	1	2	3	4	9
u. I take it as generally appropriate for the state to set standards for curriculum and for student performance.	1	2	3	4	9
v. Other teachers at this school come to me for help or advice when they need it.	1	2	3	4	9
w. My principal understands what good standards-oriented mathematics and science teaching is like.	1	2	3	4	9
x. My colleagues and I share materials that can be used to prepare students to do well on ESPA	1	2	3	4	9
y. It is possible to raise ESPA scores without really improving what students know about a subject.	1	2	3	4	9
z. Parents are involved in this school (e.g., they attend parent–teacher conferences, visit the school, etc.).	1	2	3	4	9

Math teachers only aa.–ee.

aa. Even if I try hard, I cannot teach mathematics as well as I teach most subjects.	1	2	3	4	9
bb. I understand mathematics concepts well enough to be effective in teaching elementary mathematics.	1	2	3	4	9

	Strongly Agree	Moderately Agree	Moderately Disagree	Strongly Disagree	Don't Know/ Refused
cc. I find it difficult to use manipulatives to explain math concepts to my students.	1	2	3	4	9
dd. Given a choice, I would not want the principal to evaluate my mathematics teaching.	1	2	3	4	9
ee. I do not know what to do to help students become excited about mathematics.	1	2	3	4	9

Science teachers only ff.–jj.

	Strongly Agree	Moderately Agree	Moderately Disagree	Strongly Disagree	Don't Know/ Refused
ff. Even if I try hard, I cannot teach science as well as I teach most subjects.	1	2	3	4	9
gg. I understand science concepts well enough to be effective in teaching elementary science.	1	2	3	4	9
hh. I find it difficult to use scientific models or realistic demonstrations to explain science concepts to my students.	1	2	3	4	9
ii. Given a choice, I would not want the principal to evaluate my science teaching.	1	2	3	4	9
jj. I do not know what to do to help students become excited about science.	1	2	3	4	9
kk. When it comes right down to it, a teacher really can't do much because most of a student's motivation and performance depends on his or her home environment.	1	2	3	4	9
ll. No matter how hard they try, some students will not be able to learn aspects of my subject matter.	1	2	3	4	9
mm. The attitudes and habits students bring to classes greatly affect their chances for academic success.	1	2	3	4	9
nn. Students' achievement depends to a great degree on how well they are taught.	1	2	3	4	9

	Strongly Agree	Moderately Agree	Moderately Disagree	Strongly Disagree	Don't Know/ Refused
oo. Yearly changes in test scores often reflect differences in the characteristics of students taking the test rather than changes in school effectiveness.	1	2	3	4	9
pp. The ESPA is sensitive to the curriculum and instructional improvements made in our school.	1	2	3	4	9
qq. When it comes to ESPA scores, schools with highly transient populations are at an unfair disadvantage.	1	2	3	4	9

G-7. Each pair represents opposite ends of a continuum in instructional approaches. You may agree totally with one statement or the other or find yourself somewhere in between.

A1. Statement A: I try to provide opportunities and resources for my students to discover or construct mathematical or science concepts for themselves, but I also try to lead my students to figure things out by asking pointed questions without telling them the answers.

B1. Statement B: My students really won't learn math or science unless I go over the material in a detailed and structured way. It's my job to explain, to show students how to do the work, and to give them practice doing it.

Now, thinking of a continuum of numbers where the number "1" is total agreement with Statement A and the number "6" is total agreement with Statement B. What number on the continuum would you select?

Position A1   1   2   3   4   5   6   Position B1

G-8. Here is the second set of statements:

A2. Statement A: When I teach math and science, I aim for comprehensive coverage even if it means sacrificing in-depth study.

B2. Statement B: When I teach math and science, I aim for in-depth study of selected topics and issues even if it means sacrificing coverage.

Position A2   1   2   3   4   5   6   Position B2

Now, thinking of a continuum of numbers where the number "1" is total agreement with Statement A and the number "6" is total agreement with Statement B. What number on the continuum would you select?

* * * * *

Section H

H-1. Did you receive math or science ESPA scores for your students (individual, class, or grade) from last spring (2000)?

    1. Yes   2. No   9. Don't Know/Refused

H-2. What information about **math** or **science** ESPA scores did you receive?

a. Individual student math or science scores

    1. Yes   2. No   9. Don't Know/Refused

b. Class average or proportion passing

    1. Yes   2. No   9. Don't Know/Refused

c. School average or proportion passing

    1. Yes   2. No   9. Don't Know/Refused

d. Comparison of how your school or class did relative to state average.

    1. Yes   2. No   9. Don't Know/Refused

e. Math or science cluster scores for your school (For example, in math the five clusters are number sense, operations, and properties; measurement; spatial sense and geometry; data analysis, probability, and discrete mathematics; and patterns and algebra.)

    1. Yes   2. No   9. Don't Know/Refused

f. Math or science cluster scores for your class

    1. Yes   2. No   9. Don't Know/Refused

H-3. Did you have any follow-up discussion regarding these ESPA scores for *your* students or *your* school?

    1. Yes   2. No   9. Don't Know/Refused

H-4. (If YES in H-3) With whom did you meet to discuss these ESPA scores for your students?

a. Your principal

    1. Yes   2. No   9. Don't Know/Refused

b. Your supervisor

    1. Yes   2. No   9. Don't Know/Refused

c. Other teachers

    1. Yes   2. No   9. Don't Know/Refused

d. Anyone else—Other (please specify) _____

    1. Yes   2. No   9. Don't Know/Refused

H-5. On a scale of 1 to 5 where 1 is not at all and 5 is a great deal, please indicate whether you feel ESPA scores are being used to evaluate your
teaching effectiveness in math *and/or* science?

Not at All   A Great Deal   DK/REF
  1   2   3   4   5   9

H-6. On a scale of 1 to 5 where 1 is not at all and 5 is a great deal, how accurately did these ESPA scores reflect the *math* knowledge of your
students?

Not at All   A Great Deal   DK/REF
  1   2   3   4   5   9

H-7. On a scale of 1 to 5 where 1 is not at all and 5 is a great deal, how accurately did these ESPA scores reflect the *science* knowledge of your students?

Not at All   A Great Deal   DK/REF
  1   2   3   4   5   9

H-8. For each of the following, on a scale of 1 to 5 where 1 is not at all and 5
is a great deal, how much have you changed your math and/or science
teaching practices in response to these ESPA scores?

a. I have changed class content, teaching more of some topics and
less of others.

Not at All   A Great Deal   DK/REF
  1   2   3   4   5   9

b. I have changed the order of topics taught.

Not at All   A Great Deal   DK/REF
  1   2   3   4   5   9

c. I now have students do more writing in math and/or science.

Not at All   A Great Deal   DK/REF
  1   2   3   4   5   9

d. I now have students explain their reasoning orally more frequently in math and/or science.

Not at All   A Great Deal   DK/REF
  1   2   3   4   5   9

e. I now have students use *more* manipulatives, and do experiments
or hands-on activities in math and/or science.

Not at All   A Great Deal   DK/REF
  1   2   3   4   5   9

f. I now use more open-ended questions in class and on tests.

Not at All			A Great Deal		DK/REF
1	2	3	4	5	9

g. I now do more test preparation in math and/or science, such as teaching test-besting skills or giving practice sessions with ESPA-like items.

Not at All			A Great Deal		DK/REF
1	2	3	4	5	9

h. I now use more homogenous grouping for math and/or science instruction.

Not at All			A Great Deal		DK/REF
1	2	3	4	5	9

H-9. Are there any other changes you've made to your math and/or science teaching practice in response to ESPA scores?

    1. Gave Response   2. None/Don't Know/Refused

BY OBSERVATION:

Respondent Gender: 1. Male   2. Female

INTERVIEWER RATING OF RESPONDENT:

Overall, how engaged (interested, involved, cooperative, thoughtful) would you say this respondent was during the interview?

    1. Very much engaged
    2. More engaged than disinterested
    3. About equally engaged/disinterested
    4. More disinterested than engaged
    5. Very much disinterested

Appendix C

Principal Interview Guide

1-R. What would you say are the **three** major issues that your **school** has faced in the last year or two?

USE THE FOLLOWING PROBES AS NEEDED:

Could you please tell me more about _____ ?
Please explain the nature of this issue?
What is it about _____ that made it an issue?

2-R. Now, what would you say are the **three** major issues that your **district** has faced in the last year or two?

USE THE FOLLOWING PROBES AS NEEDED:

Could you tell me more about _____ ?
Please explain the nature of this issue?
What is it about _____ that made it an issue?

3. When you are actually in the teacher's classroom watching the teacher teach, what are you looking for that indicates good or bad teaching? We are particularly interested in learning about the criteria you use to judge the work of your teachers.

4. When you evaluate teachers, how important is (READ ITEM) (is it not important at all, somewhat important, moderately important, or very important)?

	Not at all Important	Somewhat Important	Moderately Important	Very Important	DK
a. The classroom is quiet.	1	2	3	4	9
b. Teachers maximize instructional time-on-task.	1	2	3	4	9
c. The content taught is part of the Core Curriculum Content Standards.	1	2	3	4	9
d. Children are actively involved in exploring concepts of the subject being taught.	1	2	3	4	9
e. Children work with a variety of materials (e.g., writing, manipulative charts, etc.).	1	2	3	4	9
f. Students' instructional experiences are varied (e.g., whole class, cooperative learning, learning centers, etc.).	1	2	3	4	9
g. The teacher specifies the learning outcome at the beginning of each lesson.	1	2	3	4	9
h. Students' test scores.	1	2	3	4	9

5. How much have your criteria for evaluating teachers changed since the introduction of the Core Curriculum Content Standards in May 1996?

     1. None, not at all

     2. A little bit

     3. A moderate amount

     4. A great deal

     5. Don't know

6. The following is a list of individuals or groups that might hold a principal accountable. Please tell me how actively each one works to hold you accountable.

Does (NAME OF GROUP / PERSON FROM LIST) work (not at all actively, somewhat actively, moderately actively, or extremely actively) to hold you accountable?

	Level of Activity for Accountability				
	Not at all	Somewhat	Moderately	Extremely	Don't Know
ROTATE CHOICES					
a. Superintendent	1	2	3	4	9
b. School Board	1	2	3	4	9
c. Parents	1	2	3	4	9
d. The State	1	2	3	4	9

7. Now, I would like to know how important you think ESPA scores will be for each of these individuals or groups in making judgments about your performance.

Do you think ESPA will be not at all important, somewhat important, moderately important, or extremely important for (NAME OF GROUP / PERSON FROM LIST) in making judgments about your performance?

	Level of Importance for Performance Judgments				
	Not at all	Somewhat	Moderately	Extremely	Don't Know
ROTATE CHOICES					
a. Superintendent	1	2	3	4	9
b. School Board	1	2	3	4	9
c. Parents	1	2	3	4	9
d. The State	1	2	3	4	9

8a. Has your school undergone any major curriculum change in **math or science** in the last **3 years**?

    1. Yes   2. No   3. Don't know

If yes, what are these changes? Are there any others? PROBE FOR UP TO THREE TO FOUR CHANGES.

INTERVIEWERS NOTE: PROBE FOR DESCRIPTION OF CHANGE. FOR INSTANCE, DOES IT FOCUS ON CONTENT COVERED? (WHAT CONTENT?) DOES IT FOCUS ON WAYS OF TEACHING? (WHAT WAYS?) SOMETHING ELSE?

9. IF YES TO Q8a: For each of the following resources, please tell me if it has or hasn't been part of this planning process.

	YES	NO	*DON'T KNOW*
a. Release time for teachers to work together during the school day	1	2	9
b. Paid after-school time	1	2	9
c. Scheduling so grade-level teachers or school improvement teams have common preparation periods for planning	1	2	9
d. Outside experts	1	2	9
e. School-controlled budget for school improvement activities	1	2	9

10. ASK EVERYONE: How many days did you spend preparing for and supervising the last administration of the ESPA? _____ days

11. **In addition** to the time that they spend taking the ESPA, how many days do you expect to have your fourth-grade students spend taking standardized tests other than the ESPA in the **2000–2001** academic year? _____ days

12a. A variety of programs around the state offer teachers assistance in becoming better teachers of mathematics and science. Some of these programs require teachers to go to out-of-district workshops; some offer assistance in the school or district; and some combine the two. Will you please tell me the names or types of programs in which your school is currently participating?

12b-R. Questions about **the two most important** programs. RECORD ANSWERS IN GRID BELOW. Repeat b–g for each program.

12b-R-a. Which of the two programs you named is the most important? i.) _____   ii.) _____

12b-R-b. Will you please tell me how many fourth-grade teachers in your school are participating in this program? i.) _____   ii.) _____

12b-R-c. And, what is the total number of fourth-grade teachers in your school? i.) _____   INTERVIEWER NOTE: ONLY NEED TO ASK TOTAL FOR FIRST PROGRAM.

12b-R-d. How many of the non-fourth-grade full-time teachers (classroom and pullout) are participating in this program? i.) _____   ii.) _____

12b-R-e. And, what is the total number of full-time teachers in your school? i.) _____   INTERVIEWER NOTE: ONLY NEED TO ASK TOTAL FOR FIRST PROGRAM.

12b-R-f. How many days do teachers
    participate in this program?   i.) _____   ii.) _____
INTERVIEWER NOTE: AFTER-SCHOOL
SESSION COUNTS AS HALF DAY;
RELEASE DAY OR WHOLE-DAY
SUMMER SESSION COUNTS AS ONE
DAY.

12b-R-g. Does THE PROGRAM STAFF   i.) 1. Yes   ii.) 1. Yes
    provide follow-up where teachers are   2. No   2. No
    visited in the classroom?   9. Don't   9. Don't
                                                 Know   Know

13. First, what things, if any, are happening in your school to ensure that
    your students are learning the **Core Curriculum Content Standards**
    in math and science? Are there any others?

COULD YOU TELL ME MORE ABOUT THAT? COULD YOU GIVE
    ME SOME MORE DETAILS ABOUT HOW THIS WORKS?

14. What things are happening in your school to help students and teach-
    ers get ready for ESPA?

INTERVIEWERS: PROBE FOR UP TO THREE THINGS.

15a. Below is a list of things that principals can do to help students and
    teachers get ready for ESPA. How much effort did you give to each?
    How much effort did you give to (READ NAME OF ACTIVITY)
    (none, a little, a moderate amount, or a great deal)?

Activity ROTATE ITEMS			Amount of Effort Given		
	None	A Little	Mod Amt	Great Deal	Don't Know
a. Providing encouragement to teachers who are doing a good job of preparing students.	1	2	3	4	9
b. Telling teachers and students that doing well on ESPA is a high priority.	1	2	3	4	9
c. Expressing disapproval to teachers who are not working hard enough to raise ESPA scores.	1	2	3	4	9
d. Focusing on core curriculum content standards while supervising and evaluating teachers.	1	2	3	4	9

15b. Here are some additional things that are being done to help teachers and students prepare for ESPA. Using a scale from 1 to 5 where a 1 is not happening at all at your school and a 5 is happening a great deal at your school, please rate each of the following.

Using this scale from 1 to 5, to what extent is (READ ITEM) happening in your school?

15c. FOR ANY ITEM WHERE THE ANSWER GIVEN IS GREATER THAN "1"—NOT HAPPENING, ASK: Is this happening because of a school-level or a district-level initiative?

Activity ROTATE ITEMS

Extent to which this is happening in your school:

a. Helping teachers align content taught with core curriculum content standards.

Not at All				Great Deal	Don't Know
1	2	3	4	5	9

School	District	Don't Know
1	2	9

b. Arranging for professional development related to ESPA and tested subjects.

Not at All				Great Deal	Don't Know
1	2	3	4	5	9

School	District	Don't Know
1	2	9

c. Holding pep rallies, pizza parties, and other social events to motivate students

Not at All				Great Deal	Don't Know
1	2	3	4	5	9

School	District	Don't Know
1	2	9

d. Requiring teachers to integrate ESPA preparation into weekly instructional planning.

Not at All				Great Deal	Don't Know
1	2	3	4	5	9

School	District	Don't Know
1	2	9

e. Holding periodic meetings with teachers or devoting time at faculty meetings to discuss ESPA.

Not at All				Great Deal	Don't Know
1	2	3	4	5	9

School	District	Don't Know
1	2	9

f. Providing teachers with new textbooks aligned to the Core Curriculum Content Standards.

Not at All   Great Deal   Don't Know

   1   2   3   4   5   9

        School   District   Don't Know
          1   2   9

g. Providing teachers with new math manipulatives and hands-on science equipment.

Not at All   Great Deal   Don't Know

   1   2   3   4   5   9

        School   District   Don't Know
          1   2   9

h. Providing teachers with supplemental instructional materials for ESPA preparation (review books, software, etc.).

Not at All   Great Deal   Don't Know

   1   2   3   4   5   9

        School   District   Don't Know
          1   2   9

i. Requiring teachers to identify the content standards addressed in their lesson plans.

Not at All   Great Deal   Don't Know

   1   2   3   4   5   9

        School   District   Don't Know
          1   2   9

j. Holding special ESPA practice sessions before or after school or during weekends.

Not at All   Great Deal   Don't Know

   1   2   3   4   5   9

        School   District   Don't Know
          1   2   9

k. Providing students in danger of scoring low on ESPA with remedial help or tutoring during the school day.

Not at All   Great Deal   Don't Know

   1   2   3   4   5   9

        School   District   Don't Know
          1   2   9

l. Holding a special meeting with parents to inform them about the testing program.

Not at All   Great Deal   Don't Know

   1   2   3   4   5   9

        School   District   Don't Know
          1   2   9

Below are some comments about ESPA. Please tell me if you strongly agree, moderately agree, moderately disagree, or strongly disagree with each.

	Strongly Agree	Moderately Agree	Moderately Disagree	Strongly Disagree	Don't Know
16. I have received enough information about ESPA to provide curricular and instructional leadership to my teachers.	1	2	3	4	9
17. The district has one or more special initiatives to improve the quality of elementary math and science instruction.	1	2	3	4	9
18. Score differences between schools often reflect students' characteristics more than the work of the school staff.	1	2	3	4	9
19. Some schools have found ways to raise ESPA scores without really improving what students know about a subject.	1	2	3	4	9
20. ESPA provides teachers and administrators with useful information to help improve our instructional program.	1	2	3	4	9
21. ESPA provides teachers with useful information for providing more effective instruction for each student.	1	2	3	4	9
22. ESPA puts too much stress on children.	1	2	3	4	9
23. ESPA puts too much stress on teachers and administration.	1	2	3	4	9

	Strongly Agree	Moderately Agree	Moderately Disagree	Strongly Disagree	Don't Know
24. ESPA takes away time that would be better spent on instruction.	1	2	3	4	9
25. The Core Curriculum Content Standards in math and science provide useful guidance to teachers.	1	2	3	4	9
26. Educators in this school are developing ways to help children better learn the content specified by the math and science standards.	1	2	3	4	9
27. In my school, teachers are able to develop home-study programs for parents to work with their children at home.	1	2	3	4	9
28. Parents are involved in this school (they attend parent–teacher conferences, visit the school, etc.).	1	2	3	4	9
29. Students' parents do volunteer work in classrooms in this school.	1	2	3	4	9
30. Parents regularly spend time with their children on academic instruction at home (e.g., helping with homework, reading to them, etc.).	1	2	3	4	9
31. The academic programs in this school are strongly supported by local organizations, local institutions, or businesses.	1	2	3	4	9

32. When you were a classroom teacher, what grade(s) did you teach? Check all that apply.

    a. Grade K–5   b. Grades 6–8

    c. Grades 9–12   d. Other (please indicate) _____

33. When you were a classroom teacher, what subject(s) did you teach? Check all that apply.

    a. Mathematics   b. Science

    c. Language arts/literacy   d. Social studies

    e. World languages   f. Visual or performing arts

    g. Comprehensive health or physical education

    h. Other (please indicate) _____

RESPONDENT GENDER: 1. Male

                                 2. Female

Appendix D

Teacher Interview Guide

QUESTIONS FOR TEACHER INTERVIEWS

Classroom Observation

*Q01 M/S What were you trying to accomplish during today's lesson? What content or ideas were you focusing on?

*Q02 M/S What worked well with today's lesson? Why did it work well?

*Q03 M/S What, if anything, would you change about today's lesson? Why?

*Q04 M Look for instance of kids explaining mathematical ideas to each other or teacher and ask why it was done and how well it went?

*Q04S Although the Core Curriculum Content Standards and the ESPA are related, some schools are making broader changes in the content they teach and in the instructional methods they use that are likely to help in both areas and other changes more specifically designed to help children score well on the test. I'd like to ask you about both of these changes.

Ask after one observation:

*Q05 Since 1996, there has been pressure on teachers to match their teaching to the Core Curriculum Content Standards. What things, if any, are you doing to help your children learn the Core Curriculum Content Standards in math and science?

*Q06 What kinds of things do you generally do to help your students get ready for ESPA?

*Q07 What are you doing specifically to prepare students for the ESPA (i.e., test preparation)?

*Q08 Considering either the ESPA or the Content Standards, how, if at all, has that affected the topics you teach?

*Q09 How have you changed the teaching strategies you use in response to the ESPA and/or the Content Standards?

*Q10 What role has your principal played in helping you prepare for the ESPA or in changing your math and science teaching in general? (PROBES: SUPERVISION, PROFESSIONAL DEVELOPMENT)

*Q11 What role has your district played in helping you prepare for the ESPA or in changing your math and science teaching in general? (PROBES: PROFESSIONAL DEVELOPMENT, CURRICULUM REVISION)

*Q12 What do you think of the ESPA? If response primarily negative, probe with "What are the benefits of the ESPA?" If response primarily positive, probe with "What are the downsides of the ESPA?"

Ask after a different observation:

*Q13 When you want help to improve your teaching or develop new ideas, where do you usually turn? (PROBE: PROFESSIONAL DEVELOPMENT, PEERS, PRINCIPAL, INSTRUCTIONAL MATERIALS?)

*Q14M What personal or professional learning experiences since you have been a teacher/in the last 5 years,[1] stick out in your mind as strongly influencing how you think about mathematics (these experiences could be within your school, the district, or outside of the district)? How did your teaching practice change as a result?

*Q14S What personal or professional learning experiences since you have been a teacher/in the last 5 years,[1] stick out in your mind as strongly influencing how you think about science (these experiences could be within your school, the district, or outside of the district)? How did your teaching practice change as a result?

*Q15 What has the district offered to help you improve your math or science teaching in the last year? Which ones have you participated in? How

---

[1]Choose whichever is shorter.

have the offerings that you participated in been helpful? How have they been counterproductive?

*Q16 Have you and your principal developed a personal improvement plan for you in the last X years? What were the major issues to be addressed? What strategies were you to use to improve in those areas? What resources, if any, did the school/district provide? Which of those things did you actually do?

*Q17 What other things has your principal done to encourage you to improve your math and science teaching?

*Q18 What kinds of things related to math and science teaching do you talk about with other teachers in this school?

Appendix E

Interview Coding Scheme

The following coding scheme was intended to reflect the conceptual framework guiding the study from the beginning. However, it was developed inductively through a review of completed interviews. The first version was developed after interviews were completed in the spring of 2000. It was revised after reviewing interviews from the spring of 2001. These reviews helped to refine issues to address and patterns that we wanted to capture.

1. Demographic Information
    1.1   District
    1.2   Gender
    1.3   Grade level

2. Content Standards
    2.1   Teaching Methods
        2.1.1   More how and why questions / higher order thinking skills
        2.1.2   Authentic learning (relate curriculum to real life)
        2.1.3   Focus on various learning styles
        2.1.4   More hands-on (kits in science, lab work in science, manipulatives in math)
        2.1.5   More open-ended questions
        2.1.6   Having students explain their thinking / writing
        2.1.7   Relating topics and disciplines with one another
        2.1.8   Cooperative learning
        2.1.9   More drill / worksheets
        2.1.10   Less drill / worksheets
        2.1.11   Journals
        2.1.12   Writing
        2.1.13   No change

2.2.   Content

2.2.1   Emphasizing certain topics more (e.g., geometry, measurement)

2.2.2   No change in content

2.2.3   Repeating important content

2.2.4   Aligning with what has been on ESPA/what they believe will be on ESPA

2.2.5   New content

2.2.6   Less fluff

Appendix F

List of Codes for Classroom Observation Data

A booklet containing a more complete description of each code and the corresponding options was developed prior to coding the observations. All coders were trained to use the coding system, and issues regarding the codes and options were resolved during the development of the instrument and training sessions.

Code	Coding Options
I. Task demand[a, e]	1) Memorization only. 2) Procedures without connections. 3) Procedures with connections. 4) "Doing math."
II. Manipulative usage[e]	1) Demonstration by the teacher only. 2) Algorithmic-like procedural use by students only. 3) Nonalgorithmic use by student as a tool to solve problems or explore patterns. 4) Manipulatives were not used.
III. Group work	1) Absent. 2) Present.
IV. Nature of group work if present	1) Collaborative. 2) Competitive (i.e., a game with a winner).
V. Task type[b]	1) Practice of routine procedures. 2) Nonroutine types of problems.
VI. Number of problems[b, f]	1) Five or fewer. 2) More than five.
VII. Knowledge needed[b]	1) Definition/procedural. 2) Principled/conceptual knowledge.
VIII. Conjectures[c, d]	1) No conjectures of any type were observed in the lesson. 2) Observed conjectures consisted mainly of making connections between a new problem and problems previously seen or about the truthfulness of particular statements. 3) Students made generalizations about mathematical ideas.

Code	Coding Options
IX. Connections within mathematics[c, d]	1) Mathematical topics were presented in isolation of other topics, or connections among mathematical topics were present in the lesson but only mentioned briefly. 2) Connections among mathematical topics were discussed by teacher and students during the lesson, or connections were clearly explained by the teacher. 3) The mathematical topic of the lesson was explored in enough detail for students to think about relationships and connections among mathematical topics.
X. Connections to students lives[c]	1) Connections between mathematics and students' daily lives were not apparent in the lesson. 2) Connections between mathematics and students' daily lives were not apparent in the lesson, but would be reasonably clear if explained by the teacher. 3) Connections between mathematics and students' daily lives were clearly apparent in the lesson.
XI. Attempt at real-world connections	1) No attempt at connecting the mathematical content of the lesson to the real world is made at all. 2) Teacher (or student) makes a comment or two about a real-world connection but this is done in passing. 3) A short section of the time during the lesson is devoted to discussing real-world issues of everyday items appearing to make a bridge to the main activity of the lesson. 4) The lesson itself focuses on tackling a situation in the real world.
XII. Student explanations[c, d]	1) Students simply stated answers to problems or their explanations focused on execution of procedures for solving problems rather than an elaboration on their thinking and solution path. 2) Students explained their responses or solution strategies. They elaborated on their solutions orally or in written form by justifying their approach to a problem, explaining their thinking, or supporting their results.
XIII. Student Strategies[c]	1) Multiple strategies were not elicited from students. 2) Different problem-solving strategies were rarely elicited from students or only briefly mentioned by the teacher. 3) Students were asked if alternate strategies were used in solving particular problems, but this was not a primary goal of instruction 4) Discussion of alternative strategies with frequent substantive in nature and an important element of classroom instruction.
XIV. Classroom discussions[c, f]	1) The teacher was interested only in correct answers. No attempt was made to use students' responses to further discussion. 2) The teacher established a dialogue with the student by asking probing questions in an attempt to elicit a student's thinking processes or solution strategies. 3) The teacher valued students' statements about mathematics by using them to foment discussion or related them to the lesson in some way.

Code	Coding Options
XV. Instructional decisions[c]	1) A student's comment, question or observation potentially could have led to a discussion, but the teacher did not pursue it. 2) The teacher used students' inquiries comments, or observations as a guide to shape the mathematical content of the lesson. 9) No such opportunities came about in the lesson.
XVI. Reasonableness of student responses[c]	1) The teacher rarely asked students whether their answers were reasonable. If a student gave an incorrect response, another student provided or was asked to provide a correct answer. 2) The teacher asked students if they checked whether their answers were reasonable but did not promote discussion that emphasized conceptual understanding. 3) The teacher encouraged students to reflect on the reasonableness of their answers, and the discussion involved emphasis on conceptual understanding.
XVII. Conversation with peers[c, d, f]	1) There were no exchanges between peers in small groups or as a formal part of the general discourse within a large-group setting, or student exchanges with peers reflected little or no substantive conversation of mathematical ideas. 2) Most of the students asked their classmates for a description of how they solved a particular problem, discussed alternative strategies, and/or questioned how classmates arrived at a solution.
XVIII. Lesson coherence[b]	1) Discrete activities on different topics with different objectives. 2) Several activities on the same topic with potential to be unified. 3) One or more activities with an explicitly unified central idea/objective.

[a]Stein and Smith, M. S. (1998).

[b]Stigler and Hiebert (1997, 1999).

[c]Davis, Wagner, and Shafer (1997). Copyright 1999 by the Board of Regents of the University of Wisconsin System.

[d]Modification of original J. Davis et al. (1997) codes by combining two coding options.

[e]Hiebert and Wearne (1993).

[f]Based on 121 observations. Percentages may not sum to 100 due to a small number of missing values.

References

AAAS Project 2061. (1993). *Benchmarks for science literacy.* New York: Oxford University Press.

Abelman, C., & Elmore, R. F. (1999). *When accountability knocks will anyone answer?* Philadelphia: Consortium for Policy Research in Education.

Adams, J. E., & Kirst, M. W. (1999). New demands and concepts for educational accountability: Striving for results in an era of excellence. In J. Murphy & K. S. Louis (Eds.), *Handbook of research on educational administration* (2nd ed., pp. 463–490). San Francisco: Jossey-Bass.

Anyon, J. (1997). *Ghetto schooling.* New York: Teachers College Press.

Ball, D. (1990). The mathematical understandings that prospective teachers bring to teacher education. *The Elementary School Journal, 90*(4), 449–466.

Ball, D. L., & Bass, H. (2000). Interweaving content and pedagogy in teaching and learning to teach: Knowing and using mathematics. In J. Boaler (Ed.), *Multiple perspectives on mathematics teaching and learning* (pp. 83–104). Westport, CT: Ablex.

Barton, P. (2001). *Raising achievement and reducing gaps: Reporting progress toward goals for academic achievement.* National Educational Goals Panel. Retrieved March 15, 2002, from http://www.negp.gov

Bass, B. M., & Avolio, B. J. (1994). *Improving organizational effectiveness through transformational leadership.* Thousand Oaks, CA: Sage.

Berliner, D. C., & Biddle, B. J. (1995). *The manufactured crisis: Myths, fraud, and the attack on America's public schools.* Reading, MA: Addison-Wesley.

Berman, P. E. (1986). From compliance to learning: Implementing legally induced reform. In D. Kirp & D. Jensen (Eds.), *School days, rule days* (pp. 46–62). Philadelphia: Falmer Press.

Berman, P., & McLaughlin, M. (1977). *Federal programs supporting educational change: Vol. 7. Factors affecting implementation and continuation.* Santa Monica, CA: RAND.

Black, P., & Wiliam, D. (1998). Assessment and classroom learning. *Assessment in Education, 5,* 7–74.

Blase, J. (1993). The micropolitics of effective school-based leadership: Teachers' perspectives. *Educational Administration Quarterly, 24,* 143–163.

Blase, J., & Blase, J. (1999). Principals' instructional leadership and teacher development: Teacher perspectives. *Educational Administration Quarterly, 35*(3), 349–378.

Boaler, J. (2002). Learning from teaching: Exploring the relationship between reform curriculum and equity. *Journal for Research in Mathematics Education, 33*(4), 239–258.

Borko, H., & Elliott, R. (1999). Hands-on pedagogy versus hands-off accountability: Tensions between competing commitments for exemplary math teachers in Kentucky. *Phi Delta Kappan, 80*(5), 394–400.

Bossert, S. T. (1988). School effects. In N. J. Boyan (Ed.), *Handbook of research on educational administration* (pp. 341–351). White Plains, NY: Longman.

Brophy, J., & Good, T. L. (1986). Teacher behavior and student achievement. In M. Wittrock (Ed.), *Handbook of research on teaching* (3rd ed., pp. 328–375). New York: Macmillan.

Bulgar, S. (2002). *Through a teacher's lens: Children's constructions of division of fractions.* Unpublished doctoral dissertation. New Brunswick, NJ: Rutgers University Press.

Bulgar, S., Schorr, R. Y., & Maher, C. A. (2002). Teachers' questions and their role in helping students build an understanding of division of fractions. In *Proceedings of Psychology of Mathematics Education—XXVI* (pp. 161–168). Norwich, England.

Burch, P., & Spillane, J. P. (2001, April). *Subject matter and elementary school leadership: Leaders' thinking about mathematics and literacy in the context of their school reform initiatives.* Paper presented at the annual meeting of the American Educational Research Association, Seattle, WA.

Burns, J. M. (1978). *Leadership.* New York: Harper & Row.

Camara, W., & Schmidt, A. E. (1999). *Group differences in standardized testing and social stratification* (College Board Rpt. No. 99-5). New York: College Entrance Examination Board.

Campbell, P. (1995). *Project IMPACT: Increasing mathematics power for all children and teachers. Phase 1, final report.* College Park: Center for Mathematics Education, University of Maryland.

Carpenter, T. P., Fennema, E., Peterson, P. L., Chiang, C.-P., & Loef, M. (1989). Using knowledge of children's mathematics thinking in classroom teaching: An experimental study. *American Educational Research Journal, 26*(4), 499–531.

Carpenter, T. P., & Lehrer, R. (1999). Teaching and learning mathematics with understanding. In E. Fennema & T. A. Romberg (Eds.), *Mathematics classrooms that promote understanding* (pp. 19–32). Mahwah, NJ: Lawrence Erlbaum Associates.

Clotfelter, C. T., & Ladd, H. F. (1996). Recognizing and rewarding success in public schools. In H. F. Ladd (Ed.), *Holding schools accountable: Performance-based reform in education* (pp. 23–63). Washington, DC: Brookings Institution.

Cobb, P., Boufi, A., McClain, K., & Whitenack, J. (1997). Reflective discourse and collective reflection. *Journal for Research in Mathematics Education, 28*(3), 258–277.

Cobb, P., Wood, T., & Yackel, E. (1990). Classrooms as learning environments for teachers and researchers. In R. B. Davis, C. A. Maher, & N. Noddings (Eds.),

Constructivist views on the teaching and learning of mathematics (pp. 140–168). Reston, VA: National Council of Teachers of Mathematics.

Cobb, P., Wood, T., Yackel, E., & McNeal, E. (1993). Mathematics as procedural instructions and mathematics as meaningful activity: The reality of teaching for understanding. In R. B. Davis & C. A. Maher (Eds.), *Schools, mathematics, and the world of reality* (pp.119–133). Needham, MA: Allyn & Bacon.

Cohen, D., & Barnes, C. (1993). Pedagogy and policy. In D. Cohen, M. McLaughlin, & J. Talbert (Eds.), *Teaching for understanding: Challenges for policy and practice* (pp. 207–239). San Francisco: Jossey-Bass.

Cohen, D. K., & Hill, H. C. (1998). Instructional policy and classroom performance: The mathematics reform in California. *Teachers College Record, 102*(2), 294–343.

Coleman, J. S., Campbell, E. Q., Hobson, J., McPartland, J., & Mood, A. (1966). Equality of educational opportunity. Washington, DC: U.S. Government Printing Office.

Corbett, H. D., & Wilson, B. L. (1991). *Testing, reform, and rebellion*. Norwood, NJ: Ablex.

Cuban, L. (1993). *How teachers taught: Constancy and change in American classrooms*, 1890–1980 (2nd ed.). New York: Teachers College Press.

Davis, J., Wagner, L. R., & Shafer, M. C. (1997). *Classroom observation scale*. Madison: University of Wisconsin.

Davis, R. B. (1984). *Learning mathematics: The cognitive science approach to mathematics education*. Norwood, NJ: Ablex.

Davis, R. B., & Maher, C. A. (1997). How students think: The role of representations. In L. English (Ed.), *Mathematical reasoning: Analogies, metaphors, and images* (pp. 93–115). Mahwah, NJ: Lawrence Erlbaum Associates.

Dreeben, R. (1970). *The nature of teaching: Schools and the work of teachers*. Glenview, IL: Scott, Foresman.

Dworkin, M. S. (1959). *Dewey on education selections*. New York: Teachers College Press.

Editorial Projects in Education. (2001). *A better balance: Standards, tests, and the tools to succeed: Quality Counts 2001*. Bethesda, MD: Editorial Projects in Education.

Education Week on the Web. (2002a, April 3). *Accountability*. Retrieved April 15, 2002, from http://www.edweek.org/context/topics/issuespage.cfm?id=49

Education Week on the Web. (2002b, April 3). *Assessment*. Retrieved April 15, 2002, from http://www.edweek.org/context/topics/issuespage.cfm?id=41

Elmore, R. F. (1995). Teaching, learning, and school organization: Principles of practice and regularities of schooling. *Educational Administration Quarterly, 31*(3), 355–374.

Erlichson, B. A., & Goertz, M. E. (2001). *Implementing whole school reform in New Jersey: Year 2*. New Brunswick, NJ: Center for Government Services.

Fairman, J., & Firestone, W. A. (2001). The district role in state assessment policy: An exploratory study. In S. H. Fuhrman (Ed.), *From the capitol to the classroom: Standards-based reform in the states* (pp. 124–147). Chicago: University of Chicago Press.

Fennema, E., Sowder, J., & Carpenter, T. A. (1999). Creating classrooms that promote understanding. In E. Fennema & T. A. Romberg (Eds.), *Mathematics classrooms that promote understanding* (pp. 185–199). Mahwah, NJ: Lawrence Erlbaum Associates.

Firestone, W. (1989). Using reform: Conceptualizing district initiative. *Educational Evaluation and Policy Analysis, 11*(2), 151–165.

Firestone, W. A. (1990). Continuity and incrementalism after all. In J. Murphy (Ed.), *The educational reform movement of the 1980s: Perspectives and cases* (pp. 143–166). Berkeley, CA: McCutchan.

Firestone, W. A. (2003). Educational accountability. In J. W. Guthrie (Ed.), *Encyclopedia of education*, (2), 651–656. New York: Macmillan Reference.

Firestone, W. A., Camilli, G., Yurecko, M., Monfils, L., & Mayrowetz, D. (2000). State standards, socio-fiscal context and opportunity to learn in New Jersey. *Education Policy Analysis Archives, 8*(35), http://epaa.asu.edu/epaa/v8n35/

Firestone, W. A., Goertz, M. E., & Natriello, G. J. (1997). From cashbox to classroom: The struggle for fiscal reform and educational change in New Jersey. New York: Teachers College Press.

Firestone, W. A., & Mayrowetz, D. (2000). Rethinking "high stakes": Lessons from the United States and England and Wales. *Teachers College Record, 102*(4), 724–749.

Firestone, W., Mayrowetz, D., & Fairman, J. (1997). *Rethinking high stakes: External obligation in assessment policy*. Paper presented at the meeting of the American Educational Research Association, Chicago.

Firestone, W. A., Mayrowetz, D., & Fairman, J. (1998). Performance-based assessment and instructional change: The effects of testing in Maine and Maryland. *Educational Evaluation and Policy Analysis, 20*(2), 95–113.

Firestone, W. A., Monfils, L., Camilli, G., Schorr, R., Hicks, J., & Mayrowetz, D. (2002). The ambiguity of test preparation: A multimethod analysis in one state. *Teachers College Record, 104*(7), 1485–1523.

Floden, R. E., Porter, A. C., Alford, L. E., Freeman, D. J., Susan, I., Schmidt, W. H., & Schwille, J. R. (1988). Instructional leadership at the district level: A closer look at autonomy and control. *Educational Administration Quarterly, 24*(2), 96–124.

Fullan, M. (1991). *The new meaning of educational change*. New York: Teachers College Press.

Goertz, M. E. (2002). *Accountability in the states: How is it working?* (Congressional Briefing). Philadelphia: Consortium for Policy Research in Education.

Goldsmith, L. T., & Schifter, D. (1993). *Characteristics of a model for the development of mathematics teaching* (Reports and papers in progress). Newton, MA: Center for Learning, Teaching & Technology, Education Development Center.

Haberman, M. (1991). The pedagogy of poverty versus good teaching. *Phi Delta Kappan, 73*(4), 290–294.

Hafner, A. L. (1993). Teaching-method scales and mathematics-class achievement: What works with different outcomes? *American Educational Research Journal, 30*(1), 71–94.

Hallinger, P., & Heck, R. L. (1996). Reassessing the principal's role in school effectiveness: A review of the empirical research: 1980–95. *Educational Administration Quarterly, 32*(1), 5–44.

Hannaway, J. (1993). Decentralization in two school districts: Challenging the standard paradigm. In J. Hannaway & M. Carnoy (Eds.), *Decentralization and school improvement* (pp. 135–162). San Francisco: Jossey-Bass.

Hannaway, J., & Kimball, K. (2001). Big isn't always bad: School district size, poverty, and standards-based reform. In S. H. Fuhrman (Ed.), *From the capitol to the classroom: Standards-based reform in the states* (pp. 99–123). Chicago: University of Chicago Press.

Hannaway, J., & Talbert, J. E. (1993). Bringing context into effective school research: Urban–suburban differences. *Educational Administration Quarterly, 29*(2), 164–186.

Hanushek, E. (1994). *Making schools work: Improving performance and controlling costs.* Washington, DC: Brookings Institution.

Hanushek, E., & Meyer, R. H. (1996). Comments on chapters two, three, and four. In H. F. Ladd (Ed.), *Holding schools accountable: Performance-based reform in education* (pp. 128–149). Washington, DC: Brookings Institution.

Heller, M., & Firestone, W. A. (1995). Who's in charge here? Sources of leadership for change in eight schools. *The Elementary School Journal, 96*(1), 65–86.

Heubert, J. P., & Hauser, R. M. (1998). *High stakes: Testing for tracking, promotion and graduation.* Washington, DC: National Academy Press.

Hiebert, J., & Carpenter, T. P. (1992). Learning and teaching with understanding. In D. A. Grouws (Ed.), *Handbook of research on mathematics teaching and learning* (pp. 65–97). New York: Macmillan.

Hiebert, J., & Wearne, D. (1993). Instructional tasks, classroom discourse, and students' learning in second grade arithmetic. *American Educational Research Journal, 30*, 393–425.

House, E. R., Glass, G. V., McClean, L. D., & Walker, D. F. (1978). No simple answer: A critique of the Follow Through Evaluation. *Harvard Educational Review, 48*, 128–160.

Hoy, W. K., & Miskel, C. G. (1996). Educational administration: Theory, research, and practice (5th ed.). New York: McGraw-Hill.

Jencks, C., & Phillips, M. (Eds.). (1998). *The Black–White test score gap.* Washington, DC: Brookings Institute.

Jencks, C., Smith, M., Acland, H., Bane, J. J., Cohen, D., Gintis, H., Heyns, B., & Michelson, S. (1972). *Inequality: A reassessment of the effect of family and schooling in America.* New York: Harper & Row.

Kaase, K. J. (2002, April 1–5). *School accountability and student accountability: Reducing or exacerbating achievement gaps?* Paper presented at the annual meeting of the American Educational Research Association, New Orleans, LA.

Kane, M. T. (2001). So much remains the same: Conception and status of validation in setting standards. In G. J. Cizek (Ed.), *Setting performance standards: Concepts, methods, and perspectives* (pp. 53–88). Mahwah, NJ: Lawrence Erlbaum Associates.

Klein, S. P., Hamilton, L. S., McCaffrey, D. F., & Stecher, B. M. (2000). *What do test scores in Texas tell us?* (IP-202). Santa Monica, CA: RAND.

Kleine-Kracht, P. (1993). Indirect instructional leadership: An administrator's choice. *Educational Administration Quarterly, 24*(2), 187–212.

Klinzing, G., Klinzing-Eurich, G., & Teicher, R. P. (1985). Higher cognitive behaviors in classroom discourse: Congruency between teachers' questions and pupils' responses. *The Australian Journal of Education, 29*(1), 63–75.

Knapp, M. S. (1995). *Teaching for meaning in high-poverty classrooms.* New York: Teachers College Press.

Kober, N. (2001). *It takes more than testing: Closing the achievement gap.* Washington, DC: Center on Education Policy.

Koretz, D. M. (1986). *Educational achievement: Explanations and implications of recent trends.* Washington, DC: Congressional Budget Office.

Koretz, D. M. (1987). *Trends in educational achievement*. Washington, DC: Congressional Budget Office.

Koretz, D., Mitchell, K., Barron, S., & Keith, S. (1996). *Final report: Perceived effects of the Maryland School Performance Assessment Program*. Los Angeles: National Center for Research on Evaluation, Standards, and Student Testing.

Labaree, D. F. (2000). Resisting educational standards. *Phi Delta Kappan, 82* (1), 28–33.

Leithwood, K., & Duke, D. L. (19991). A century's quest to understand school leadership. In J. Murphy & K. S. Louis (Eds.), *Handbook of research on educational administration* (2nd ed., pp. 45–72). San Francisco: Jossey-Bass.

Leithwood, K., Jantzi, D., & Steinbach, R. (1999). *Changing leadership for changing times*. Buckingham, England: Open University Press.

Linn, R. L. (2000). Assessments and accountability. *Educational Researcher, 29* (2), 4–15.

Little, J. W. (1982). Norms of collegiality and experimentation: Workplace conditions of school success. *American Educational Research Journal, 19* (3), 325–340.

Little, J. W. (1989). District policy choices and teachers' professional development opportunities. *Educational Evaluation and Policy Analysis, 11* (2), 165–180.

Lortie, D. (1975). *Schoolteacher: A sociological analysis*. Chicago: University of Chicago Press.

Loucks-Horsley, S., Hewson, P. W., Love, N., & Stiles, K. E. (1998). *Designing professional development for teachers of science and mathematics*. Thousand Oaks, CA: Corwin.

Louis, K. S., & Kruse, S. D. (1995). *Professionalism and community: Perspectives on reforming urban schools*. Thousand Oaks, CA: Corwin.

Louis, K. S., & Miles, M. B. (1990). *Improving the urban high school: What works and why*. New York: Teachers College Press.

Louis, K. S., Toole, J., & Hargreaves, A. (1999). Rethinking school improvement. In K. S. Louis & J. Murphy (Eds.), *Handbook of research on educational administration* (2nd ed., pp. 251–276). San Francisco: Jossey-Bass.

Ma, L. (1999). *Knowing and teaching elementary mathematics*. Mahwah, NJ: Lawrence Erlbaum Associates.

Madaus, G. F., & Clarke, M. (2001). *The adverse impact of high stakes testing on minority students: Evidence from 100 years of test data* (ERIC Document Reproduction Service No. ED450183). New York: Century Foundation Press.

Maher, C. A. (1998). Kommunikation och konstruktivistisk undervisning [Communication and constructivist teaching]. In A. Engrstom (Ed.), *Matematik och reflektion* (pp. 124–143). Lund, Sweden: Studenlitteratur.

Maher, C. A., Martino, A. M., & Davis, R. B. (1994). Children's different ways of thinking about fractions. *Proceedings of Psychology of Mathematics Education XVIII*. Lisbon, Portugal.

Martino, A., & Maher, C. A. (1999). Teacher questioning to promote justification and generalization in mathematics: What research practice has taught us. *Journal of Mathematical Behavior, 18* (1), 53–78.

McDonnell, L. M. (1995). Opportunity to learn as a research concept and policy instrument. *Educational Evaluation and Policy Analysis, 17* (3), 305–322.

McGrath, J. E. (1982). Dilemmatics: The study of research choices and methods. In J. E. McGrath, J. Martin, & R. A. Kulka (Eds.), *Judgment calls in research* (pp. 69–102). Beverly Hills, CA: Sage.

McLaughlin, M. (1987). Lessons from experience: Lessons from policy implementation. *Educational Evaluation and Policy Analysis, 9*(2), 171–178.

McLaughlin, M. W. (1990). The Rand Change Agent study revisited: Macro perspectives and micro realities. *Educational Researcher, 19*(9), 11–16.

McNeil, L. M. (2000). *Contradictions of school reform: Educational costs of standardized testing.* New York: Routledge.

McNeil, L., & Valenzuela, A. (1999). The harmful impact to the TAAS system on testing in Texas: Beneath the accountability rhetoric. Retrieved February 15, 2001, from http://www.law.harvard.edu/civilrights/conferences/testing 98

Mehrens, W. A. (1998). Consequences of assessment: What is the evidence. *Educational Policy Analysis Archives, 6*(13). Retrieved April 15, 2002, from http://olam.ed.asu.edu/ epaa/v6n13.html

Miles, M., & Huberman, A. M. (1994). *Qualitative data analysis: An expanded sourcebook.* Thousand Oaks, CA: Sage.

Monfils, L., Camilli, G., Firestone, W. A., Yurecko, M., & Mayrowetz, D. (2000, April). *Multidimensional analysis of scales developed to measure standards based instruction in response to systemic reform.* Paper presented at the annual meeting of American Educational Research Association, New Orleans, LA.

National Alliance of Business. (2000). *Improving performance: Competition in American public education.* Washington, DC: Author.

National Center for Education Statistics. (1998). *Digest of educational statistics, 1998.* Washington, DC: Author.

National Center for Education Statistics. (2000a). *Digest of Educational Statistics, 2000.* Washington, DC: Author.

National Center for Education Statistics. (2000b). *Statistics in brief: Overview of public elementary and secondary school districts: School year 1998–99.* Washington, DC: Author.

National Commission on Excellence in Education. (1983). *A nation at risk: The imperative for educational reform.* Washington, DC: U.S. Department of Education.

National Commission on Mathematics and Science Teaching for the 21st Century. (2000). *Before it's too late.* Washington, DC: Education Publications Center, U.S. Department of Education.

National Council of Teachers of Mathematics (1989). *Principles and standards for school mathematics.* Reston, VA: Author.

National Council of Teachers of Mathematics. (1995). *Assessment standards for school mathematics.* Reston, VA: Author.

National Council of Teachers of Mathematics. (2000). *Principles and standards for school mathematics.* Reston, VA: Author.

National Research Council. (1996). *National Science Education Standards.* Washington, DC: National Academy Press.

Nelson, B. S., & Sassi, A. (2000). Shifting approaches to supervision: The case of mathematics supervision. *Educational Administration Quarterly, 36*(4), 513–553.

New Jersey State Department of Education. (1996). *Core Curriculum Content Standards.* Trenton, NJ: Author.

Newmann, F. M., & Associates. (Eds.). (1996). *Authentic achievement: Restructuring schools for intellectual quality.* San Francisco: Jossey-Bass.

Newmann, F. M., Bryk, A. S., & Nagaoka, J. K. (2001). *Authentic intellectual work: Conflict or coexistence.* Chicago: Consortium on Chicago School Research.

Newmann, F. M., King, M. B., & Rigdon, M. (1997). Accountability and school performance: Implications from restructuring schools. *Harvard Education Review*, 61(1), 41–69.

No Child Left Behind Act of 2001, Pub. L. No. 107-110, 115 STAT. 1425 (2001).

O'Day, J., & Smith, M. S. (1993). Systemic reform and educational opportunity. In S. H. Fuhrman (Ed.), *Designing coherent educational policy* (pp. 250–312). San Francisco: Jossey-Bass.

Odden, A., & Dougherty, V. (1982). *State programs of school improvement: A 50-state survey*. Denver, CO: Education Commission of the States.

Pennell, J. R., & Firestone, W. A. (1997). *Changing practices through teacher networks: Matching program features with teacher characteristics and circumstances. Teachers College Record, 34*(5), 209–235.

Piciarello, H. (1968). *Evaluation of Title I*. Washington, DC: American Institute for the Advancement of Science.

Pirie, S., & Kieren, T. (1994). Growth in mathematical understanding: How can we characterize it and how can we represent it. *Educational Studies in Mathematics, 26*(2–3), 165–190

Porter, A. (1989). External standards and good teaching: The pros and the cons of telling teachers what to do. *Educational Evaluation and Policy Analysis, 11*(4), 343–356.

Raudenbush, S. W., & Bryk, A. S. (2002). *Hierarchical linear models: Applications and data analysis methods* (2nd ed.). Thousand Oaks, CA: Sage.

Raudenbush, S. W., Bryk, A., Cheong, Y. F., & Congdon, R. (2000). *HLM5: Hierarchical linear and nonlinear modeling*. Chicago: Scientific Software International.

Razze, J. S. (2001). *The influence of New Jersey policy, standards, and assessments on elementary science teaching*. Unpublished doctoral dissertation, Rutgers University, New Brunswick, NJ.

Resnick, L. B., & Resnick, D. P. (1992). Assessing the thinking curriculum: New tools for educational reform. In B. R. Gifford & M. C. O'Connor (Eds.), *Changing assessments: Alternative views of aptitude, achievement, and instruction* (pp. 37–75). Boston: Kluwer Academic.

Richardson, V., Anders, P., Tidwell, D., & Lloyd, C. (1991). The relationship between teachers' beliefs and practices in reading comprehension instruction. *American Educational Research Journal, 28*(3), 559–586.

Robelen, E. W. (2002). An ESEA primer. *Education Week*. Retrieved July, 24, 2002, from http://www.edweek.com/ew/newstory.cfm?slug=16eseabox.h21&keywords=ESEA%20Primer

Romberg, T. A., & Kaput, J. J. (1999). Mathematics worth teaching, mathematics worth understanding. In E. Fennema & T. A. Romberg (Eds.), *Mathematics classrooms that promote understanding* (pp. 3–18). Mahwah, NJ: Lawrence Erlbaum Associates.

Rosenblum, S., & Louis, K. S. (1981). *Stability and change: Innovation in an educational context*. New York: Plenum.

Rosenholtz, S. J. (1989). *Teachers' workplace: The social organization of schooling*. New York: Longman.

Rosenstein, J., Caldwell, J., & Crown, W. (Eds.). (1997). *New Jersey Mathematics Curriculum Framework*. New Brunswick, NJ: Rutgers University.

Rothman, R. (1995). *Measuring up: Standards, assessment, and school reform*. San Francisco: Jossey-Bass.

Schmidt, W. H., McKnight, C. C., & Raizen, S. A. (1996). *A splintered vision: An investigation of U.S. science and mathematic education*. East Lansing, MI: U.S. National Research Center for the Third International Mathematics and Science Study.

Schorr, R. Y. (2000). Impact at the student level. *Journal of Mathematical Behavior*, 19, 209–231.

Schorr, R. Y. (2002). *Looking at change in the teaching of mathematics*. Paper presented at the Annual meeting of the American Educational Research Association, New Orleans, LA.

Schorr, R. Y. (2000). Motion, speed, and other ideas that "should be put in books." *Journal of Mathematical Behavior*.

Schorr R. Y., & Firestone, W. A. (2001). *Changing mathematics teaching in response to a state testing program: A fine-grained analysis*. Paper presented at the annual meeting of the American Educational Research Association, Seattle, WA.

Schorr, R. Y., & Koellner-Clark, K. (2003). Using a modeling approach to consider the ways in which teachers consider new ways to teach mathematics. *Mathematical Thinking and Learning: An International Journal*, 5(2), 191–210.

Schorr, R. Y., & Lesh, R. (1998). Using thought-revealing activities to stimulate new instructional models for teachers. In S. Berenson, K. Dawkins, M. Blanton, W. Coulcombe, J. Kolb, K. Norwood, & L. Stiff (Eds.), *Proceedings of the 20th Annual Meeting of the North American Chapter of the International Group for the Psychology of Mathematics Education* (pp. 723–731). Columbus, OH: ERIC Clearinghouse for Science, Mathematics, and Environmental Education.

Schorr, R. Y., & Lesh, R. (2002). A models and modeling perspective on classroom-based teacher development. In R. Lesh & H. Doerr (Eds.), *Beyond constructivism: A models and modeling perspective on teaching, learning, and problem solving in mathematics education*. Mahwah, NJ: Lawrence Erlbaum Associates.

Schorr, R. Y., & Lesh, R. (2003). A modeling approach for providing teacher development. In R. Lesh & H. Doerr (Eds.), *Beyond constructivism: A models and modeling perspective on teaching, learning, and problem solving in mathematics education* (pp. 141–157). Mahwah, NJ: Lawrence Erlbaum Associates.

Schorr, R. Y., Maher, C. A., & Davis, R. B. (1997). Does teaching mathematics as a thoughtful subject influence the problem-solving behaviors of urban students? *Proceedings of the 21st International Conference for the Psychology of Mathematics Education*(4), 136–143. Lahti, Finland.

Shafer, M., & Romberg, T. A. (1999). Assessment in classrooms that promote understanding. In E. Fennema & T. A. Romberg (Eds.), *Mathematics classrooms that promote understanding* (pp. 159–184). Mahwah, NJ: Lawrence Erlbaum Associates.

Shulman, L. (1987). Knowledge and teaching: Foundations of the new reform. *Harvard Education Review*, 57(1), 1–22.

Silver, E. A., & Stein, M. K. (1996). The QUASAR Project: The "revolution of the possible" in mathematics instructional reform in urban middle schools. *Urban Education*, 30, 476–521.

Simon, M. A., & Tzur, R. (1999). Exploring the teacher's perspective from the researchers' perspectives: generating accounts of mathematics teachers' practice. *Journal for Research in Mathematics Education*. 30(3), 252–264.

Simon, M. A., Tzur, R., Heinz, K., Kinzel, M., & Schwan-Smith, M. (2000). Characterizing a perspective underlying the practice of mathematics teachers in transition. *Journal for Research in Mathematics Education, 31*(5), 579–601

Smerdon, B. A., Burkam, D. T., & Lee, V. E. (1999). Access to constructivist and didactic teaching: Who gets it? Where is it practiced? *Teachers College Record, 101*(1), 5–34.

Smith, B. (2000). Quantity matters: Annual instructional time in an urban school district. *Educational Administration Quarterly, 36*(5), 652–662.

Smith, M. L. (1991a). Meanings of test preparation. *American Educational Research Journal, 28*(3), 521–542.

Smith, M. L. (1991b). Put to the test: The effects of external testing on students. *Educational Researcher, 20*(5), 8–12.

Smith, M. L. (1996). *Reforming schools by reforming assessment: Consequences of the Arizona Student Assessment Program.* Tempe: Southwest Educational Policy Studies, Arizona State University.

Smith, M., & O'Day, J. (1991). *Putting the pieces together: Systemic school reform.* New Brunswick, NJ: Consortium for Policy Research in Education.

Smylie, M., Conley, S., & Marks, H. M. (2002). Building leadership into the roles of teachers. In J. Murphy (Ed.), *The educational leadership challenge: Redefining leadership for the 21st century* (pp. 162–188). Chicago: University of Chicago Press.

Smylie, M. A., & Hart, A. W. (1999). School leadership for teacher learning and change: A human and social capital perspective. In J. Murphy & K. S. Louis (Eds.), *Handbook of research on educational administration* (pp. 421–443). San Francisco: Jossey-Bass.

Sowder, J., & Phillip, R. (1999). Promoting learning in middle-grades mathematics. In E. Fennema & T. A. Romberg (Eds.), *Mathematics classrooms that promote understanding* (pp. 89–108). Mahwah, NJ: Lawrence Erlbaum Associates.

Spillane, J. (1996). School districts matter: Local educational authorities and state instructional policy. *Educational Policy, 10*(1), 63–87.

Spillane, J. (1998a). A cognitive perspective on the role of the local educational agency in implementing instructional policy: Accounting for local variability. *Educational Administration Quarterly, 34*(1), 31–57.

Spillane, J. (1998b). State policy and the non-monolithic nature of the local school district: Organizational and professional considerations. *American Educational Research Journal, 35*(1), 33–63.

Spillane, J. (2000). *District leaders' perceptions of teacher learning.* Philadelphia: Consortium for Policy Research in Education.

Spillane, J. P., & Thompson, C. L. (1997). Reconstructing conceptions of local capacity: The local education agency's capacity for ambitious instructional reform. *Educational Evaluation and Policy Analysis, 19*(2), 185–203.

Spillane, J. P., & Zeuli, J. S. (1999). Reform and teaching: Exploring patterns of practice in the context of national and state mathematics reforms. *Educational Evaluation and Policy Analysis, 21*(1), 1–27.

Stecher, B. M., & Barron, S. I. (1999). *Quadrennial milepost accountability testing in Kentucky.* Los Angeles: CRESST.

Stecher, B. M., & Mitchell, K. (1995). *Portfolio-driven reform: Vermont teachers' understanding of mathematical problem-solving and related changes in classroom practice*

(Tech. Rpt. No. 400). Los Angeles: National Center for Research on Evaluation, Standards, and Student Testing.

Stein, K. S., Smith, M. S., Henningsen, M. A., & Silver, E. A. (2000). *Implementing standards-base mathematics instruction: A casebook for professional development.* New York: Teachers College Press.

Stein, M. K., & D'Amico, L. (2000). *How subjects matter in school leadership.* Paper presented at the annual meeting of the American Educational Research Association, New Orleans, LA.

Stein, M. K., & Smith, M. S. (1998). Mathematical tasks as a framework for reflection. *Mathematics Teaching in the Middle School, 3*(4), 268–276.

Stigler, J. W., & Hiebert, J. (1997). Understanding and improving classroom mathematics instruction. *Phi Delta Kappan, 79*(1), 14–21.

Stigler, J. W., & Hiebert, J. (1999). *The teaching gap: Best ideas from the world's teachers for improving education in the classroom.* New York: The Free Press.

Stodolsky, S. S., & Grossman, P. L. (1995). The impact of subject matter on curricular activity: An analysis of five academic subjects. *American Educational Research Journal, 32*(2), 227–249.

Sullivan, P., & Clarke, D. (1992). Problem solving with conventional mathematics content: Responses of pupils to open mathematical tasks. *Mathematics Education Research Journal, 4*(1), 42–60.

Supovitz, J. A., Mayer, D. P., & Kahle, J. B. (2000). Promoting inquiry-based instructional practice: The longitudinal impact of professional development in the context of systemic reform. *Educational Policy, 14*(3), 357–384.

Swanson, C. B., & Stevenson, D. L. (2002). Standards-based reform in practice: Evidence on state policy and classroom instruction from the NAEP state assessment. *Educational Evaluation and Policy Analysis, 24*(1), 1–24.

Tabachnick, B., & Zeichner, K. (1984). The impact of the student teaching experiment on the development of teacher perspectives. *Journal of Teacher Education, 21*, 165–167.

Thompson, A. G. (1985). Teachers' conceptions of mathematics and the teaching of problem solving. In E. A. Silver (Ed.), *Teaching and learning mathematics problem solving: Multiple research perspectives* (pp. 281–294). Hillsdale, NJ: Lawrence Erlbaum Associates.

Tobin, K., Tippins, D., & Gallard, A. J. (1994). Research on instructional strategies for teaching science. In D. L. Gabel (Ed.), *Handbook of research on science teaching and learning: A project of the National Science Teachers Association* (pp. 45–93). New York: Macmillan.

Tschannen-Moran, M., Woolfolk Hoy, A., & Hoy, W. K. (1998). Teacher efficacy: Its meaning and measure. *Review of Educational Research, 68*(2), 202–248.

Weick, K. (1976). Educational organizations as loosely coupled systems. *Administrative Science Quarterly, 21*(1), 1–19.

Welch, W. W. (1979). Twenty years of science curriculum development: A look back. In D. C. Berliner (Ed.), *Review of research in education* (Vol. 7, pp. 282–306). Washington, DC: American Educational Research Association.

Westinghouse Learning Corporation and Ohio University. (1969). *The impact of Head Start: An evaluation of the effects of Head Start on Children's cognitive and affective development.* Washington, DC: Office of Educational Opportunity.

Whitford, B. L., & Jones, K. (2000). Kentucky lesson: How high stakes school accountability undermines a performance-based curriculum vision. In B. L. Whitford & K. Jones (Eds.), *Accountability, assessment, and teacher commitment: Lessons from kentucky's reform efforts* (pp. 9–24). Albany: State University of New York Press.

Wolcott, H. F. (1977). *Teachers vs. technocrats: An educational innovation in anthropological perspective.* Eugene: Center for Educational Policy and Management, University of Oregon.

Yin, R. (1994). *Case study research: Design and methods* (2nd ed.). Beverly Hills, CA: Sage.

Zhang, L. (2002, April). *Examining achievement gap between Black and White students: A longitudinal study.* Paper presented at the annual meeting of the American Educational Research Association, New Orleans, LA.

Zieky, M. J. (2001). So much has changed: How the setting of cutscores has evolved since the 1980s. In G. J. Cizek (Ed.), *Setting performance standards: Concepts, methods, and perspectives.* Mahwah, NJ: Lawrence Erlbaum Associates.

Author Index

E

Editorial Projects in Education, 4, 11, 15, 52, 65, *223*
Elliott, R.., 12, *222*
Elmore, R. F., 13, 100, *221, 223*
Erlichson, B. A., 15, *223*

F

Fairman, J., 11, 12, 96, 113, 114, 115, 116, 118, 138, 139, 170, *223, 224*
Fennema, E., 20, 67, *222, 223*
Firestone, W., 114, 116, *224*
Firestone, W. A., 4, 6, 11, 12, 14, 20, 21, 39, 45, 65, 66, 94, 96, 109, 113, 114, 115, 116, 118, 138, 139, 170, 173, *223, 224, 225, 227, 228, 229*
Floden, R. E., 114, 115, *224*
Freeman, D. J., 114, 115, *224*
Fullan, M., 12, 63, 64, 91, 167, *224*

G

Gallard, A. J., 27, *231*
Gintis, H., *225*
Glass, G. V., 144, *225*
Goertz, M. E., 6, 15, 109, *223, 224*
Goldsmith, L. T., 21, *224*
Good, T. L., 39, *222*
Grossman, P. L., 52, *231*

H

Haberman, M., 68, *224*
Hafner, A. L., 68, *224*
Hallinger, P., 66, 92, *224*
Hamilton, L. S., 145, *225*
Hannaway, J., 68, 92, 118, *224, 225*
Hanushek, E., 64, 65, *225*
Hargreaves, A., 66, 92, *226*
Hart, A. W., 94, *230*
Hauser, R. M., 143, 167, *225*
Heck, R. L., 66, 92, *224*
Heinz, K., 21, *230*
Heller, M., 92, 94, *225*
Henningsen, M. A., 24, *231*
Heubert, J. P., 143, 167, *225*
Hewson, P. W., 13, 66, 67, 168, *226*
Heyns, B., *225*
Hicks, J., 45, 66, *224*

Hiebert, J., 3, 7, 20, 21, 24, 29, 169, 174, 228, *225, 231*
Hill, H. C., 39, 66, *223*
Hobson, J., 143, 144, *223*
House, E. R., 144, *225*
Hoy, W. K., 67, 95, *225, 231*
Huberman, A. M., 119, *227*

J

Jantzi, D., 13, 94, 95, *226*
Jencks, C., 144, *225*
Jones, K., 12, *232*

K

Kaase, K. J., 146, *225*
Kahle, J. B., 66, *231*
Kane, M. T., 145, *225*
Kaput, J. J., 28, *228*
Kieren, T., 31, *228*
Keith, S., 11, *226*
Kimball, K., 92, *224*
King, M. B., 13, *228*
Kinzel, M., 21, *230*
Kirst, M. W., 6, 65, 73, 95, *221*
Klein, S. P., 145, *225*
Kleine-Kracht, P., 94, *225*
Klinzing, G., 31, *225*
Klinzing-Eurich, G., 31, *225*
Knapp, M. S., 68, *225*
Kober, N., 144, *225*
Koellner-Clark, K., 19, 20, 21, 66, *229*
Koretz, D., 11, *226*
Koretz, D. M., 144, *225, 226*
Kruse, S. D., 81, 94, *226*

L

Labaree, D. F., 9, *226*
Ladd, H. F., 65, *222*
Lee, V. E., 39, *230*
Lehrer, R., 20, *222*
Leithwood, K., 13, 66, 93, 94, 95, *226*
Lesh, R., 13, 19, 20, 21, 66, *229*
Linn, R. L., 6, *226*
Little, J. W., 115, 137, *226*
Lloyd, C., 63, *228*
Loef, M., 67, *222*
Lortie, D., 81, *226*
Loucks-Horsley, S., 13, 66, 67, 168, *226*
Louis, K. S., 66, 81, 92, 94, *226, 228*

Subject Index

Note: *t* indicates table